No More Corncraiks

Other books of similar interest from Scottish Cultural Press

Parish Life in Eighteenth-century Scotland, Maisie Steven
1 898218 28 5

Edinburgh a la Carte: a history of food in Edinburgh, Michael Turnbull
1 898218 87 0

Discover Scotland's History, A. D. Cameron
1 898218 76 5

Picnic on the Culbin Sands by William Buckler, c.1840

The 10th Earl of Moray with some of his family, stoically ignoring the rain as they enjoy their picnic

(By kind permission of the Earl of Moray)

No More Corncraiks

Lord Moray's Feuars in Edinburgh's New Town

Ann Mitchell

SCOTTISH CULTURAL PRESS
EDINBURGH

First Published 1998 by
Scottish Cultural Press
Unit 14, Leith Walk Business Centre
130 Leith Walk
Edinburgh EH6 5DT
Tel: 0131 555 5950 • Fax: 0131 555 5018
e-mail: scp@sol.co.uk

British Library Cataloguing in Publication Data
A catalogue record for this book is available from the British Library

ISBN: 1 84017 017 4

Printed and bound by
Cromwell Press Ltd, Trowbridge, Wiltshire

Contents

List of Illustrations

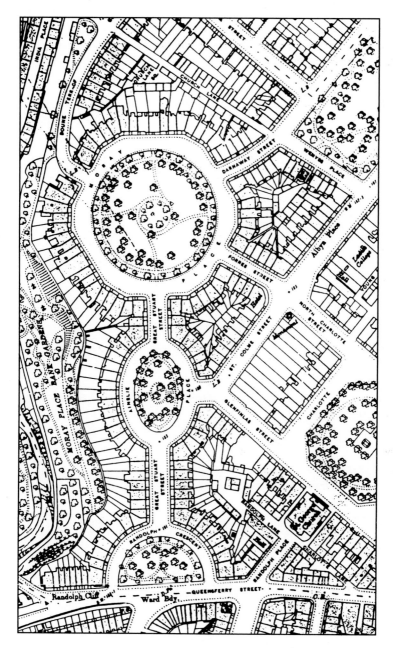

Detail from a 1914 map showing the Moray Feu

Graduating from Oxford University in 1943, Ann Mitchell lived in Oxford until her marriage in 1948 – and has lived in Edinburgh with her husband since then, and in Edinburgh's New Town since 1953. From 1958 to 1976 she undertook voluntary work – mainly in administration – with Edinburgh and Scottish marriage guidance councils. After divorce-related research, she graduated M.Phil. in Social Administration from the University of Edinburgh in 1980, and from 1980–84 she was a research associate investigating children's experiences of parental divorce, leading to the publication of several books.

She has served on the committees of a number of voluntary organisations concerned with the welfare of children, and from 1986 to the present she has helped adults, who were adopted as children, find out more about their natural families.

Over the years Ann Mitchell has become increasingly interested in local history, leading to the publication of *The People of Calton Hill* (Mercat Press) in 1993. She has four children and six grandchildren.

Acknowledgements

I am extremely grateful to the Earl of Moray for allowing me to use a family painting as a frontispiece and for giving me information about the 10th Earl and his family.

My warm thanks go to many people. In particular, Ann Hope was an inspiration, in her knowledge of the Scottish Institution, of the Hope family and of other nineteenth-century Moray feuars. Audrey James generously lent me the diaries of her great-aunt Dr Alice Ker; Felicity Ashbee kindly allowed me to quote from the letters of her great-aunt Jessie Carrick; Fearne Jardine Paterson kindly lent me a copy of the Recollections of her great-grandfather George Balfour-Kinnear and compiled a family tree for me; April Murphy told me of the autobiography of her great-great-great-grandmother Eliza Fletcher and enthusiastically gave me a great deal of information about the Fletchers of Saltoun and of Dunans; Tony Chambers allowed me to reproduce a photograph of a painting of his great-great-grandfather's family; Jack Mackenzie-Stuart helped me to photograph the statue of the Dean sailor in his little garden (previously tended by my mother-in-law). David Gillon (chairman of the Moray Feuars) and Grace Durham both helped to make this book known to present Moray feuars, several of whom provided me with historical and anecdotal background.

I should also like to thank Leslie Hodgson for giving me files about people connected with St John's Episcopal church; Jessie Sym for reminiscing with me; Archie Turnbull for comments on an early draft; Kirstie Colam for suggesting useful contacts; Susanna Kerr of the Scottish National Portrait Gallery; and the staff of the Edinburgh Room, Edinburgh Central Library (and especially Andrew Bethune) for their usual cheerful helpfulness.

Finally, the book could not have been written without the constant encouragement and constructive suggestions from my husband, Angus.

Picture Credits

Corncraik by Mike Langman, reproduced with permission of the Royal Society for the Protection of Birds, title page; the Earl of Moray, frontispiece; *Crombie's Modern Athenians*, pp. 1, 23, 111; Thomas Shepherd: *Edinburgh in the Nineteenth Century*, pp. 6, 72; Graham Metcalfe, p. 24; April Murphy, p. 31; Grant: *Old and New Edinburgh*, pp. 43, 122, 125, 142, 176, 203; W. S. Dalgleish: *Memorials of the High School*, p. 43; Anthony Chambers, p. 57; Iain Gordon Brown: *Elegance and Entertainment in the New Town*: the Harden Drawings, p. 61; St George's School for Girls, p. 65; Audrey James, p. 69; the Registrar General for Scotland, p. 79; Aberdeen University Library, p. 134; William Hole: *Quasi Cursores*, pp. 99, 100, 136; the University Maga, 1838, p. 160; Felicity Ashbee, p. 166.

Introduction

Francis, 9th Earl of Moray, bought Drumsheugh House (on the north-western outskirts of Edinburgh) from the Heriot Trust in 1782. His son, another Francis and the 10th Earl, succeeded to the title and the house in 1810. The house, sometimes called Moray House, stood where Randolph Crescent garden now is, and facing what became Great Stuart Street.

The 10th Earl's first wife Lucy Scott had died in 1798, leaving him with two very young sons. Three years later he married his first cousin, Margaret Jane, daughter of Sir Philip Ainslie of Pilton. They had four sons and four daughters, all of whom lived to adulthood.

James Gillespie Graham, architect

After his death in 1848, four of the Earl's sons succeeded, in turn, to the earldom, but they all (as well as their other two brothers) died unmarried. The earldom then devolved on a cousin in 1895.

Watching the spread of Edinburgh's New Town, the Earl planned to sell for further development the thirteen-acre property on which his house stood. In November 1821, *The Scotsman* 'understood' that Lord Moray had decided to feu the grounds to the west and north of Charlotte Square. He had his house pulled down in 1822.

The Earl took tremendous care to ensure a sympathetic lay out of streets and houses on the awkward sloping site and engaged the services of James Gillespie (later, on his marriage to Margaret Graham, Gillespie Graham) as architect. The site lay between the main road from Edinburgh to Queensferry and the area of the New Town to the north of Queen Street. It was bounded on the south by Charlotte Square and on the west by the picturesque Water of Leith.

James Gillespie (1777–1855) designed a polygon with a diameter of 325 yards (Moray Place), an oval (Ainslie Place) and a crescent (Randolph Crescent), each to be joined to the next by a short street in two parts (Great Stuart Street) with an interesting spur to the north east (Doune Terrace). Other streets were on the periphery.

The Conditions of Roup

The articles and conditions of roup (i.e. auction) and sale of the grounds of Drumsheugh, published in July 1822, were meticulously detailed. They stipulated that the houses should be built on a regular plan and conform to an elevation prepared by James Gillespie. They specified the siting of the chimneys, the breadth of the sunken areas (twelve feet), and the width of the pavement (ten feet). The ground marked as 'stable ground' was to be used only for stables, coach-houses or washing houses, with access lanes of four feet in width at the back of adjoining houses.

Purchasers of feus would be responsible for the expense of paving the streets and constructing the sewers. Purchasers were bound to have their houses built to street level by Martinmas 1824 and completely roofed in by Whitsunday 1825. Feuars were not, at any time, to convert their houses into 'shops or warerooms for the sale of goods or merchandize of any kind; but to use them as dwelling-houses only …with the exception of the east front to the Queen Street gardens,' where shops were to be allowed (i.e. in Wemyss Place).

These restrictions did not exclude hotels.

The Earl's land was sold, in lots upon which buildings were to be erected, on 7 August 1822, at the Royal Exchange, opposite St Giles Cathedral. In that week, Edinburgh was in a fever of preparation for the visit of George IV.

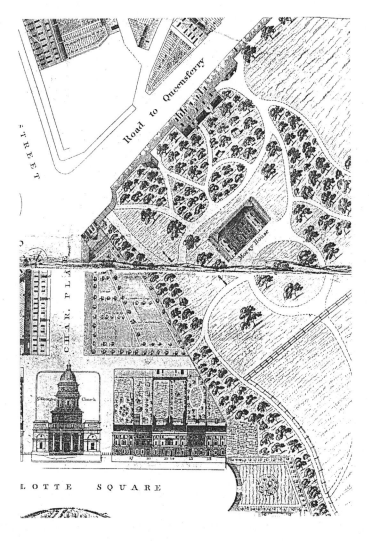

Kirkwood's plan and elevation, 1819, showing the Earl of Moray's 'Moray House'

Pleasure Ground

Imaginative use was to be made of the steep ground between the houses and the Water of Leith, by laying out a private garden for the use of residents. The Earl 'resolved to preserve the beauty of the bank on the south side of the river... and to reserve the same as pleasure ground for the benefit of himself and his feuars.' Feuars whose lots were connected to the pleasure ground were not to build stables or other out-houses on their own back gardens. In addition, there were to be gardens in the centre of Moray Place, Ainslie Place and Randolph Crescent.

Building Progresses

By June 1824, an anonymous diarist could report (Book of the Old Edinburgh Club, vol. 29, p. 150) that: 'In Lord Murray's (sic) ground, besides the large polygon there are buildings going on in Ainslie Place, St Colme Street, Forres and Darnaway Street.'

Less enthusiastic was Lord Cockburn who described the 'beginning of a sad change' when the Earl of Moray's ground was broken up for building. He had, he wrote in his *Memorials*, considered that 'it would be some consolation if the buildings were worthy of the situation; but the northern houses are turned the wrong way, and everything is sacrificed to the multiplication of feuing feet.' Lord Cockburn had enjoyed listening 'to the ceaseless rural corn-craiks nestling happily in the dewy grass.'

According to the diarist again, the houses were not all completed by Whitsunday 1825, as stipulated by the Earl. He wrote, in June 1826, 'Moray Place wants just five stances of being completed all on the south side. A great part of it is now inhabited; among the occupiers are the Solicitor-General (Dr Hope), Mr Hunter of Thurstan, Mrs Oswald of Dunnikier etc. The north side of Ainslie Place is wholly roof'd in but only one or two houses are inhabited. Forres Street will be completed this season and St Colme Street wants just two stances on the west. There are only three houses in Glenfinlas Street and four buildings in Randolph Crescent. Darnaway Street wants the south side.'

J. H. A. Macdonald (Lord Kingsburgh, Lord Justice Clerk) wrote in his *Life Jottings of an Old Edinburgh Citizen* that even in the 1840s 'Moray Place, Ainslie Place, Randolph Crescent were by no means complete. Many corners and gaps were left unbuilt on and were only gradually filled up.'

The Architect

James Gillespie was the son of a sheriff-substitute at Dunblane. On his marriage to an heiress, Margaret Anne Graham of Orchill, he added her surname to his. They lived in Albany Street while he was working on the plans for the Moray Estate. The houses were not all built when his wife died in 1825, after giving birth to their second daughter. He lived at various addresses after that, and married his second wife Elizabeth Campbell who was considerably younger than he was. Soon after his death in 1855, at his home in York Place, his widow and her sister lived at 1 Ainslie Place, where Mrs Gillespie Graham remained for ten years.

Who lived in these new houses?

Others have written about the architecture, but there has been no history of the people who lived in the houses built on the Moray Feu. *No More Corncraiks* takes an in depth look at some of the inhabitants during the nineteenth century. Many of them were tenants and not owners of their homes.

These pages allow the reader to perambulate along each street in turn, pausing at every house to learn something about past inhabitants. A directory is also included, listing all the nineteenth-century householders in the Feu.

Author's note:

In the absence of their menfolk, wives sometimes took their husband's rank, e.g. Mrs Colonel … or Mrs Doctor … . A 'Writer' was a solicitor.

Moray Place

The fifty feus in Moray Place were offered for sale at a public roup on 7 August 1822. The feuing plan shows that thirty-two were immediately sold, at least twenty-seven of them to purchasers who subsequently lived in the houses which were built on their land.

Between 1824 and 1826 all of the houses in the west section (numbers 19 to 36) were occupied, as well as most of the north-east section. All of the houses in Moray Place were lived in by 1832. *Number 1* is at the north-east of Moray Place, and the numbers continue in a counter-clockwise direction. Houses on the corner sites are smaller than others, because the higher floors belong to houses in the intersecting streets.

North West angle of Moray Place, 1829

Number 1

for Baillie, 1832 to 1836, see *14 Randolph Crescent*
for Kieser, 1851, see *1 Great Stuart Street*

Dr William Graham (1800–1886), the founder of the Scottish Institution (see *no. 9*) joined his brother Henry, a WS, at no. 1 in 1856. He lived there until the school closed in 1871: a plaque outside the house records his contribution to the secondary education of girls.

No. 1 was the home of Maj. Gen. John Kirkland from 1872 to 1877 and of Maj. Gen. Charles Irvine of the Indian Army from 1879 to 1904. General Kirkland retired from the Coldstream Guards in 1869. He had served in the Crimean campaign and in 1857 he raised the Second Battalion of Foot, providing 1068 recruits within seven weeks.

Number 2

Donald and Alexander Smith moved into no. 2 in 1826. Donald was manager of the Western Bank of Scotland and Alexander was also a banker. They were soon joined by two more brothers, David WS and William, a merchant. David Smith moved to *3 Doune Terrace* in 1832 and then to *2 Ainslie Place* in 1846.

In March 1833 Alexander attended an auction, at 16 Picardy Place, of paintings belonging to the late Lord Eldin (John Clerk of Penicuik). On the third and last day of the sale, the floor of the drawing room gave way under the weight of about a hundred people who were precipitated into the library below. According to a 67-year-old survivor, John Howell, people were saved from more serious injury because their fall was delayed by the slowly sagging drawing room carpet. However, Alexander Smith fell on his back and was killed. The auction was stopped when the bidding for a Teniers' *View of an Interior* had reached sixty guineas. The auctioneer's clerk, in his terror, escaped by scrambling up the chimney.

Captain William Balfour RN of Trenaby in Orkney retired from the navy in 1840 and three years later came to 2 Moray Place. He was Vice-Lieutenant of Orkney: he married twice, both wives being Orcadians, and had eight children by his first wife and seven by his second. In 1806 he married, as his first wife, Mary Balfour Manson; their son Thomas became MP for Orkney at the age of 21. Capt.

Balfour obtained a grant of supporters from the Lord Lyon King of Arms in 1843, as a representative of the Lairds of Munquhanny. (Heraldic supporters are figures on either side of a shield in a coat of arms, and are granted to chiefs of important clans.) This was an ancient family whose first recorded ancestor was Siward of Balfour Castle, Fife in the eleventh century (see also *9 Doune Terrace*).

for Blackburn, 1867 to 1877, see *9 Great Stuart Street*

Alexander Kinnear (1833–1917) lived at no. 2 from 1877 until his death. His first cousin, George Balfour-Kinnear, was then living at *9 Doune Terrace*. He made his name when retained by the liquidators on the collapse of the City of Glasgow Bank in 1878: he was elevated to the bench in 1882, where he was known for his courtesy and patience. In 1897, after eight years as chairman of the Scottish Universities Commission, he was appointed Baron Kinnear. The Commission had earlier had its offices at *35 Moray Place*, from 1859 to 1863. Lord Kinnear never married but his three sisters lived with him, one of whom, Georgina Kinnear, had been headmistress of the Park School in Glasgow.

Number 3

One of the new householders in 1825 was Duncan Campbell (1786–1842), created baronet of Barcaldine in 1831. Sir Duncan was one of those who had a family home elsewhere as well as a town residence. In the Peninsular War battle of Talavera in 1809 he had acted as ADC to his cousin General Campbell (afterwards Sir Alexander Campbell, baronet) and Duncan Campbell had three horses shot under him. After his death in 1842, the castle and barony of Barcaldine in Argyllshire, which had been in his family since the 1670s, were sold. They were bought back in 1896 by his grandson, Sir Duncan Campbell, third baronet.

Duncan Campbell obtained an estimate from William Trotter for furnishing his Moray Place house. (William Trotter, 1772–1833, was one of the foremost makers of fine furniture and probably furnished many of the houses in the New Town. He had premises in Princes Street, above the present Waverley Market and, perhaps for that reason, he was in favour of further building on the south side of Princes Street. He lived in Abercromby Place and was Lord Provost for two years from 1825.)

The fascinating estimate shows every detail of the furniture proposed for fifteen rooms as well as for the servants' quarters below stairs. The dining room would have 'a set of very fine pillar and claw dining Tables of best Spanish wood with moulded edge, claws and legs on fine brass socket castors'. For the large front drawing room he would provide twelve rosewood chairs, two chairs 'with stuft seats and backs', and a handsome Grecian sofa and ottoman as well as a variety of occasional tables.

William Trotter even prescribed the colours of the curtains (rich crimson damask, bound with lace and finished with plummet fringe, for the dining room), and the Venetian blinds. Forty-nine pieces of flock paper were needed for the drawing room, and 529 feet of gold moulding. The children (of whom there were eventually twelve) were provided with a schoolroom and a nursery. The latter was to have three crib bedsteads and two tent bedsteads each 4 ft 6 ins wide: one wonders how many children slept in such a wide bed! The cost of the whole furnishings was estimated to be £1953 8s 4d. (Scottish Record Office GD 170/537.)

Sir Duncan rented his house at no. 3 from 1830 to 1835 to Patrick Orr WS (who then spent five years at *no. 15*), before Sir Duncan returned for a further three years. (For Orr, see *3 Darnaway Street*.)

for Moncrieff, 1838 to 1842, see *15 Great Stuart Street*
for Gordon, 1842 to 1847, see *9 Doune Terrace* (Kinnear)

Lord Deas (1804–1887) lived at no. 3 for only four years from 1857, having come from Heriot Row, where he later died. He was elevated to the bench in 1853 after two years as Solicitor-General. He had first made his mark as a student. In 1827 he was awarded an MA degree *extra ordinem*, on the strength of an essay he wrote on the national character of the Athenians. He was full of dry humour and pawky old sayings. It was said that he made the boast that he would clear Glasgow of its hooligans so that he could go for a walk, leaving his watch on a lamp-post (surely a strange ambition!) and on coming back find it still there. Consequently, he was the terror of the thieves of Glasgow, who thought their luck was out when they saw him on the bench. He had hair 'white as the driven snow'. His son Francis, advocate, lived at *9 St Colme Street* from 1870 for five years, followed by his brother Sylvester, a WS, with his wife and five children.

After retiring from Java in 1862, Robert William Thomson lived at no. 3 for the next ten years. Destined for the pulpit, but disliking classical studies, he had turned to civil engineering. Being employed on the demolition by blasting of Dunbar Castle, he conjured up the idea of firing mines by electricity. Next he was a railway engineer; then he invented India rubber tyres, but they were too expensive for general use. He took out a patent for a 'fountain pen' in 1849.

Thomson went to Java in 1852, where he designed machinery for manufacturing sugar. The Dutch authorities would not allow him to leave a crane by the waterside overnight in case the natives fell over it, so he designed the first portable steam crane. While in Moray Place, he invented a locomotive traction steam engine with broad India rubber tyres on the driving wheels, for use on the roads of Java for transporting sugar.

Number 4

James Burnett (1801–1876), later 10th baronet of Leys, spent twenty years here from 1840. In 1837 he had married Lauderdale, sister of Dean Ramsay (see *23 Ainslie Place*) and youngest daughter of the Dowager Lady Ramsay, with whom they lived at *7 Darnaway Street* for three years. The marriage was the second for both of them. James was a WS and, later, Sheriff Principal of Kincardineshire.

Number 5

Sir David Baxter (1793–1872), first baronet of Kilmaron and Balgarvie was the head of one of the largest mercantile businesses in the world, based on jute and yarn-spinning in Dundee. He introduced power-loom weaving which was a great success. He and his wife came to live in Edinburgh in 1861, first for one year at *11 Randolph Crescent* and then at *5 Moray Place* until his death, after which his widow remained there until 1884. They had no children but kept a large complement of resident servants including, at each of three censuses, a butler, footman, coachman, lady's maid and up to nine others: even a groom in 1871.

In 1863, the year in which he was made a baronet, Sir David presented a magnificent park, to be known as Baxter Park, to the people of Dundee. On that day a procession four miles long with six men abreast marched through the streets to the park. Later, he established a chair of engineering at Edinburgh University, to which he had the right to make the first appointment. He chose Fleeming

Jenkin (see *3 Great Stuart Street*). He also gave £4000 to provide an official residence for the Principal of the University of Edinburgh. In his will, he bequeathed £20,000 to augment the salaries of Professors in the Faculty of Arts. After his death his relatives founded University College, Dundee, which was connected with St Andrews University until it became a separate university in the 1960s.

Number 6

John Learmonth of Dean (1789–1858), a partner in his family's firm of coachmakers at 4 Princes Street, lived at 6 Moray Place from 1826 to his death. He was the last Lord Provost of the old Town Council, 1831–1833, years of parliamentary, municipal and university reform. He did not have much opportunity for civic developments because of the virtual bankruptcy of the City of Edinburgh, following long-standing confusion over its finances.

He chaired a meeting in 1833 to discuss the erection of a monument to Sir Walter Scott, who had died in the previous year.

**The Dean Bridge, with Ainslie Place, Great Stuart Street,
Randolph Crescent and Randolph Cliff**

The foundation stone was laid in East Princes Street gardens in 1840. Whitson, in *Lord Provosts of Edinburgh*, reported that 'after unsuccessfully contesting two parliamentary elections, John Learmonth abandoned public life and devoted himself to the development of his estates'. The Dean Bridge over the Water of Leith, designed by Telford and costing £30,000, was erected largely at Learmonth's own expense in 1833. He later sold the land of Dean to a cemetery company.

Number 7

Several members of the Monypenny family lived at no. 7 from 1825 for most of the next fifty years. Alexander, who was a WS and died in 1844, was one of the three trustees for the creditors of Sir Walter Scott. He had also been Depute Clerk for the Admission of Notaries from 1814 to 1832. Alexander's sister Deborah and brother William (a collector of Customs in Kirkcaldy) lived with him. According to the street directories, no one lived in the house from 1848 to 1860 when William, by then described as a landed proprietor of Ardit, became the householder. Another brother, David, sat as a Lord of Session as Lord Pitmilly. All died childless. An ancestor, John de Monypenny of Pitmilly, swore fealty to King Edward I in 1296.

Number 8

This house was occupied by George Wauchope from 1827 until his death in 1848 and by his widow Eliza (sister of David Anderson, of *no. 24*) from 1853 for a further ten years. George, who previously lived at 100 George Street, was a wine merchant in Leith. He was the fourth of five sons (and seven daughters) of Captain John Wauchope of Niddrie.

After George Wauchope's death, the widowed Eliza, with her eldest son Andrew's wife Anne and four of their daughters (they later had four more) were at *5 Randolph Cliff* until 1853. Meanwhile no. 8 Moray Place was occupied by Mrs Margaret Bewicke, aged 88. She was the daughter and co-heiress of Robert Spearman, and widow of Calverley Bewicke, both of Northumberland.

Patrick (later Lord) Fraser (1819–1889) lived at no. 8 from 1863 until 1889 when he was found dead in his study chair at his country home of Gatton House, Melrose. He was the author of *The Conflict of*

Laws in Cases of Divorce (1860). This arose from his involvement with the Yelverton case concerning the validity of a marriage between William Charles Yelverton (later 4th Viscount Avonmore) and Miss Maria Theresa Longworth. Major Yelverton had read aloud the Church of England marriage service at the lady's Edinburgh lodgings in 1857; they were then more formally married at a Roman Catholic ceremony in Ireland and subsequently lived together. Litigation continued from 1857 to 1868, while Miss Longworth tried to prove that her marriage was valid, the House of Lords eventually deciding that it was not. Miss Longworth received much public sympathy. Yelverton had meanwhile married the widow of Professor Edward Forbes in Edinburgh in 1858.

After Lord Fraser's death his widow continued to employ a Frenchwoman, who had been governess to the family for over twenty years, as well as seven servants, including a coachman and a page.

Number 9

Here was the Scottish Institution, a school for girls founded in 1834 by Dr William Graham (who later lived at *no. 1*) 'to unite the ordinary and the ornamental branches of education with such a liberal course of instruction in the physical sciences as has not previously been attempted in schools, and at such a fee as to render the branches thus combined accessible to the great majority of the respectable class of society.' The school moved from *15 Great Stuart Street* to 9 Moray Place in 1841.

Dr Graham's aim was to provide 'young ladies' with an education in English and geography, writing, accounts and languages, as well as in music and drawing. Under the same roof they could also learn chemistry, botany, natural philosophy and geology. Parents were urged to send their daughters from the age of ten.

In one of his lectures (published in 1876), William Graham considered it important for young ladies to prepare for their leisure after leaving school by becoming familiar with literature and 'our leading authors'. Some parents were dubious about the value of such reading in time which could, they thought, be better given to 'accomplishments' such as music and drawing. He believed that an educational institution should correct 'the erroneous views which parents have of the education of their children.'

TWENTY-THIRD SESSION.

The Scottish Institution

FOR

THE EDUCATION OF YOUNG LADIES,

9 MORAY PLACE, EDINBURGH.

The Institution Re-opens on the 1st of October 1856.

BRANCHES TAUGHT IN THE ESTABLISHMENT.

1. HISTORY AND GEOGRAPHY, GRAMMAR, COMPOSITION, ELOCUTION, AND ENGLISH LITERATURE...................... ..... } Dr GRAHAM, 78 Queen Street.
2. JUNIOR ENGLISH DEPARTMENT, INCLUDING READING, GRAMMAR, DERIVATION, HISTORY, AND GEOGRAPHY...... } Dr GRAHAM and Mr MACLAREN.
3. WRITING, ARITHMETIC, AND BOOK-KEEPING.............. { Mr GREEN, 37 George Street, and Mr A. TROTTER, 63 Frederick Street.
4. SINGING (INCLUDING PSALMODY)..............
5. THEORY OF MUSIC, AND ELEMENTS OF COMPOSITION... ... . } Signor BUCHER, 1 Great Stuart Street.
6. PIANOFORTE............. .... { Mr CHARLES HARGITT, 56 Queen Street, and Assistants.
7. DRAWING AND PERSPECTIVE... .... { G. SIMSON, R.S.A., 54 Frederick Street. Mr D. SIMSON, 25 India St., and Assistants.
8. LESSONS ON PHYSICAL SCIENCE, INCLUDING ASTRONOMY, USE OF GLOBES, BOTANY............................. } Mr ANDERSON, 7 Gayfield Square.
9. MATHEMATICS................
10. FRENCH LANGUAGE AND LITERATURE... { Dr DUBUC, 121 George Street. Mademoiselle LAMY.
11. ITALIAN LANGUAGE AND LITERATURE.. Signor RAMPINI, 10 Gloucester Place.
12. GERMAN LANGUAGE AND LITERATURE.. Dr AUE, 48 Frederick Street.
13. DANCING AND EXERCISES..................... Mademoiselle ANGELICA, 1 Albyn Place.

OCCASIONAL LECTURES ON SCIENCE.

LADY SUPERINTENDENT..............MISS MURRAY, 46 Moray Place.
FRENCH GOVERNESS............ .........MADEMOISELLE LAMY.

FEES.

FOR THE WHOLE SESSION.......................£21 0 0
Payable in advance as follows :—
For each of the first three Quarters..£6 6 0
For the last Quarter of the Session (for Annual Pupils only)........... 2 2 0
Pupils not attending the whole Session, each Quarter.................... 6 6 0
When three of the same family attend, the third is only charged Three Guineas a Quarter, or Twelve Guineas per Annum, exclusive of the charge for Musical Instruments.
For the use of Instruments for each Pupil attending Music, per Qr... 0 10 6

PREPARATORY CLASS FOR JUNIOR PUPILS.

The Fee for this Course for the whole Session is Twelve Guineas.

All letters to be addressed to Dr GRAHAM, the Secretary; or to Miss MURRAY, at the Institution, 9 Moray Place.

Advertisement for the Scottish Institution

14

Attention was paid to recreation and health and the girls, attended by monitors, had 'the privilege of walking in the extensive private grounds contiguous.'

Unfortunately Dr Graham had to compete with traditional prejudices about education for women. In 1867 John Hughes Bennett, Professor of Medicine, told the audience at a prize-giving ceremony, 'I think the manner in which food ought to be prepared is a very useful thing in female education. ...I do not think the learned professions are the field on which they are likely to succeed. I should decidedly advise them, however ambitious they may be, not to become doctors of medicine.' Dr Graham was a founder member (and, later, President) of the Educational Institute of Scotland which in recent years has had its offices at *46–48 Moray Place*.

As Treasurer of the Clyde Navigation Trust, George Readman was appointed General Manager of the Clydesdale Bank from 1852 until 1880, in which year he and his wife moved into 9 Moray Place. He became managing director in 1886, for one year. On taking over the Clydesdale Bank he introduced a series of innovations and, in particular, he rejected the tradition in Scottish banking of almost complete secrecy by publishing general figures. He also introduced an experiment of time deposits, withdrawable after one month's notice and attracting a higher rate of interest. However, other banks objected and he had to stop the experiment.

There had been many years of conflict between Scottish and English banking, and the Clydesdale Bank under George Readman did much to reduce this conflict.

He was generous to charities but picked them with care. He wrote to Dr Barnardo in 1890, refusing to make a donation because Barnardo's activities were then concentrated in the south of England, and he believed that Englishmen were slow to respond to Scottish appeals.

After his death in 1894, his son James, an advocate who became father of the Bar, lived at *20 Moray Place*. Another son, George, also an advocate, lived at *20 Great Stuart Street* from 1872 to 1881, then at *4 St Colme Street* and finally at *10 Darnaway Street* from 1889 to 1897.

Number 10

Robert Handyside (1798–1858), who married Helen Bruce of Kennet in 1848, would have met his wife when he had lodgings for a year from 1832 at *no. 35*, only four doors from her home at *no. 39*. As an advocate he had lodgings there with two friends, both Writers to the Signet, John Alison and Peter Wilson. He then moved with his landlady to *23 Ainslie Place* for two years before going to India Street and Hope Street. On his marriage he and his wife lived at *4 Great Stuart Street* for six years before going to 10 Moray Place. In 1853 he was appointed Solicitor-General and then a Lord of Session as Lord Handyside. After his death, Helen's brother Hugh and sister Margaret left *no. 39* and came to live with her at no. 10, where they lived until 1867.

Major-General (later, General Sir) Frederick Hamilton (1815–1890) was Commander of the Forces in Scotland 1866–1868, while living at 10 Moray Place. He then left Scotland, on appointment as Commander of the Brigade of Guards. He had been a page of honour to George IV and William IV.

Number 11

for Fox Talbot, 1861, see *13 Great Stuart Street*

Number 12

John Hope (1794–1858), a great-great-grandson of the first Earl of Hopetoun, started his family's long connection with Moray Place when he moved to no. 12 from Queen Street in 1826 after his marriage. He was then Solicitor-General for Scotland, having been appointed at the age of 29. Six years later he moved to *no. 44* for two years and then to *no. 20* until his death from 'a sudden attack of paralysis' in 1858. He had been Lord Justice Clerk for the last seventeen years of his life. When he was Dean of the Faculty of Advocates, Lord Cockburn wrote of him, 'Our high-pressure dean screams and gesticulates and perspires more in any forenoon than the whole Bar of England in a reign.'

John Hope's son William was one of the first recipients of the Victoria Cross when it was instituted in 1856, for his courage on the field at the Battle of Inkerman in the Crimea in 1854. He was unsuccessfully recommended for a second Victoria Cross when he stood on the top of a wooden windmill which had been set on fire by a Russian shell and which was being used as storage for ammunition. Using a chain of volunteers who passed wet blankets and buckets of water to him, he succeeded in extinguishing the fire, thereby preventing much loss of life – and of ammunition – as well as quelling any panic.

In 1832, Charles Hope (1763–1851), later Lord Granton, followed his son John at no. 12 where he lived until his death. He was, successively, Lord Justice Clerk, Lord President of the Court of Session and Lord Justice-General, a man of imposing presence with a magnificent voice which, according to Cockburn, 'was surpassed by that of the great Mrs Siddons alone'. When he retired from the Bench in 1841, he was paralysed in his lower limbs and his step-grandson, Lord Kingsburgh (another Lord Justice Clerk) wrote: 'I have seen him wheeled down a gangway put out from his door to his carriage, and his servant practically hoisting him in.'

Lord Granton, who married his cousin Lady Charlotte Hope in 1793, had four sons and eight daughters. None of the daughters married and, at the 1841 census, seven of them still lived with their widowed father (and three of them at the 1851 census). The family had seven or eight servants and, in spite of 'two fully lighted sunk storeys', an extension of two storeys was built at the back of the house, to accommodate them. The extension is now a separate house. Lord Granton used the whole of his ground floor as a library and occasionally, it is said, as a court. It was described as the largest room of the kind in any house in Edinburgh.

Dr Robert Ferguson (1828–1912), headmaster of the Edinburgh Institution, lived at no. 12 from 1869 to 1892. The Edinburgh Institution for languages and mathematics was founded in 1832; it was a revolutionary idea to proclaim that a liberal education could be obtained without exclusively concentrating on the classics. The school expanded rapidly, with over 200 pupils within three years. The school moved from Hill Street to 8 Queen Street in 1853, where it remained until 1920 when it moved to Melville Street, becoming Melville College.

Dr Ferguson and his much younger wife had six children and, at first, sixteen boarders from his school, aged 10 to 16. Dr Ferguson was tall, handsome, black-bearded, humorous but strict. He sometimes came to school absent-mindedly without a collar or tie, which a boy would be sent to fetch from his home. The boys nicknamed him 'Chalky'. He used pieces of chalk the size of a small orange with which to cover the blackboard and wiped his chalky fingers on his black coat. He rubbed the blackboard with a duster which he then flapped in the direction of the boys he was questioning until the air was full of chalk dust.

The Education Commissioners of 1868 regarded the Edinburgh Institution as probably the best privately-owned school in Scotland. Dr Ferguson was a pioneer in the teaching of science, by introducing chemistry, physics and electricity into the curriculum. Unfortunately an explosion in his science laboratory in 1897 led to the loss of his right leg, a severe handicap for a man who, at the age of seventy, loved walking and golfing.

Number 13

Sir Alexander Ramsay-Gibson-Maitland (1820–1876) spent four years at no. 13 from 1865. He had succeeded his grandfather as 3rd baronet in 1848, and assumed the additional surname of Ramsay in 1865, on inheriting estates at Barnton. From 1868 to 1876 he was MP for the county of Edinburgh.

Robert Cross, who lived at no. 13 from 1896, was one of the few non-professional residents. He worked for J. and J. Cunningham, manufacturers of sulphuric acid, artificial manure and oil cakes.

Number 14

George Mercer of Gorthy, a landed proprietor (and a Deputy Lieutenant of Perthshire) lived at 14 Moray Place from 1842 to 1863. In 1851 his three unmarried sons and five unmarried daughters all lived with him and his wife. One son had already retired (by age 38) from the Ceylon Civil service, while the next was Colonial Treasurer of Hong Kong. Such a large family of adults had nine servants in 1851 and 1861: at the latter date, there were two lady's maids for the then five ladies of the family.

In 1864, Robert MacFarlane (1802–1880) moved into no. 14 as a widower with seven children: he remained there until his death. He began his career as a solicitor and then worked in Jamaica before returning to Edinburgh and going to the Bar. He took the title of Lord Ormidale when he became a Lord of Session in 1862. His youngest son George (another advocate) became head of the household and, in 1891, married a neighbour. She was Mary, daughter of James Hunter, a captain of Bombay Rifles who had retired to *no. 49* in 1884. They then moved to *3 St Colme Street* for Jameson, from 1892, see *3 St Colme Street*

Number 15

for Orr, 1835 to 1840, see *3 Darnaway Street*

Sir George MacPherson-Grant, baronet, was MP for Sutherland for much of his life. He and then his widow lived at no. 15 from 1840 for fifteen years. The house had earlier been occupied by his wife's brother, David Carnegy of Craigo, Forfarshire.

for Hill, 1856 to 1862, see *32 Moray Place* (Anderson)

Number 16

William Robertson, Deputy Keeper of the Records of Scotland, and his wife and son came from Great King Street to no. 16 in 1825, remaining there until 1854.

Number 17

In 1826 Charles Scott came from Dublin Street to no. 17, described as being on the corner of Moray Place and Doune Terrace. He bought 'the whole of the rustic storey, the front half of the sunk flat below, and the east half of the second or double sunk storey.' After his death, his widow remained in the house until 1848.

Number 18

Number 18, which faces onto the very short stretch of street connecting to Doune Terrace and is built above *no. 17*, was the only house to be built as flats. A Miss Young brought her boarding school there from Howe Street for five years from 1828. At the same time, Charles MacBean took in lodgers for two years.

In 1851 there were five separate households occupying the two flats at no. 18. One householder from 1851 to 1865 was John Melrose, master grocer and tea-dealer. He was a son of Andrew Melrose who had several grocery establishments in Edinburgh, the main one being at 93 George Street. The first cargo of tea to arrive at any port other than London came to Leith in 1833 from Canton. Andrew found it necessary for his health to spend his nights in the country so, after shutting his shop at night, he drove home in his carriage to Pittendreich, near Lasswade, while his wife accompanied him on a white pony.

Melrose's teas were advertised for sale 'in tin canisters and sealed packets (never in lead packets)'. The name of 'Melrose' was synonymous with 'tea' until well after the Second World War.

John Melrose was a deeply religious man. His brother William thought him more suited for a minister's life than one of business and described him as 'methodical, hard-working and conscientious but hardly an innovator'. Quietly and unostentatiously he gave largely and freely and usually anonymously to the support of religious and philanthropic work. He used to invite his employees to his house, one at a time, and read the scriptures to them and pray with them, until one employee rebelled and the practice was discontinued.

Alexander Bissett, a master plasterer, was listed at no. 18 in the 1851 census with his family. He died in 1857 of a long-standing heart disease. His widow was not at no. 18 at the 1861 census but had returned by 1871. Bissett does not appear in any street directory, nor is he listed among the plasterers.

Not many artists lived in Moray Place. One who did was Alexander Fraser (1828–1899), in one of the flats at no. 18 from 1877 to 1886. The son of an artist, his first experiment in art had been while he was still at school: he stippled the background in the works of an itinerant portrait painter. At the age of seventeen he enrolled at the Trustees' Academy in Edinburgh, where he claimed that he learned nothing. He said that he learned more from working with nature, from copying in galleries and from fellow students. He was mainly a landscape painter, being particularly skilled at evening scenes.

A goldsmith, Thomas Smith, had a flat at no. 18 for eleven years from 1886. He was a partner in Marshalls, jewellers, at 87 George Street. In 1867 he had spent six weeks in the USA and Canada, and he took part in an important trial in New York. He had been one of the victims of Lord 'Glencairn' or 'Gordon', a swindler. He went to the USA to help with identifying the criminal. He was in New York for the inauguration of a statue by John Steell of Sir Walter Scott in Central Park, a replica of the one in Princes Street.

Number 19

David Octavius Hill (1802–1870) spent six years at no. 19 from 1837. This house was opposite to *no. 18* and was built above *no. 20*. Hill was a founder-member and Secretary of the Scottish Academy of Painting (later the Royal Scottish Academy). He was a prolific landscape painter: while living in Moray Place he published a series of sixty pictures illustrating *The Land of Burns.*

To commemorate the disruption of the Church of Scotland in 1843, he painted a vast picture with over 500 clerical and lay portraits of the leading participants. He spent 23 years working on the painting, which is now in the Free Church Assembly Hall. This was the first time that photography had been used as an aid to a portrait painter. His brother Alexander, a printseller and bookseller, lived opposite to him at *no. 18* for two years.

After leaving Moray Place, D. O. Hill lived at Rock House, Calton Hill, until he died of palsy in 1870. In 1850 he was appointed as one of the Commissioners of the Board of Manufactures, a body which had under its direction the Government School of Art and the National Gallery of Scotland. He had been instrumental in inducing the government to erect the National Gallery in Edinburgh. His second wife was Amelia Paton, the sculptor, whose bronze bust of him is on his grave in the Dean cemetery.

for Windsor Hotel, 1859 to 1873, see *no. 20*
for Froebel, 1878 to 1895, see *no. 20*

Number 20

A private hotel was operating at no. 20 for two years from 1830, having previously been in Drummond Place. The *Edinburgh Advertiser* reported in March 1830: 'The Earl and Countess of Glasgow left Falconer's Hotel, Moray Place, on Monday last for Kelburn.' In newspaper advertisements, Hugh Falconer assured potential guests that, 'as there is no tavern business done at the establishment, it may be relied on as the first Family Hotel in the kingdom' and that it was 'not only the most fashionably elegant and comfortable [hotel] in town but also, contrary to the general expectation, the most moderate in its charges.'

The Rev. Professor John Lee (1779–1859), who was to become Principal of the University of Edinburgh from 1840 until his death in

1859, came to no. 20 for one year only in 1833, before moving to 12 Charlotte Square. His first wife had died in that year, leaving seven sons and four daughters. He had already been minister of the Canongate Kirk and of Lady Yester's Church and in 1835 was appointed minister of the Old Kirk of Greyfriars.

John Lee was the first Principal of the University since 1620 who also held a chair: he became Professor of Divinity and Moderator of the General Assembly of the Church of Scotland in 1843. He was experienced in combining two posts, having earlier simultaneously held chairs in St Andrews and in Aberdeen, a difficulty which he solved by sending his lectures daily by post to Aberdeen, where they were delivered by proxy.

Principal Lee was a great book collector but often could not find, in his personal library of 20,000 volumes, a book which he required. He would borrow another copy from a friend. If he did not return home when expected, the female members of his household used to search for him from bookstall to bookstall. On a visit to London he returned home followed by a hired wagon containing 372 copies of a rare edition of the Bible. It was said that he acquired a great deal of miscellaneous information, much of it 'of no use to him or to anybody else.'

for Hope, 1834 to 1858, see *no. 12*

The Windsor Hotel occupied both *19* and 20 Moray Place from 1859 to 1873, although it is not clear how these two houses could have been combined. The proprietor for the first three years was Frederick Hornyick who, at the 1861 census, had eight resident servants. The hotel had then only two 'boarders', Thomas and Charlotte Fothringham, aged 24 and 21, he being described as a landed proprietor and she as an earl's daughter. They had been married in June 1860. Thomas's father James had lived at *5 Ainslie Place* from 1836 to 1841 and uncles Thomas and Frederick had lived at *23 Moray Place* from 1825. The older Thomas died there, unmarried, in 1830 at the age of 28. Charlotte was the daughter of Sir James Carnegie, baronet, who would have been the Earl of Southesk, but for an attainder of 1715, reversed in 1855 after his death.

The next proprietor of the hotel was Miss Margaret Brown whose teenage niece and two nephews were with her in 1871. In addition to eight servants of her own, she then had a William Scott, landowner, with his wife and young daughter, as hotel guests but with their own four servants and his three visitors who, in turn, had another six servants with them.

Numbers *19* and 20 Moray Place next became a boarding and day school for young ladies from 1878 to 1895. It was opened by Karl and Joanna Froebel, whose three daughters taught music, one of them having been a pupil of Madame Clara Schumann, widow of the composer. Karl was a nephew of Friedrich Froebel, whose name is well-known as a founder of kindergarten education where children learn through play from the age of two.

Karl Froebel (1807–1894) had taken a tutorship in England in 1831 and founded a Lyceum for Young Ladies in Hamburg in 1848. The kindergarten system was introduced to England in 1854. Twenty years later Karl Froebel published an *Explanation of the Kindergarten* in which he extolled the emotional, intellectual and social advantages of encouraging children to learn by observation and by experiment. He considered that a skilled and trained governess would gain great mental satisfaction from the progress of her pupils.

The Rev. Dr John Lee

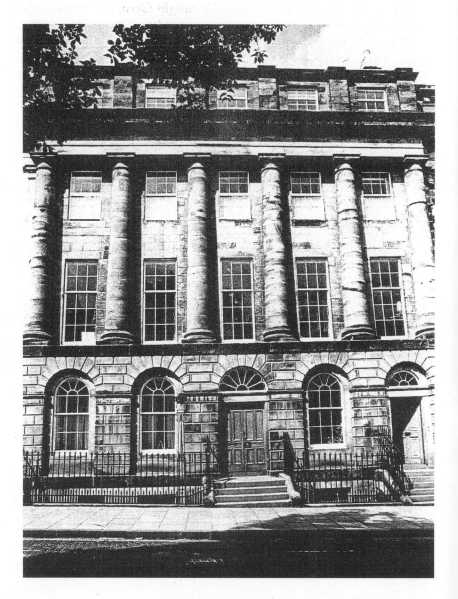

The Earl of Moray's House
(© Graham Metcalfe)

Karl and Joanna Froebel advertised 'select classes for young ladies' in the 1860s in Edinburgh. He taught German, French, logic, mental philosophy and mathematics, while his wife taught German, French and music. She also 'received a few young ladies as parlour boarders' in South Frederick Street and later in Howe Street before moving to Moray Place.

Although Karl Froebel considered that 'the temporary removal of children to boarding school can only weaken home influences,' the Froebels had seven girls aged 11 to 18 as boarders in 1881 but only three in 1891.

Among the last pupils to attend this school were Kitty and Clementine Hozier, sent there because of their parents' matrimonial difficulties. Clementine, who was born in 1885 and who later married Winston Churchill, told her daughter Mary Soames many years later that she remembered lessons in the dining room, with crumbs on the floor and an all-pervading smell of finnan haddock. The sisters were unhappy and homesick. When their mother found where they were, she took a room at *no. 18* and, standing at her window, would wave to her daughters in their classroom.

for Readman, from 1895, see *no. 9*

Number 21

for Kinnear, 1846 to 1852, see *9 Doune Terrace*

Francis Brown Douglas (1814–1886), who was Lord Provost of Edinburgh for three years from 1859, came to no. 21 in 1852. He had given up his practice at the Bar, having inherited a considerable private income, and devoted himself to public affairs. He was an unsuccessful Liberal candidate at two parliamentary elections.

The Brown Douglas family had nine living-in servants at each of the next three censuses. Six daughters and three sons were all brought up there and the large complement of servants continued after their father's death in 1886. One of his grand-daughters, Rosemary Brown Douglas, told me in 1993, at the age of 87: 'I remember when they had eight domestics including two men, one a butler with a lovely long white beard. We used to stay with them for Christmas about eighty years ago.' That house is now one of the few whole houses still in use as a family home.

Number 22

for Walker-Drummond, 1826 to 1828 and 1840 to 1844, see *no. 32*
for Mackenzie, 1832 to 1837, see *9 Doune Terrace*

Another judge, Lord Cunninghame (1783–1854) came to no. 22 in 1837, moving next door to *no. 23* three years later. He was an agricultural reformer who was briefly Solicitor-General. On the bench, he dealt with some of the most important church questions leading to the Disruption in 1843.

The Hon. Bouverie Francis Primrose (1813–1898) lived at no. 22 from 1849 for nearly fifty years. He was the second son of the fourth Earl of Rosebery. He was only two years old when his parents were divorced. He and his wife (sister of the first Earl of Lichfield) had six sons and four daughters to fill their house. Primrose was Receiver-General of the Post Office in Edinburgh and then Secretary to the Board of Manufactures. He was one of the original trustees of Fettes College in 1863. After the school had been opened in 1870, he gave the prizes at a speech day and described one prize-winner (the son of a distinguished father in England) as 'the son, so I believe, of quite respectable parents'. He was affectionately called 'Old Boo' by the boys.

Number 23

Three brothers of the Fothringham family were early Moray feuars. The eldest, Thomas (Colonel, Scots Fusilier Guards) with Frederick, WS, and their mother moved to 23 Moray Place from George Street in 1825. Thomas died unmarried in 1830, but his mother and brother remained until 1838. Meanwhile, another brother James Scrymscoure Fothringham was at *5 Ainslie Place* from 1836 for the last year of his life. His wife Mary Anne (daughter and heiress of Patrick Scrymscoure of Tealing) and their five young children remained there until 1841.

Their surname was taken from the Manor and Castle of Fotheringay, which were held in the twelfth century by the Royal family of Scotland as part of the Honour of Huntingdon. Mary Queen of Scots was imprisoned and executed there in 1587. An ancestor, Sir Alexander Fotheringham, was taken prisoner by the English at Alyth and sent to England in 1645 and was then a prisoner at the Tolbooth in Edinburgh. His nephew Thomas dropped the 'e' in Fotheringham, and his son Archibald was attainted in 1715.

for Cunninghame, 1840 to 1878, see *no. 22*

Number 24

The first name to be listed in Moray Place in the annual street directory was that of Sir Patrick Murray of Ochtertyre, baronet (1771–1837). He lived at number 24 from 1824 for four years. He probably rented this house from Francis Jeffrey who bought the feu in 1822 but did not live there until 1828. Sir Patrick next spent two years at *no. 36* and was then at *4 Great Stuart Street* until his death. After working as an advocate, he was a Baron of the Court of the Exchequer in Scotland (i.e. a judge). One of his daughters later married James Bonar of Kimmerghame, whose brother John was a neighbour at *13 Moray Place* in 1825.

The literary critic and judge, Francis Jeffrey (1773–1850), had his town house at no. 24 from 1828 until his death in 1850. His country home, where he spent all his summers, was at Craigcrook Castle – rented for £75.17s. a year – then beyond the north boundary of Edinburgh city. His chief claim to fame is as founder and editor of the *Edinburgh Review* from 1802 to 1829. He described this journal as standing on two legs, one being the criticism of current literature and the other being Whig politics. Sir Walter Scott was an early contributor.

Francis Jeffrey combined his literary life with law and politics, becoming Lord Advocate in 1830. The next year he was defeated as Whig parliamentary candidate for Edinburgh City and the crowds thronging the streets were disappointed. Two years later, after the Reform Act had transferred the right of electing from the Town Council to the citizens of Edinburgh, he was elected to the seat.

In 1834 he was raised to the bench as Lord Jeffrey. He then had to breakfast at 8 a.m., for the courts sat at 9 a.m. This gave him short nights, for he did most of his writing between 10 p.m. and 2 or 3 in the morning. He always wrote in haste and Lord Cockburn commented, 'a more illegible hand has rarely tormented friends'. Equally critical was Sydney Smith, a witty contributor to the *Review*, who once told Jeffrey 'I have tried to read your manuscript from left to right and Mrs Sydney from right to left, and we neither of us can decipher a single word of it.' Sydney Smith also drew attention to Francis Jeffrey's small stature: 'He hasn't body enough to cover his mind decently with.'

Francis Jeffrey and his second wife Charlotte Wilkes, an American, provided hospitality in 1828 to Thomas Carlyle who was moving house and wrote 'the flitting to Craigenputtock took place in May. We stayed a week in Moray Place (Jeffrey's fine new house there) after our furniture was on the road.' The Jeffreys held open house on Tuesday and Friday evenings, where anyone worth meeting would be present.

Elizabeth Grant of Rothiemurchus described Lord Jeffrey, after his death, as 'charming as a host, delightful as a guest'.

Both Lord Jeffrey and his friend Lord Cockburn had streets in the Old Town named after them.

Madeline Lady Agnew spent the last eight years of her life, from 1850, at 24 Moray Place, after one year at *13 Ainslie Place* following her husband's death. She was the daughter of Sir David Carnegie, baronet, and the widow of Sir Andrew Agnew, 7th baronet of Lochnaw. Her husband had been MP for Wigtown County: he led the Sabbatarian party in the House of Commons and each year introduced bills for the 'better observance' of the day of rest. He strenuously opposed the running of trains on Sundays over lines in which he was concerned as a shareholder. They had ten children, five of whom lived with their mother in Moray Place. One son, Sir Stair Agnew, KCB, became Queen's Remembrancer for Scotland and then Registrar General for Scotland.

David Anderson of Moredun, on the southern outskirts of Edinburgh, lived at 24 Moray Place with his three unmarried sisters from 1858 until his death in 1881. He was one of the original trustees of Fettes College from 1861. He then had eight resident servants, including a coachman, a footman and a page aged 16. When the Union Bank of Scotland opened a branch in Edinburgh in 1843, David Anderson was one of the first Directors.

Another sister, Eliza Wauchope, lived at *no. 8* from 1827 to 1863. Yet another sister, Mrs Grace Brown, lived at Ainslie House (see *11 St Colme Street*). David Anderson's nephew, David Wauchope was the householder of no. 24 from 1887 to 1896.

Number 25

Francis Abbott arrived in Edinburgh in 1847 on his appointment as Secretary to the General Post Office in Scotland, having previously worked at the GPO in Lombard Street, London. At 25 Moray Place he had far more spacious living accommodation than his predecessor, Sir Edward Lees, who had had an official house within the GPO, then half-way along the south side of Waterloo Place. Twice widowed while living in Moray Place (until 1894), Francis Abbott latterly had his daughter and son-in-law (Thomas Prevost, a retired colonel) living with him, as well as a complement of five resident servants.

Those who bridged the gap between the centuries included Patrick William Campbell WS, at no. 25 from 1894, who was responsible for producing the *History of the WS Society.*

Number 26

for Brodie, 1848 to 1889, see *2 Randolph Crescent*

Number 27

In the mid to late 1870s several judges or future judges came to Moray Place hard on each other's heels. John Trayner who, as Lord Trayner, became Lord Commissioner of Justiciary in 1887, had his home at no. 27 from 1878, after seven years at *10 St Colme Street.*

Number 28

The 10th Earl of Moray, although the feudal superior of the whole estate (owner of the land, to whom a house owner had to pay feu duty annually), may never have lived in the house which he designated for himself.

His house at no. 28 was one of thirteen to be occupied in 1825: these were mostly on the west side. His descendants are uncertain whether the Earl ever took up residence, although he is listed in the street directories from 1825 to 1831. On the other hand, the Earl might sometimes have needed a town house when he and his wife and children came to Edinburgh by ferry from their home at Donibristle in Fife for any reason.

However, the Earl's second wife was in poor health and they had to live for much of the time on the continent in a warmer climate. She died in 1837. Towards the end of 1830, the Earl advertised his house at no. 28 'to be sold or let unfurnished' as 'equally suited for a family of distinction or for an Hotel.' The accommodation consisted of 'on the lowermost or sunk floor, five rooms for servants, with closets, besides kitchen, washing-house and laundry, which are detached; on the dining room floor there are three public rooms, with butler's pantry; on the next floor there are three drawing rooms, with a bedroom, and the two uppermost floors afford eleven bedrooms with closets.' Furthermore, the house was 'abundantly supplied with water, it has two staircases, and is in complete repair.'

After apparently being unoccupied for two years, the Earl of Moray's house at 28 was rented in 1833 by Andrew Coventry, an advocate who came from Argyle Square and who was joined a year later by his mother Martha. She was the widow of Professor Andrew Coventry of Shanwell, who had held what was probably the first chair of agriculture in any university, but his subject was not then available for graduation. The family already had a foothold in Moray Place, for Professor Coventry's older son George Coventry, Rector of St Peter's Episcopal Church, Roxburgh Place, lived at *no. 49* from 1830 to 1847.

In 1843 Andrew Coventry bought the next door house at *no. 29*, living there until his death in 1878. He also bought a stable and coach house in Church Lane (now Gloucester Lane). His mother remained in one half of no 28, the other half being then occupied by Mrs Janet Playfair of Dalmarnock.

When Martha Coventry died in 1856, her widowed daughter Mrs Esther Maitland-Makgill-Crichton became the householder of 28B until 1869. She then went to Melville Street and Heriot Row, but on the death of her brother Andrew Coventry in 1878 she took over his house at *no. 29* until her death in 1892, ending nearly sixty years of one family's residence in Moray Place.

By that time, both of Esther's daughters, both widowed, lived with her. The elder daughter, another Martha, had married Miles Angus Fletcher in 1871 and had been widowed only two months later. His great-niece April Murphy (née Fletcher) wrote to me:

> Miles had a severe head injury as a result of a riding accident. He decided to emigrate and set out on 18 April 1871 ... decided to settle at Holy Cross, Minnesota, USA. He bought a property there and built some kind of shanty, hoping that Martha Maitland-Makgill-Crichton could join him. She sailed from Liverpool on 10 August and they were married in the Cathedral of St Paul on 14 September. In November his wife became very ill, and he set out to walk twelve miles across the

open plain to look for a nurse for her. He did not find one and on the way back he was overtaken by a violent snowstorm and never returned, being lost in the snow. His body was found on the third day of the search.

Miles Angus Fletcher and Martha Maitland-Makgill-Crichton

Perhaps the largest family to live in Moray Place was that of George Young (1819–1907). He was an advocate who became successively Solicitor-General for Scotland, Liberal MP for Wigtown Burghs, Lord Advocate and, in 1874, a judge of the Court of Session. His country house was at Silverknowes, on the north side of Edinburgh. When his family grew too large for *no. 47*, where they lived for fifteen years from 1854, they moved to no. 28, the house originally built for the Earl of Moray. Eventually there were sixteen children, of whom four sons also had a legal career. In spite of so much child-bearing, Lady

Young lived to the age of 70, dying in 1901. Lord Young lived at no. 28 until 1907.

Census returns at ten yearly intervals from 1861 to 1891 show that there were from nine to twelve resident servants in the Young household. According to Eric Linklater, in his book *Edinburgh*, there were 25 indoor servants, many of whom must have lived elsewhere and come in by the day.

George Young enlarged the house by having a billiard room built on at the back which could be reached via stairs from the dining room, as well as from the servants' quarters in the basement. He also installed an iron spiral staircase to the drying green from the flat roof of the extension. Carved panels of acanthus, putti, squirrels and flowers, which were placed up the main stairs of the house, were a gift to Lord Young from a grateful client; this was Mr Winans, an American millionaire who had made his money in fire-arms and was much given to litigation. He had property in Ross-shire and is known for bringing (and losing) a trivial case against a crofter whose children's pet lamb was said to have trespassed a short way onto his land.

Solicitors scrambled to retain George Young as an advocate. Madeleine Smith's acquittal in 1857, on a charge of murdering her lover Emile L'Angelier in Glasgow by poisoning him with arsenic, was thought to have been largely the result of Young's preparation of her defence when he was junior counsel. The verdict was 'not proven' and public opinion tended to the view that she was probably guilty but that L'Angelier had deserved his fate. However, it is said that George Young later took on so many cases that he often did not look at his papers until he was in court, where he picked up points from his juniors.

Mention should be made of the subsequent use made of no. 28 as the first Catholic teacher-training college in Scotland, later to become Craiglockhart College. Six nuns arrived in April 1918. One of them, Mother O'Connell, recalled in 1960:

> The house had been unoccupied for eleven years and a thick carpet of sooty dust, which penetrated everything, lay on all the floors. We had no hot water, no gas, no electricity. The kitchen stove was out of order and all the cooking had to be done on an ordinary bedroom fireplace. Only one part of a meal could be cooked at a time. What ingenuity had to be used in the menu!

After being a student hostel for one year, the college opened in September 1919, with 24 students. A year later the college moved to the former Hydropathic at Craiglockhart. During that year, the resident students slept at *9 Ainslie Place* to which, one of them later recalled, they were escorted daily through the gardens at the backs of the houses.

Arthur Hope WS, great-great-grandson of Lord Granton (at *no. 12*) and his wife Ann brought up their five children at no. 28 during and after the Second World War. One of their sons, David (Baron Hope) was Lord President of the Court of Session from 1989 to 1996, was the third Lord Justice-General in the family and is now a Lord of Appeal.

Number 29

for Coventry, 1843 to 1878 and Maitland-Makgill-Crichton, 1878 to 1892, see *no. 28*

A few officers of the HEICS retired to Moray Place. The first was Lt. Gen. John Cuninghame who lived at no. 29 from 1826 until his death in 1843, aged over 80. He had served with the 44th and 48th Regiments of Native Infantry, leaving his wife in Edinburgh. By the end of his life they had four male and three female resident servants.

Number 30

for Tod, 1844 to 1857, see *14 Ainslie Place*

Mrs Catherine Forrest kept a 'boarding institution for young ladies' at no. 30 from 1857 to 1872, but the description of 'young' covered widows and unmarried women aged 85 down to 26! She had ten boarders in 1861 and seven in 1871.

She was followed, at no. 30, by a wool broker from Tanfield, Robert Girdwood, who lived there with his family for 14 years from 1872.

Number 31

Charles Hope (1766–1844), who was Professor of Chemistry and Chemical Pharmacy at the University of Edinburgh for nearly fifty years from 1795, was a son of John Hope, Professor of Botany. He moved from Charlotte Square to 31 Moray Place late in 1824 and was joined by his widowed solicitor brother James and nephew John, who both came from Queen Street. Professor Hope was a very successful demonstrator of experiments to classes of over 500 students. Until 1823, his students were given no access to his laboratory and no opportunity for practical instruction. In 1826 he was sanctioned by the Senatus to give a popular course of lectures on chemistry to young ladies. In 1838, over two hundred 'gentlemen of rank and learning' attended an 'entertainment' given for Prof. Hope in the Assembly Rooms: Lord Meadowbank was in the chair.

Charles Hope's brother James WS (who died in 1842), was for forty years agent in Scotland for Commissions for Highland Roads and Bridges. On 1 January 1825 he wrote from 31 Moray Place: 'I have changed my quarters, driven from my former by want of room, approach of buildings, shops etc. I am now 500 yards to the north-west of my former house, a new place formed in the fields to which we used to look with admiration, but now studded with houses. We are on the top of a bank above a ravine.' During the cholera epidemic of 1832 he recorded: 'We are still in this place, free from the pestilence which surrounds us – a circumstance almost miraculous considering that it has raged for a fortnight within five miles of us.' Aware of the risk of spreading infection, he proposed improvements to the 'pleasure ground' in the centre of Moray Place, so that 'children are not of NECESSITY thrown into close intercourse with other children when fever and other infectious complaints are prevalent.'

Communication was so important between James Hope and his consulting engineer Thomas Telford, and between the Commissioners in London and the landowners in Scotland, that the Secretary of the GPO in Edinburgh conveyed bulky packages of maps and plans without charge.

After Prof. Hope's death in 1844 his nephew John Hope WS, a philanthropist, continued to live in the house at no. 31 until he died in 1893. He never married but always had a housekeeper, a man servant and a housemaid. He financed night schools for both boys and girls, and provided a public park for the children of Stockbridge. He organized children's outings to the Botanic Gardens, to Robert Forrest's statuary on Calton Hill (see Mitchell: *The People of Calton Hill*) and to the zoo (then in Broughton Park). He generously supplied medical attention, food, clothing and holidays to young people who could not afford them.

John Hope was a strict Sabbatarian and also hated tobacco: when East Princes Street gardens were opened to the public, he arranged for a ban on smoking there. He actively advocated temperance. He strenuously and inadvisedly imposed his own views when canvassing the residents of Rose Street in the 1836 local elections. *The Scotsman* reported that 'had the electors been his menial servants he could not have treated them with greater contempt. ...He was three or four times seized, with the view of being turned out of the room, and he was once floored on the staircase when laying hold of a voter.'

For thirty years he never drank tea or coffee (being stimulants). Instead, he ate oranges. He inaugurated the British League of Juvenile Abstainers in 1847 and, from among the members, he founded the cadet corps in which the boys enjoyed military-type drilling exercises. They wore a specially designed uniform of red Garibaldi shirt and blue knickerbockers, with leggings of brown sail cloth.

John Hope set up the Hope Trust, knowing that his family had no need of his money. On his death, he left over £400,000 to propagate the principles of Protestantism and temperance, including the use of unfermented wine at communion services.

Number 32

Marion, sister of Charles and James Hope of *no. 31*, had married James Walker of Dalry House, a Principal Clerk of Session, in 1797. Eight years later, James Hope married his sister's stepdaughter Jane Walker. Mrs Marion Walker, as a widow, lived next door to her brothers at 32 Moray Place from 1826 to 1838. Furthermore, her stepson, Patrick Walker-Drummond, lived at *no. 22* for two years from 1826 and again from 1840 for four years. On marrying an heiress, Margaret Drummond, he had added her surname to his and he subsequently inherited his father-in-law's baronetcy by a special limitation.

Jane Hamilton kept a boarding-house for ladies at no. 32 from 1838 to 1846: in 1841 she had six ladies as well as two teenage children of her own.

Findlay Anderson, a retired civil servant of the EIC, succeeded his brother John, a WS, at no. 32 from 1858 to 1871. His seven children had a governess from New Zealand. He would have had shared interests with James Hill, an indigo planter from the East Indies, who moved from *6 Darnaway Street* with his family to *15 Moray Place* for six years from 1856. Mrs Hill's brother Ewan Macdonell was visiting the Hills with his family at the 1861 census: he was a doctor in the Indian Civil Service.

for Christison, 1874, see *no. 40*

Number 33

Mrs Mary Sprot of Clapham, a widow and 'a fund-holder and annuitant' moved house many times. She arrived in Edinburgh in 1841 and lived successively at *nos. 33* and *40 Moray Place*, Atholl Crescent, *24 Ainslie Place*, *34 Moray Place* for two years until 1855 and finally at *4 Randolph Crescent*, where she died in 1857 aged 78. She employed from five to seven servants, including a coachman and a footman.

The Dowager Duchess of Gordon spent a year at no. 33 from 1848. She was formerly Miss Elizabeth Brodie of Arnhall. Her husband, the 5th and last Duke, had died in 1836, nine years after succeeding to the Dukedom. He had raised the 92nd, or Gordon, Highlanders in 1794, and was promoted to General in 1819. He was Keeper of the Great Seal of Scotland and Governor of Edinburgh Castle and died childless at Gordon Castle, aged 66, when the title became extinct.

Lord Fullerton, a judge, died in 1853 only three weeks after retiring, and after living for only four years at no. 33. He was a contemporary and friend of Lords Moncreiff, Jeffrey, Cockburn and Cranston. It was said that 'his logic was at once intelligent and acute, and he combined with rare felicity great firmness with great soundness of understanding.'

Number 34

David Hume (1756–1838), a nephew of the philosopher of the same name, lived at no. 34 for the last ten years of his life, after which his two nieces lived in the house for a further ten years. He had been Professor of Scots Law at Edinburgh University and was a well known writer on criminal jurisprudence. He became a Principal Clerk of the Court of Session, where he was a colleague of Sir Walter Scott. David Hume was a Baron of Exchequer until the Court of

Exchequer merged with the Court of Session in 1830.

James Douglas of Cavers spent the last six years of his life, from 1855, at no. 34. His mother, Grace, was a sister of the 10th Earl of Moray. In 1858 his son, another James, married Mary Agnew of *24 Moray Place*, sixteen years his junior. She joined the family at no. 34 but remained childless.

for Watson, 1879 to 1883, see *6 St Colme Street*

Lord Adam, another Lord of Session, moved from one house to another in the Moray Feu. He was at *no. 44* for five years from 1865 and, after about twelve years at *10 Great Stuart Street*, he finally settled at 34 Moray Place with his wife and five unmarried daughters until his death in 1914. He was said to be a great orator.

Number 35

In 1829 the house at no. 35 (not yet lived in, as far as I can ascertain) was advertised for sale 'completely finished and furnished in the best style'. Possibly the demand for such grand houses had fallen because, a year later, early in 1830, the upset price was reduced to £2,900 and, if not sold, the house would be let. It had eighteen fire apartments (i.e. with fireplaces), kitchen, and closets and 'besides private grounds, the house has also the privilege of the extensive pleasure grounds in the centre and to the north-west of Moray Place.'

Mrs Drummond took in lodgers at no. 35 from 1832 for one year only before removing to *Ainslie Place* (*no. 23* and then *no. 3*). She must have been a successful landlady since two of her lodgers moved with her. One was Peter Wilson WS and the other, Robert Handyside, an advocate who later became a judge.

The house again became a lodging-house from 1855 to 1863, when William Moir was landlord. In 1861 he had two widows as lodgers, one with a companion and a servant of her own and the other with four young adult daughters.

for Blair, from 1877, see *15 Randolph Crescent*

Number 36

for Murray, 1828 to 1830, see *no. 24*
for Wood, 1871 to 1874, see *10 St Colme Street*

Alexander Ure (1853–1928), the son of a distinguished Lord Provost of Glasgow, came to no. 36 on his marriage in 1879. Seven years later he moved to Heriot Row. As well as being an advocate he had to travel to Glasgow where he was a lecturer in constitutional law and history. He was a keen yachtsman and a great walker. He once walked from Edinburgh to London and, on another occasion, from London to Land's End.

Ure was Liberal MP for Linlithgowshire from 1895, after which judicial promotion came rapidly. He became Lord Advocate, Lord President of the Court of Session and Lord Justice-General. In 1914 he was raised to the peerage as Baron Strathclyde. When he resigned from the bench in 1920 he refused a pension since he had sufficient private means.

The house at no. 36 was given to the Queen in 1954 by the Lord Provosts of Edinburgh, Glasgow, Perth, Dundee and Aberdeen. Since then, the Queen has granted grace-and-favour tenancies from 1954 to 1969 to the Very Rev. Dr Charles Warr, Dean of the Order of the Thistle; from 1970 to 1971 to Lord Reith, former Director-General of the BBC; from 1972 to 1977 to Sir Angus MacKintosh, a retired diplomat; and from 1977 to 1995 to the Very Rev. Ronald Selby Wright, Minister Emeritus of the Canongate Kirk.

Great Stuart Street enters here

Number 37

John Goodsir (1814–1867) became Professor of Anatomy in 1846 and briefly made his home at no. 37. At the age of sixteen, as an apprentice dentist, he had pulled out a tooth for Daniel O'Connell, the prominent Irish politician. In 1835 he joined his father's practice in Anstruther as a physician and dentist. Five years later, he returned to Edinburgh, where he had studied. He and his brothers and some friends rented half of a top flat in Lothian Street for £17 a year and there they established 'The Universal Brotherhood of the Friends of Truth'. Resident with them were two young anatomical assistants, who acted as 'grooms-in-waiting', and a housekeeper.

W. A. Knight later described him in *Some Nineteenth Century Scotsmen*, as 'a tall gaunt figure, six feet three in height, with a grave face, his broad high forehead almost concealed by dark brown hair, a long prominent nose, deep eyes, large mouth and chin, stooping shoulders and downcast visage.'

Goodsir became curator, first of the museum of the College of Surgeons, and then of the University Museum of Anatomy. Disappointed at failing to be appointed assistant surgeon to the Royal Infirmary (to enable him to teach in surgical wards), he saw no company, slept on a sofa in the midst of his papers, ate irregularly and restlessly moved house three times in as many years.

'Wanting in rhetoric, devoid of gesture, and dealing out monotonous sentences for upwards of an hour together, were severe drawbacks to his success.' Nevertheless, he was a popular lecturer whose class increased from 275 to nearly 500 pupils. Symptoms of spinal paralysis appeared in 1850, gradually making walking and standing almost impossible. He was stoical: when demonstrating a sphenoid bone to his class, the door he was leaning against suddenly opened, and he fell backwards still holding his sphenoid. On being helped up, he continued with his lecture.

The Rev. Dr William Hanna (1808–1882), who spent a year at no. 37 in 1850, was the biographer of Dr Thomas Chalmers, the leader of the 1843 secession from the Church of Scotland. Dr Hanna, who married Thomas Chalmers' daughter Anne, was the Church of Scotland minister at Skirling in Peeblesshire and was closely involved with the disruption. He and his congregation left the established Church of Scotland and joined the new Free Church.

After Thomas Chalmers's death in 1847, William Hanna resided for a time in Edinburgh, having arranged a temporary exchange with another clergyman in order to have time to write his father-in-law's biography. He also then became the editor of the *North British Review* for several years. In 1850 he came to Edinburgh permanently, as minister of St John's Free Church.

Number 38

for Kerr, 1831 to 1843, see *4 Forres Street*

Number 39

Throughout the nineteenth century, Moray Place continued to attract both men and women of independent means.

Mrs Alexander Bruce of Kennet in Clackmannanshire moved to no. 39 from Albany Street in 1828. Her son Hugh, an advocate, and two unmarried daughters moved with her. They were soon joined by another son, William, a wine merchant of Leith, who had lived in Rose Street. Two other sons had died in 1817, one of them as a midshipman. Mrs Bruce had a complement of nine resident servants in 1841 (including four men) and in 1851 (including two men).

Mrs Bruce outlived her husband by 43 years. Her son Robert Bruce of Kennet claimed the barony of Balfour of Burleigh but died in 1864 before the case was decided. However his son Alexander became the sixth Lord Balfour of Burleigh and was later Secretary for Scotland and a Cabinet Minister from 1895 to 1903. An Act of Parliament in 1869 had removed the attainder attached to the fifth Lord Balfour for his part in the 1715 rebellion in support of the Old Pretender: he had earlier escaped from prison in his sister's clothes a few days before he was to have been beheaded for the murder of a schoolmaster.

Helen, one of Mrs Bruce's daughters, married a neighbour, Robert Handyside (see *no. 10*).

Number 40

Another eminent doctor was Robert Christison (1797–1882), Professor of Medical Jurisprudence and then of Materia Medica. After six years at *3 Great Stuart Street* with his brother John and twelve at *5 Randolph Crescent*, he settled at 40 Moray Place from 1847 until his death.

As medical adviser to the Crown, he was the medical witness in almost every important case in Scotland from 1829 to 1866, starting with the trial for murder of the resurrectionists Burke and Hare. He broke new ground by distinguishing between wounds inflicted before and after death.

Soon after his appointment to his chair in 1822, Christison realised that he needed to be able to read German. He later wrote, 'I spent one entire day in studying a good German grammar superficially. ...Next day, with the help of a dictionary proper, I began to read Schiller's *Dreysigjähriger Krieg*. ...In fourteen days I was able to read ten pages in an hour.' He had time for these studies because medical jurisprudence was a purely voluntary subject for young lawyers, twelve of whom attended his first lectures, dwindling to five and then to one. Ten years later he had a class of ninety students. Robert Christison became an expert on poisons, and his hazardous experiments of the effects of poison on himself were often observed.

'He nearly became a martyr to science by swallowing a large piece of the Calabar bean while dressing one day but, warned by his sensations, saved himself by promptly using his shaving water as an emetic' (Grant: *Story of the University of Edinburgh*). To the end of his life he was implacably opposed to the admission of women students to the medical school, in spite of considerable pressure from Dr Sophia Jex-Blake.

Honours were heaped on him. He was twice President of the Royal College of Physicians of Edinburgh, then President of the Royal Society of Edinburgh and President of the British Medical Association. He was created baronet in 1871. In that year, as a relaxation, he wrote his *Recollections* on 471 pages of notepaper with firm, small, exquisite handwriting, but unfortunately he never got further than 1830.

Sir Robert was a good singer and a keen mountaineer. He was very fit and at one time could race up Arthur's Seat from Hunter's Bog in less than five minutes.

From 1860, he observed and forecast the weather. In December of that year, a foot of snow fell in Edinburgh in fourteen hours, followed by temperatures of minus 4 degrees Fahrenheit. He noted that the appearance of the aurora borealis every few years indicated heavy rain in the afternoon of the second day afterwards. In January 1868 a hurricane-like storm ripped up his cupola in Moray Place, destroying more than half of the glass.

His son, Alexander, succeeded to the house after retiring as a surgeon-general in the Bengal Army. Sir Robert's twin brother Alexander retired to *32 Moray Place* in 1874, dying later that year, after being minister of Foulden parish in the Borders for many years. Of his seven sons, one died in infancy, one at sea and four in Australia and one was killed by pirates in China.

for Sprot, see *no. 33*

Number 41

William Forbes Mackenzie of Portmore, was at no. 41 from 1831 to 1835. The son of a Deputy Keeper of the Signet, he was an advocate who was later MP for Peeblesshire for fifteen years. He was known as the author of the (Forbes Mackenzie) Act of 1853 which provided for the closing of public-houses on Sundays and at 10 p.m. on weekdays.

The Misses Margaret, Anna and Catherine Weir kept a boarding school at no. 41 from 1835 to 1850, having six resident girl pupils at the 1841 census. They and their mother (widow of a Leith merchant) had previously had boarding schools in Northumberland Street and Hillside Crescent respectively. They probably combined these schools at *40 Moray Place* in 1832 before the daughters moved next door. Possibly Miss E. Weir who had a boarding school from 1846 for two years at *no. 33* was another sister.

William Thomas Thomson was the manager of Standard Life Assurance and of Colonial Life Assurance, both at 3 George Street, when he was elected first chairman of the Faculty of Actuaries, established in 1856. A year later he and his wife moved into 41 Moray Place, where they lived for nine years. He was 'a man of enthusiastic temper and of considerable mental capacity.' He held decided opinions and replied to a letter from a colleague, 'I shall not enter upon your general arguments as I would require to do so at considerable length to show that they are in many respects fallacious and for this I cannot at present afford the time.' The office of Chairman was redesigned President, and his son E. C. Thomson succeeded him in that role.

The publisher Thomas Boyd (1818–1902), senior partner of Oliver and Boyd, moved in 1867 from 11 Regent Terrace to 41 Moray Place, where he died in 1902. He was three times Master of the Merchant Company and was responsible for educational reforms, converting four 'hospitals' or orphanages into Merchant Company day schools. His scheme was used as a model by the English endowed schools commissioners.

Thomas Boyd was Lord Provost for five years from 1877 and chaired the committee which raised £320,000 for a new Royal Infirmary, which soon became the largest and best equipped hospital in Europe. The 240 patients were brought by cabs and other conveyances from the old Infirmary in Infirmary Street to Lauriston Place in 1879.

Thomas Boyd was knighted by Queen Victoria in 1881 on the occasion of the 'Wet Review' of Scottish Volunteers in the Queen's Park. From 1882 he was Chairman of the Fishery Board for Scotland for two five-year periods. To help her with her large family (three sons and six daughters) his wife had eight resident servants at the 1881 census.

Moray Place

Professor Sir Robert Christison

Archibald Bryce

43

Number 42

for Grove, 1861, see *7 Doune Terrace*

Dr Hamilton Bryce (1824–1904) and his wife came to live at no. 42 in 1867, and remained there for thirty years. They had six children, five boys (including a pair of twins) and a girl.

Dr Bryce had established the Edinburgh Collegiate School in 1867 at 27 and 28 Charlotte Square. He had previously been a classics teacher for 16 years at the Royal High School, where he considered that the classes, of up to 150 boys, were too large. He founded his school with classes limited to thirty, trained boys how to learn by themselves and provided lessons in modern languages and natural science as well as classics.

Dr Bryce used English, rather than Latin or Greek, as the basis for a good education. At his school, daily public readings of works by English authors were important, as were poetry recitations and a debating society. He provided a laboratory, a gymnasium, a playground and a cricket field. There were clubs for football, cricket, bicycling and golf, with particular emphasis on golf.

In 1871, Dr and Mrs Bryce had thirteen boys as boarders, aged 11 to 16. Eight years later the boarders moved to *1 Doune Terrace*.

The Principal of the University was a member of the school's honorary committee. Many boys did so well that they were able to by-pass a university education and go straight into the Indian Civil Service, Woolwich Royal Academy or the Royal Military Academy. Dr Bryce opened a preparatory department in 1878 at Viewpark in Bruntsfield.

Forres Street enters here

Number 43

This was the home for two years from 1891 of the Misses Manuel and the Misses Bartholomew, milliners and dressmakers.

Number 44

for Hope, 1832 to 1834, see *no. 12*
for Adam, 1865 to 1870, see *no. 34*

Number 45

Miss Eliza Banks had a ladies' school here from 1837 for ten years, with two resident teachers and seven girl boarders.

Number 46

James Skene of Rubislaw (1775–1864) lived at no. 46 for five years from 1832. He had earlier practised at the Scottish Bar: there he had been a close friend of Sir Walter Scott. A keen horseman, he became a cornet of the Edinburgh Light Horse in 1797, a regiment largely organised by Walter Scott. He abandoned his legal career to concentrate on drawing and painting. Scott described him as 'for a gentleman, the best draughtsman I ever saw.'

For some years, Skene was curator of the library and museum of the Royal Society of Edinburgh. He made his first sketches, as a child, with whiting on a cellar door in Riddell's Court, after his widowed mother had moved to Edinburgh with her seven children. Later, he executed over 200 sketches and watercolours, recording many buildings in Edinburgh's Old Town and the beginnings of the New Town. In 1838 he and his wife moved to Greece, to be near two of their children and he produced hundreds of sketches in the Greek islands. Coming from a well-off family he could afford to travel extensively.

Shortly before the Skenes moved to Moray Place from Princes Street, their daughter Felicia, aged eleven, and her sister used to welcome in their home the young Duc de Bordeaux (grandson of Charles X of France, in exile at Holyrood) and his sister Louise. They also visited the royal children in the Palace of Holyroodhouse where, one evening, they played a game in which they had to illustrate the word 'courtship'. Felicia drew a ship with a huge flag which she decorated with imaginary flowers. The French exiles were enchanted, for they said she'd drawn fleur-de-lis, although she said she had never heard of such a flower.

During their last two years in Moray Place, the so-called Earl of Stirling lived with the Skenes, before moving to Carlton Terrace. From that address he stood trial for, and was found guilty of, pretending to be the Earl of Stirling by means of forged documents.

From 1824 he had styled himself Earl of Stirling, alleging that his mother was the great-granddaughter of the fourth son of the first earl, and he voted at elections of Scottish peers.

Claiming to be Hereditary Lieutenant and Lord Proprietor of the Province of Nova Scotia, he offered for sale one million acres of 'most excellent land' in New Brunswick and created his friend and adviser Thomas Banks a baronet. He must have been a colourful character during his short stay in Edinburgh, before departing ignominiously to die in America (see Mitchell: *The People of Calton Hill* for further detail).

The Scottish Institution boarding house for 24 to 28 girls aged 10 to 15 was at no. 46 from 1837 to 1857, under the supervision of Miss Margaret Murray, and later at Ainslie House. A few boarders were accommodated by Miss Helen Johnson at *12 Moray Place* from 1865 for four years.

Mrs Margaret Mackichan, a widow, had a boarding school at no. 46 from 1867 to 1876 with two resident teachers and twelve schoolgirls as well as two middle-aged ladies of independent means as boarders in 1871.

In 1876, John McLaren, son of a former Lord Provost and MP for Edinburgh, brought his German wife Ottilie to no. 46, where they brought up three daughters and three sons. He had lived nearby in rooms in *Darnaway Street* after being called to the Bar in 1856. He became Lord Advocate and, briefly, Liberal MP for Wigtown in 1880. In the next year he was elected MP for Edinburgh in place of his father who stood down. Almost immediately, and very reluctantly, he accepted a place on the bench where he remained for thirty years. He used to drive up to Parliament Square in his stately red-upholstered landau and pair.

Lord McLaren had nearly died from a chill at the age of twelve and was then too weak to go to school. He studied at home and especially with his father who was involved in the free trade movement and who married, as his third wife, a sister of John and Jacob Bright, both MPs. In 1868 Lord McLaren published *The Law of Scotland Relating to Wills*. In spite of his poor health he completed this treatise by sitting up the whole of every alternate night. He later studied astronomy and was President of the Scottish Meteorological Society. His daughter Ottilie became a sculptor and her bust of Lord Young was placed in Parliament House. His sister, Dr Agnes McLaren (1831–1913) was one of the first women doctors and a suffragette.

Number 47

Members of the Moncreiff family arrived at no. 47 in 1825. Sir James Wellwood Moncreiff, 9th baronet (1776–1851), had previously lived in Northumberland Street. As Lord Moncreiff he became a distinguished judge who, throughout his life, was active in Whig politics. Lord Cockburn wrote of him, 'I am not aware how his moral nature could have been improved. A truer friend, a more upright judge, or a more affectionate man could not be.' On the other hand, Omond's *Lord Advocates of Scotland* gave a different picture of him saying that, at the end of his life, he sat on the bench 'with a frosty look on his face, as if he did not wish to hold much intercourse with his fellows.'

Among Sir James's five sons and three daughters, the Rev. Henry Wellwood Moncreiff (1810–1883), later 10th baronet, lived in the family house until his father's death in 1851: he became Moderator of the Free Church General Assembly in 1861. From 1854 to 1869 the house was occupied, probably as a tenant, by George Young, an advocate who later, as Lord Advocate, lived at *no. 28* for many years.

William Moncreiff (1813–1895), yet another son of Sir James, returned in 1870 to his family home at no. 47 where he lived until his death. He was a Chartered Accountant (see also *15 Great Stuart Street*).

for Young, 1854 to 1869, see *no. 28*

Number 48

Daniel Ainslie came here as a 42 year old widower in 1849, having retired as an East Indian merchant. His mother, his two unmarried sisters and his son and daughter (with their governess) were with him. The family always had six resident servants, one being a coachman John Bathgate who was there for four consecutive censuses from 1851 to 1881. At various times, the Ainslies also had a livery servant, a groom, a butler, a footman or a page. Daniel Ainslie died here in 1890.

Number 49

for Coventry, 1830 to 1847, see *no. 28*
for Hunter, from 1884, see *no. 14*

Number 50

for Horn, 1837 to 1847, see *7 Randolph Crescent*
for MacWhirter, 1853 to 1857, see *4 Ainslie Place*
for Henderson, 1857 to 1860, see *19 Ainslie Place*

CENSUS RETURNS

Twenty householders (including fourteen women) described themselves as independent in 1841; otherwise the law was in a majority of those giving professions, with four judges, five advocates and seven solicitors. By 1851 sixteen (including nine women) were landed proprietors or annuitants, with two judges, three advocates, twelve solicitors and miscellaneous occupations such as church, civil engineer, East India Company and teacher. The pattern continued much the same, except that the number of solicitors decreased to three in 1871 and 1881 and the number of advocates steadily increased to six. About a quarter of all the householders were in the legal profession for the rest of the century.

The number of people living in Moray Place at the census dates increased from 444 in 1841 to 537 in 1871, and then decreased to 383 in 1891.

Children

There were 81 children under sixteen in 1841, boarders of the Scottish Institution accounting for seventeen of them.

The census with the greatest number of children was in 1871, when there were 108, mainly because of two houses being used for school boarders for the Edinburgh Institution and the Edinburgh Collegiate School.

Some families were very large. George Lloyd, giving his occupation as 'independent', had twelve children with one born practically every year, and nine servants – and yet they lived at *no. 25* in 1841 for only one year. Also in 1841, at one of the two households of *no. 18*, Alexander Gowan SSC had eight very young children, including twins aged one and a baby of one month, and eight resident servants. At the same time, there were two pairs of twins in the young family of John Horsley, of the East India

Company, at *no. 21*.

The number of children in Moray Place dropped to only 25 in 1891, when three-quarters of the households were childless. Even so, the garden in the centre of Moray Place must have provided a popular meeting place for these children and their twelve nurses.

Governesses

When the first families came to Moray Place, they could send their sons to the Royal High School, the Edinburgh Academy (opened in 1824) or the Naval and Military Academy in Lothian Road. Education for girls was not yet thought to be desirable, apart from such subjects as music and drawing. Girls were often taught at home. There were only two governesses in Moray Place in 1841, but there were seven at each of the next three censuses. Probably some families would have shared a governess, with children going to a neighbour's house for their lessons. Governesses often came from overseas; their places of birth included Switzerland, France, Germany and New Zealand. The occupation of governess was an acceptable one for a young lady, but could also be a lonely one, for she was not a member of the family circle, nor was she a servant.

Resident Servants

While many households had no young children, all had servants. At each of the six censuses the houses had an average of five resident servants each, the total numbers ranging from 219 in 1841 to 264 in 1871. The number of servants in any one house varied from one to twelve.

At every census, most households had a housekeeper or a cook or – occasionally – both, and also at least one housemaid. Families with small children had a nurse with or without a nursery maid. Additionally, lady's maids, laundry maids (or laundresses) and kitchen maids were frequently to be found. Lady's maids were sometimes foreign, coming from France, Germany or Switzerland. The number of table maids gradually increased from three to 18. Over the years, there was an occasional sick nurse, door maid (in 1891), stillrooom maid (in 1871), scullery maid (1881 and 1891) and sewing maid (1871 and 1881).

In 1841 there were 35 resident male servants, reducing to 18 in

1891. Male servants were usually butlers or footmen; there were also from two to four pages at each census. Rather surprisingly, at each census there were two or three families with a resident coachman, and one or two had grooms. The terms of Lord Moray's feu forbade the building of any stables attached to the houses. Carriages or horses would have been stabled a short distance away, in mews properties with living accommodation above them. The wives and daughters of coachmen living in the mews might well have worked as non-resident servants in Moray Place houses.

Moray Place Householders

1.
1827 Col. Anstruther (& James, WS)
1832 Charles Baillie, advocate
1836 Mrs Cathcart
1841 Lady Christian Douglas
1844 Mrs H. Baxter
1846 Mrs Elizabeth Baxter; Samuel Laing
1847 Mrs Fleming
1849 Lt. Col. Bruce
1856 Dr William Graham
1872 Maj. Gen. Kirkland
1875 Miss Borthwick
1877 & Miss Nicholson
1879 Maj. Gen. Charles Irvine, Indian Army

2.
1826 Donald & Alexander Smith, bankers
1827 & David Smith, banker, to 1832
1832 & William Smith, banker
1837 Mrs Hastie & John Hastie
1843 Capt. William Balfour RN
1860 Adolph Robinow
1867 R. B. Blackburn, advocate
1877 Alexander S Kinnear, advocate
1878 & Mrs Robert Lockhart

3.
1825 Duncan Campbell of Barcaldine
1830 Patrick Orr WS
1835 Sir Duncan Campbell of Barcaldine
1838 Robert R Bell, advocate; Benjamin R Bell, advocate; James Moncreiff, advocate
1842 Mrs Gordon
1848 Archibald Young, advocate; William Young WS
1857 Lord Deas

1863 R. W. Thomson
1873 Arthur Alison, advocate
1896 & R. B. Alison WS; A. J. Alison, advocate

4.
1832 Mrs Col. Fraser
1835 Charles Brownlow esq.
1836 Lt. D. Bremner; Gidion Needham esq.
1837 Daniel McPhail, lodging keeper; George Gillanders WS; Roderick McKenzie esq. of Flowerburn
1841 James H. Burnett WS
1856 Sir James H. Burnett of Leys
1861 James Boyd
1893 Robert Stewart
1899 Harry Cheyne WS

5.
1826 Thomas J. Fordyce esq. of Ayton
1837 John Douglas esq.
1841 Mrs Gordon
1843 Mrs Douglas
1847 Col. Sir Ord Honeyman, Bt.
1851–56 Thomas DuBoulay
1861 Mrs Douglas
1862 Sir David Baxter of Kilmaron
1884 James D. Lawrie, stockbroker

6.
1826 John Learmonth of Dean, Lord Provost
1860 Capt. George Sinclair
1863 John Middleton
1868 R. C. Williamson
1892 Mrs R. C. Williamson; A. C. Williamson, advocate

7.
1825 Alexander Monypenny WS
1829 & James Dalgleish WS
1845 Miss Monypenny
1851 Thomas Brown
1860 W. T. Monypenny of Ardit
1874 Mrs Austin
1888 & Robert D. J. Mein Austin

8.
1827 George Wauchope esq.
1851 Mrs Bewicke
1853 Mrs George Wauchope
1863 Patrick Fraser, advocate

9.
1827 Mrs Fairlie
1833 Rev. R. H. Brandling
1841 Scottish Institution
1872 William W. Gibson
1875 William Ross CA
1881 George Readman, advocate

10.
1826 James W. Hunter esq. of Thurston
1842 A. Campbell esq., Blythswood
1847 James W. Hunter
1854 Hon. Lord Handyside
1859 Mrs Handyside; & Miss Bruce & Hugh
Bruce, advocate
1867 Maj. Gen. Frederick W. Hamilton
1868 John Buchanan
1881 Mrs Buchanan; Thomas Ryburn
Buchanan MP; John Young Buchanan
1900 Sir Kenneth Mackenzie, Bt.; King's &
Ld. Treasurer's Remembrancer

11.
1828 Robert Wardlaw Ramsay esq. of
Tillicoultry & Whitehill
1837 Lady Ann Wardlaw Ramsay
1839 George Dickson esq.
1844 Mrs Buchanan of Auchintorslie
1851 Mr Robertson, civil engineer
1854 Alexander Crombie of Thornton
1861 H. Fox Talbot, photographer
1862 John B. Innes, WS
1890 H. M. Horsburgh, CA
1892 David A. Paterson

12.
1826 John Hope, Solicitor-General for
Scotland
1832 Charles Hope, Lord President, Court of

Session
1860 Mrs Stein
1865 Miss Helen M. Johnson
1869 Robert M. Ferguson, Ph.D.,
1892 Miss Melville; George F. Melville

13.
1825 John Bonar, younger, of Kimmerghame
1829 James Hunt esq. of Pittencrieff
1861 Lady Elizabeth Moore; John Middleton
1865 Sir Alexander C. G. Maitland, Bt. MP
1871 John Fraser
1887 Sir John Don Wauchope
1889 T. Oliver Fraser & Mrs John Fraser
1891 Alexander Lawson
1896 Robert Cross

14.
1826 John Binny esq. of Forneth
1842 George Mercer esq. of Gorthy
1865 Hon. Lord Ormidale
1879 & George L. Macfarlane, advocate
1892 Andrew Jameson, KC
1894 & John Gordon Jameson, advocate

15.
1825 David Carnegy esq. of Craig
1835 Patrick Orr WS
1840 Sir G. MacPherson-Grant Bt.
1847 Dowager Lady M. Grant
1856 James Matthew Hill
1862 William Younger
1868 Andrew Williamson

16.
1825 William Robertson
1856 Hon. Mrs Mackenzie
1879 Miss Mackenzie

17.
1826 Charles Scott esq.
1842 & Mrs Scott
1848 David Cowan WS
1866 Alexander Howe WS

18.
1827–40 Misses Smith
1828–31 Charles Macbean, lodgings
1828–33 Miss Young, boarding school
1832–33 William R. Henderson esq.
1833–36 John Anderson WS
1833–36 John Sinclair, British Linen Bank
1836–41 J. B. Shand
1836–42 John Gowan, solicitor

1836–40 Thomas Lindsay, wright
1840–42 Mrs Monteith
1841–43 Alexander Hill, bookseller
1842–46 Alexander Gowan, solicitor
1843–50 James Brown esq.
1843–44 J. B. Gracie WS
1846–62 Mrs Irvine, lodging keeper
1850–62 John McCandlish WS
1851–65 John Melrose
1862–65 Mrs Stewart
1862–80 Miss MacGregor
1863–64 J. Alexander
1865–73 E. R. Aitchison, accountant
1866–67 James McKenzie
1868–70 George Yule, waiter, lodging keeper
1869–71 John Macdougall Gibson, advocate
1871–73 Charles A. Millie, advocate
1872–74 Thomas Armstrong, teacher
1873–76 George Beatson
1874–77 P. Devine, photographer
1874–95 Miss Drummond, dressmaker
(no. 18a from 1884)
1876–   David Henderson, & D. Henderson
junior
1886–96 T. Smith
1896–99 E. M. Montague
1897–99 Charles Hunter Stewart, MB, D.Sc.
1899–   James Watt, WS
1899–   Mrs Bayne

19.
1828 Mrs William Russell; George Hill,
solicitor
1835 Hugh Bremner WS; David Whigham WS
1837 Alexander Hill, bookseller
1837 David Octavius Hill
1843 -
1862 (with no. 20) Windsor Hotel
1873 -
1892 William Murray, advocate
1898 George Tod
1899 & Mrs MacWatt

20.
1828 James Stuart of Duncarn
1830 Falconer's Hotel
1833 Rev. Dr John Lee
1834 John Hope of Granton
1859 Windsor Hotel
1878 Karl Froebel
1895 Mrs Strethill Wright
1895 James B. Readman D.Sc.

21.
1833 Capt. James Carnegie
1836 Mrs Gillespie of Kirkton
1841 Mrs John Horsley
1846 James Kinnear WS
1852 Francis Brown Douglas, advocate

22.
1826 Francis Walker Drummond of
Hawthornden
1832 Mrs Henry Mackenzie; James Mackenzie
WS
1837 Hon. Lord Cunninghame
1840 Sir Francis Walker Drummond Bt
1844 J. B. Gracie WS
1846 A. Alison of Blair Castle
1849 Hon. Bouverie Francis Primrose
1899 Charles Scott Dickson QC MP

23.
1825 Mrs Ogilvy Fotheringham; Frederick
Fotheringham jun.; WS Col. Thomas Ogilvy
Fotheringham
1838 W. F. Lindsay Carnegie esq.
1840 Hon. Lord Cunninghame
1852 John Cunninghame of Duloch
1878 Sir Archibald Campbell Bt, advocate

24.
1824 Sir Patrick Murray of Ochtertyre
1827 Francis Jeffrey, Lord Advocate
1850 Lady Agnew
1858 David Anderson of Moredun
1882 The Misses Anderson
1887 David B. Wauchope
1896 & D. A. Wauchope

25.
1825 John Aytoun esq. of Inchdairney
1841 George Lloyd esq.
1844 Mrs Blackburn, senior of Killearn
1846 Mrs Horsley
1847 Francis Abbott
1894 P. W. Campbell WS

26.
1825 Mrs Oswald; Lt. Col. Oswald of
Dunnikier
1848 John C. Brodie WS
1868 William Stuart Walker of Bowland
1872 John Clerk Brodie WS
1889 J. Sharp Callender, merchant

27.
1825 Sir John Erskine
1828 Miss Whyte Melville
1877 Misses Jackson
1878 John Trayner, advocate

28.
1825 Earl of Moray
1833–43 Andrew Coventry, advocate
1834 & Mrs Dr Coventry
1856 Mrs Maitland-Makgill-Crichton (no. 28b)
1869 George Young QC MP
1895 & Charles Young WS & Edward Young WS

28a.
1838 Mrs Playfair of Dalmarnock
1856 Misses Playfair
1864 W. J. Sands WS

29.
1826 Lt. Gen. John Cunningham(e)
1843 Andrew Coventry, advocate
1878 Mrs Maitland-Makgill-Crichton
1892 William Younger

30.
1825 C. D. Riddell, advocate
1838 Mrs Murray Allan of Havering
1840 C. D. Riddle esq.
1843 Alex. Cunninghame of Balgounie
1844 J. R. Tod WS
1857 Mrs Forrester, lodging keeper
1872 Robert Girdwood
1887 J. Comrie Thomson, advocate
1899 Thomas McKie, advocate

31.
1825 Prof. Thomas C. Hope; James Hope WS; John Hope WS
1894 Hope Trust; also, from 1886, David Campbell SSC

32.
1826 Mrs James Walker senior of Dalry
1838 Miss Hamilton
1846 John Anderson WS
1858 & Finlay Anderson EIC
1872 Mrs Johnston
1874 Rev. Alexander Christison
1884 James Brown

33.
1832 Sir James Miles Riddell, Bt.
1841 Mrs Sprot of Clapham
1846 Miss E. Weir, boarding school
1848 Duchess of Gordon
1849 Lord Fullerton
1854 Misses Abercrombie
1859 John Macnair, brewer
1892 Henry Johnston QC

34.
1826 Hugh Cowan; John Russel CS
1829 Hon. Baron Hume
1840 Miss Hume of Ninewells & Miss Agnes Hume
1848 Miss Campbell & Miss Mary Campbell
1851 Misses Swinton
1853 Mrs Sprot
1855 James Douglas of Cavers
1865 Mrs Russell of Blackbraes
1873 George Bliss MacQueen
1879 William Watson MP, Lord Advocate
1883 Hon. Lord Adam

35.
1832 Mrs Drummond, lodging keeper; John Alison WS; Peter Wilson WS; Robert Handyside, advocate
1834 Miss Lang
1846 Sir Charles Hastings
1850 Miss Taylor; Mrs Lancaster
1855 William Moir, lodging keeper
1863 F. L. M. Heriot, advocate; Mrs Heriot senior of Ramornie
1871 Miss Robertson, lodging keeper
1877 Alexander Blair, advocate

36.
1828 Sir Patrick Murray of Ochtertyre
1830 Mrs Fleming; John F. Stoddart, advocate
1838 Miss Purves
1847 C. F. Shand, advocate
1852 Mrs Bethune
1859 Scottish University Commission
1861 Thomas Saltern
1863 Mrs General Pitman
1871 Alexander Wood MD, FRCP
1875 W. J. Laidlay, advocate
1879 Alexander Ure, advocate
1886 George Dods MB, LRCSE
1889 John S. Pitman WS
1894 Miss Boswell

37.
1830 Mrs Col. Maitland
1832 Mrs Burnly
1833 Miss Benson
1838 David Manson SSC
1842 Mrs Joseph Lacon
1846 Prof. John Goodsir
1847 J. Thomson of Gogar Burn
1848 Thomas Thomson WS
1851 Rev. Dr Hanna
1852 Capt. James Thomson of Glendouran
1877 R. R. Mitford
1878 Richard V. Campbell, advocate

38.
1831 Lt. Col. Lord Robert Kerr
1844 Mrs Anderson
1850 John Gibson junior, WS; H. George
      Gibson WS
1868 Mrs Collins

39.
1828 Mrs Bruce of Kennet; Hugh Bruce,
      advocate; William Bruce, wine merchant
1859 Mrs Admiral Douglas
1861 John Kirkpatrick, advocate

40.
1832 Mrs Robert Weir
1837 lodgings
1841 Misses Harriman
1843 George McKillop
1846 Mrs Sprot
1847 Prof. Robert Christison
1862 & David Christison, MD
1867 & John Christison WS
1886 Sir Alexander Christison Bt

41.
1831 William Forbes Mackenzie of Portmore;
      James Hay Mackenzie WS
1835 Misses Weir, boarding school
1851 D. J. S. Thorburn
1857 William Thomas Thomson, actuary
1867 Thomas Jamieson Boyd
1903 Sir James Guthrie PRSA

42.
1832 James Anstruther WS
1861 Francis Grove RN; Miss Somerville
1868 A. Hamilton Bryce
1880 & G. Ferguson Bryce WS
1887 & George Hamilton Bryce (to 1889)
1898 William Bain, British Linen Bank

43.
1828 Miss Taylor
1831 Alexander Munro Binning WS; George
      Munro Binning, advocate
1836 William Dyce esq.
1838 Mrs General Farquharson
1846 Misses Skelton
1851 Mrs James H. Bell
1852 F. W. L. Gordon
1855 Charles Wilson MD, FRCPE
1858 & J. Dove Wilson, advocate
1864 Rev. E. Burch Field of Moreland; James
      Hamilton Field
1879 R. W. Campbell
1888 C. C. Nisbet WS
1891 Misses Manuel; Misses Bartholomew
1897 John H. Tait, advocate; A. H. M.
      Jamieson, advocate

44.
1826 D. S. Threshie WS
1832 John Hope, Dean of Faculty
1838 Mrs Taylor
1841 Mrs General Durham
1850 Mrs Thomas Bruce
1851 -
1859 C. Tennant Couper, advocate
1862 Miss Chiene
1865 James Adam; A. Cowan Scott, teacher of
      music
1867 & William Inglis, advocate
1870 Mrs Elder
1873 -
1878 Miss Burdon Sanderson
1881 G. P. de Martin, Director, Foreign
      Language Institute
1885 David Paulin, Scottish Life Assurance
1892 Mrs G. G. Mackay
1893 James Hutcheson, MD, FRCS; Miss Hall

45.
1829 Roderick McLeod of Cadboll
1833 Misses (or Mrs?) Cruikshanks
1837 Miss Banks
1847 Alexander Dunlop
1855 Mrs David Boyd
1857 John Hill
1858 George A. Haig
1862 John Holt Skinner
1871 Alexander H. Lee
1876 Andrew Wylie of Prinlaws
1879 Colin G. Macrae WS (Knighted 1900)

46.
1832 James Skene of Rubislaw; William F. Skene WS; George Skene, advocate
1835 & Earl of Stirling
1837 Miss Murray
1858 Robert Stewart of Carfin
1867 Mrs Mackichan, boarding school
1876 John McLaren, advocate

47.
1825 James Moncreiff, advocate; William Moncreiff, accountant
1854 George Young, advocate (later MP)
1870 William Moncreiff, CA

48.
1830 J. Corse Scott esq. of Sinton
1849 Daniel Ainslie
1890 Mrs Swinton
1894 John Erskine Guild WS; Robert Harrower Guild, stockbroker
1899 Miss Ella Brickmann; Miss Snow

49.
1829 William Redfern
1830 Rev. George Coventry of Shanwell
1844 Mrs H. Gordon
1847 James Buchanan
1884 James Hunter

50.
1832 Thomas Hutchins, surgeon-dentist
1837 Robert Horn, advocate
1847 Miss Cantly
1851 A. K. Mackenzie
1853 Dr Macwhirter
1857 Prof. William Henderson
1860 Mrs Jane H. Thomson; Miss Isabella E. Lee
1867 & A. H. Lee
1869 Lt. Col. J. Shearman
1871 Mrs Thomson & Miss Lee
1900 Maj. Gen. Sir Robert Murdoch Smith

Doune Terrace

The heir to the earldom of Moray takes the courtesy title of Lord Doune: hence the name of Doune Terrace. The Terrace is to the north of Moray Place, overlooking the residents' 'pleasure ground'. It has only ten houses, *number 10*, at the west end, being detached from the others, and built underneath the back of *18 Moray Place*.

Number 1

Robert Chambers (1802–1871), writer and publisher, came to no. 1 from Ann Street in 1846, with his wife Annie and several children (they eventually had eight daughters and three sons, three others having died in infancy).

Robert, like some of his siblings, was born with six fingers on each hand and six toes on each foot. A surgeon 'reputed to be a man of skill' cut off the upper joint of the extra toes 'in the most cruel and unprofessional-like manner, by means of a pair of scissors'. It was not surprising that Robert could never find shoes to fit.

He had always been fascinated by books. At the age of ten he discovered his father's *Encyclopaedia Britannica* in a chest in the attic, and it was 'what the gift of a whole toy-shop would have been to most children'. At the age of sixteen he set up a bookstall in Leith Walk, stocked with his old school books, as well as some books from his father and some pocket Bibles. He did well enough to move up to India Place and then Hanover Street and he also began to write. Sir Walter Scott was impressed by the first edition of Robert's *Traditions of Edinburgh* in 1823 and 'wondered where the boy gets all his information'.

Robert was closely associated with his brother William in the publication of *Chambers' Journal* from 1832, with the aim that 'every Saturday, when the poorest labourer … draws his humble earnings, he shall have it in his power to purchase … a meal of healthful, useful and agreeable mental instruction,' giving cheap access to literature. At first the *Journal* consisted of two pages, costing a penny halfpenny. The circulation quickly rose to 50,000 and, by 1844, to 84,000. The *Journal* continued for well over a hundred years, ceasing publication in 1956. William Chambers was Lord Provost of

The family of Robert Chambers, *c.***1844.**

James (3), Amelia (6), Anne (9), Mary (11), with William (1), Anne Chambers (wife), Janet and Eliza (8) and Nina (14). Robert, the eldest son, is missing, presumably away at school. Three children had already died in infancy. Phoebe and Alice were yet to be born.

Edinburgh from 1865 to 1869.

In 1844, fifteen years before Darwin published his *Origin of the Species*, Robert Chambers published *Vestiges of the Natural History of Creation*, keeping his authorship secret to avoid awkward questions of politics and theology.

Before coming to Doune Terrace, Robert Chambers had already published thirty books. He also played the flute and his wife was 'born with music in her' (John Lehmann: *Ancestors and Friends*) and played the harp. All of their daughters were musical: Amelia composed songs, Nina was a brilliant pianist and the twins Jenny and Lizzie danced while Mary sat drawing.

Robert and Annie frequently entertained visitors. After visits from Sir Edward Bulwer Lytton or Sir James Young Simpson, the children might be found either hypnotised into trance-like attitudes or halfway up the curtains, or unconscious on the floor with chloroform-soaked handkerchiefs over their mouths. Thomas De Quincey often spent Sunday evenings at 1 Doune Terrace and kept a pair of 'wonderfully small and neat' wellington boots there. This was in case he could not return to his lodgings within the Sanctuary of Holyrood, because of fear of debt collectors.

The menu at a 5 p.m. dinner party given by Robert Chambers in honour of the poet George Outram consisted of hotch potch, cockie leekie, crappit heads (stuffed haddock), salmon, scallops, haggis, poor man o'mutton and several sweets including 'strawberries and cream, in soup plates'.

R. C. Lehmann (Robert Chambers' grandson) recorded stories of family life in the Chambers household in *Memories of Half a Century*. In it, Mary recalled her twentieth birthday in 1855: 'None of them gave me a present (although I gave them all due warning some days before so that they might have sufficient time to prepare the presents) except Mamma and Annie. Mamma gave me a pair of scissors, a thimble, a lovely coral stud for my neck, and a beautiful ring. Annie gave me a very pretty jug, Bob gave me his blessing (wretch!) and Pa gave me a long lecture on the Dean Bridge.'

Nina married Frederick Lehmann, whose brother Rudolf married her sister Amelia. Nina visited her parents in 1858 and wrote 'Papa is quite fidgety in the mornings till I bring down the boys (aged two and a half and seven months)... You should have seen us at breakfast, Papa with Randy on his knee getting bits of egg, sups of tea and crumbs of roll.' Two years later, Nina told of a visitor, Miss

Y, whose false teeth (a double set of 28 teeth) were found under her chair after she had gone. They were put on the mantel piece and decently covered with *The Scotsman* but exposed to view whenever a member of the family took down the newspaper to read it.

Another daughter, Eliza, who married Robert Priestley (later, knighted and MP), wrote *The Story of a Life-Time;* in this she described going to Dr Graham's school over a shop in Queen Street and then to his Institution in *Moray Place,* 'just round the corner of our Terrace, which was so exposed to the winds of heaven that we were often in winter battened up against the area railings in speeding along to our classes.'

When living briefly in London after 1861, Robert Chambers was asked why he rented pews at two different churches. He replied, 'because when I am not in the one, it will always be concluded by the charitable that I am in the other.' He retired to St Andrews and died there in 1871.

A boarding department of the Edinburgh Collegiate School in Charlotte Square was opened in 1879 at no. 1. The Rector, Dr Bryce (who lived at *42 Moray Place*), appointed Mr E. Johnston Smith MA to be in charge. Mr and Mrs Smith came from Chalmers Street and had previously had boarders living with them. They came to Doune Terrace with four very young sons of their own as well as ten boys as boarders. They left in 1888.

Frank Hardy, a young schoolmaster of the Edinburgh Academy, lived at no. 1 with his sister, both being unmarried, from 1891 for three years. They took in as boarders one schoolmaster and four boys aged nine to eighteen. Hardy was universally known as 'Twank' because someone in his family had been unable to pronounce 'Frank'. He taught classics, history and English literature at the Academy for 42 years and was an official housemaster from 1895, first in Buckingham Terrace and soon afterwards in a new house in Kinnear Road. Before the First World War he taught many boys horse riding: he also enjoyed reminiscing about his visits to Canadian cattle ranches and would demonstrate, in the classroom, how to rope a steer using his master's high stool as the target (Magnusson).

for Ker, 1888, see *no. 10*

A fishmonger of Castle Street, John Anderson, brought his family to live at 1 Doune Terrace in 1894. If the Andersons were away from home, a friend of their cook used to come from her home in nearby St Stephen Street to have a bath.

Number 2

for Kinnear, 1838 to 1841 and for Gordon, 1847 to 1853, see *no. 9*

Robert Romanes and his wife lived at no. 2 for only three years from 1854. He was the son of James Romanes, silk mercer and tartan manufacturer to Queen Victoria, who did much to popularise the wearing of tartan. Neither Robert nor his brother carried on the family business which is still in Princes Street. At his death in Peebles, Robert's occupation was given as 'gentleman': more usual then, than now, as an occupation.

A few houses were used as educational establishments. Miss Elizabeth Somerville was the proprietor of a boarding school for young ladies at no. 2 for four years from 1857. At the 1861 census there were two resident governesses (one music teacher and one French teacher) and ten girls aged thirteen to eighteen.

Number 3

David Smith WS, who had lived at *2 Moray Place* from 1826 with three of his brothers, moved in 1832 to 3 Doune Terrace, where he also had his office in partnership with James Kinnear WS, whose home was at *no. 9*. The house was crowded, as David Smith's mother and his sisters Ann, Marion (Menie) and Euphemia (Phemie) and brother Tom all lived with him. Six other brothers, bankers and merchants, lived elsewhere in Edinburgh. Having married in his late thirties, David Smith moved to *2 Ainslie Place* in 1846, remaining there for twelve years.

Tom Smith used to take George, the eldest of James Kinnear's children (see *no. 9*), to his attic bedroom at no. 3 to snap a pair of flintlock horse pistols. Tom later sailed for China and was never heard of again: it was suspected that the ship was taken by Chinese pirates, because his signet ring was recovered in a Chinese port.

for Balfour-Kinnear, from 1887, see *no. 9*

LIST OF THE WINES
OF MESSRS. J. COCKBURN & CAMPBELL, EDINBURGH,
Sold by their Agent, Mr. J. C. Miller,
No. 16, Riding House Lane, Langham Place, London,

WHO, AT THE ANNEXED PRICES, DELIVER THEIR WINES AT ANY PLACE IN ENGLAND TO WHICH THERE ARE PUBLIC
CONVEYANCES, TAKING ON THEMSELVES EVERY RISK AND EXPENSE.

	Price ♥ doz. when bought in large quantities, bottles included.	Price ♥ doz. when bought in small quantities, bottles included.			Price ♥ doz. when bought in large quantities, bottles included.	Price ♥ doz. when bought in small quantities, bottles included.
French Claret		45s.	**Spanish** Sherry		36/	38s.
Ditto, 1825	60/	64s.	Ditto		41/	45s.
Ditto, 1825	72/	76s.	Ditto		49/	53s.
Ditto, 1825	84/6	90s.	Ditto, East India, very Old			70s.
Hermitage, Red		90s.	Paxarete, pints			43s.
Ditto, White		90s.	Mountain, pints			38s.
Coté Roti		90s.	**Md.** Madeira, East India	64/		68s.
Champagne, Red and White		87s.	Ditto, West India	54/		58s.
Ditto, Sillery		87s.	Hock			64s.
Sauterne, Barsac, and Grave		63s.	**Rhenish** Ditto			90s.
Frontignan, pints		40s.	Moselle			56s.
Portugal Port, newly Bottled	36/8	40s.	Musbach (Palatine Wine)			45s.
Ditto, Old Bottled	43/	45s.	Marsala	26/		28s.
Ditto, ditto	48/	50s.	Brandy, Old Pale			72s. — 90s.
Lisbon		34s.	Ditto, dark coloured			72s. — 85s.
Bucellas		40s.	Scotch Whiskey			20s. Gallon.
Teneriffe		34s.	Other Spirits, Curacoa, &c.,			
Cape		26s.	prices according to quality			

56 dozens to a Pipe of Port, 52 dozens to a Butt of Sherry, 22½ dozens to a Hhd. of Claret.

Price List of Messrs. Cockburn and Campbell, 1834

Robert and Mary Harden

Number 4

Miss Marion Turnbull had a boarding school for young ladies at no. 4 for ten years from 1852. Possibly she met competition from Miss Somerville at *no. 2*. In 1861, Miss Turnbull had two resident governesses as well as seven girls aged thirteen to seventeen (Census).

Number 5

A family which had a long connection with Doune Terrace was that of John Cockburn (1784–1862), wine merchant, who brought his family to no. 5 from India Street in 1828. After his death in 1862 his widow Eliza continued to live in the house until 1885. The Cockburns had at least ten children, but the three youngest, aged 1, 3 and 5 at the 1841 census may have died in childhood, since they were absent at the 1851 census. To look after such a large family, there was a governess and eleven resident domestic servants (nine female and two male) in 1841. The number of servants was later slightly reduced – eight in 1851 (including a 14 year old boy) and in 1861 (including a page and a coachman). As a widow, Mrs Cockburn still had seven resident servants in 1871 (including a 12 year old page and a coachman) and in 1881 (with two lady's maids for herself and her two unmarried daughters and a page).

John Cockburn, a brother of the judge, Lord Cockburn, founded the firm of Cockburn and Campbell in 1831, acquiring premises with a large cellarage in St Andrew Square. His partner, James Campbell, was a grandson of Sir Ilay Campbell, Lord President of the Court of Session. The firm's centenary report in 1931 makes interesting reading. The order books from 1831 showed wine being sent by boat from Leith to ports in England and by canal to Glasgow and thence by steamboat to Stranraer. In October 1832, 50 dozen bottles of East India sherry and 22 dozen of 1825 claret were sent to Downing Street, for Earl Grey, the Prime Minister. 'East India sherry' had been shipped from Spain to India and back again. In the sixteenth century trading ships sailing to the East Indies used to carry casks of sweet sherry lashed to their decks. It was discovered that, after travelling through the tropics, the heat and humidity had matured the wine to a great smoothness.

Soon after this, Sir Robert Peel (later, Prime Minister) wrote to order one butt (52 dozen bottles) of sherry: 'corresponding with the sample bottle which had the Yellow seal – marked in the catalogue Very Superior £116 per butt' and six dozen claret of 1825 vintage to be sent to Drayton Manor. After two days reflection he wrote to order 'two butts instead of one of the sherry and ten dozen Superior Port, not too long in the bottle.'

Sherry was the favourite wine for several decades, representing nearly half of the wines sold by the firm by mid-century. Port came second and claret third in popularity. There was only one order for whisky in the first three months after trading began in 1831, and the only liqueur sold was curaçao.

A great deal of alcohol was consumed, though possibly less than in the eighteenth century. In his *Memorials* Lord Cockburn wrote that, before 1800, judges quite openly drank strong port, 'to the great envy of the parched throats in the gallery.' He commented, 'not that the Ermine was absolutely intoxicated, but it was certainly sometimes affected.'

However, in 1841, Lord Cockburn wrote to his brother: 'My dear John – Have you any PERFECT whisky? ABSOLUTELY PERFECT for instant use? Lord Dunfermline [at *11 Ainslie Place* 1831–33] and another person dine here on Monday, who rejoice in no other liquor, and who are super-eminently fastidious. If you have none which ought to make them ashamed of all they ever tasted, send me none. If you have such as they have no notion of, send me a gallon or even a single bottle. Ever, H. Cockburn' (Introduction to *Memorials*, 1910 edition).

Students, as well as judges, were thirsty. In 1845 a twenty-year old at Merton College, Oxford (Mr Wyndham C. Anstruther, who later succeeded to his father's baronetcy) received his order of ten dozen claret, six dozen port, six dozen sherry, one dozen brandy and one dozen Islay whisky.

Number 6

Middle-class Edinburgh families often liked their sons to serve in India in the Honourable East India Company Service in a civil or military capacity. The men were frequently separated from their wives and children, who remained in Scotland. For this reason, they retired as soon as they could afford to do so.

Robert Harden and his wife Mary had their home at 6 Doune Terrace from 1831 when he was only 27. He had retired as a lieutenant in the Indian Army in 1829, after ten years service in Madras. He remained in the house until 1875, by which time Mary had died and he had remarried. Among the visitors who stayed with the Hardens was Frederick Barker who had married Robert's sister Jane. He had left Derbyshire to become the second bishop of Sydney, New South Wales in 1854. As primate of Australia and a stalwart evangelical, he established seven new dioceses including Perth and Brisbane.

Robert's mother, Jessy Allan, had lived, before her marriage to John Harden, in Queen Street and she kept a detailed journal from 1801 to 1811 for the benefit of her sister Nancy Ranken in India. The journal was delightfully and profusely illustrated by her husband John, an accomplished artist and musician.

for Balfour-Kinnear, from 1875, see *no. 9*

Number 7

An early arrival in Doune Terrace was Captain Francis Grove RN, whose first wife Emily Ure had died young, leaving him with four small sons and two daughters. He brought them and his second wife Mary Roberts to no. 7 in 1841. His brother Thomas, who was also in the Royal Navy, had lived there for the three previous years.

Francis Grove had been shipwrecked near Ceylon in 1813, at the age of fourteen, the year in which he joined the Navy. He subsequently served in the East Indies, the Mediterranean (being involved in the bombardment of Algiers in 1818), North America and South America. He and his wife left Doune Terrace in 1851 but briefly returned to the area when they rented *42 Moray Place* in 1861.

Number 8

James Steuart WS, after one year at *3 Albyn Place*, bought 8 Doune Terrace from the builders in 1827 and spent over sixty years there. His wife died young, leaving him with five children: three of their four sons also became lawyers. Unusually, some resident servants stayed with the family for many years. One, Marion Aitken, who was probably a nurse to the children in 1841, became a lady's maid to the only daughter and was still in the household in 1861. A butler in 1861 was succeeded by a male 'domestic servant' and then, in 1881, by two male invalid attendants for the 78 year old James

Steuart. After his death in 1886, his widowed son Archibald had the house until 1902.

Number 9

James Kinnear (1811–1849), partner of David Smith at *no. 3*, lived at no. 9, where he was a tenant from 1834, with his wife Mary and her brother Thomas Balfour, advocate. James and Mary had seven children.

Thomas Balfour became MP for Orkney in 1831, at the age of 21. He died in 1838, unmarried, while on a visit to James and Mary Kinnear. His father, Captain William Balfour RN, later lived at *2 Moray Place.*

In 1838, probably because of a misunderstanding, the owner of 9 Doune Terrace sold the house, although James Kinnear had been prepared to pay a higher price than the one accepted. So he took a

Elizabeth Mitchell and her contemporaries *c.*1896

lease of *no. 2* for the next three years and then lived at Murrayfield House before buying *21 Moray Place* in 1846. Unfortunately he did not have much time in which to enjoy his home there. He died at Cadiz in 1849, having been ordered south for health reasons. His widow sold *21 Moray Place* to Francis Brown Douglas in 1852 for £2650 and moved over the Dean Bridge to 3 Clarendon Crescent. A daughter of James and Mary Kinnear, Fearne, married Prof. William Edmonstoune Aytoun of *16 Great Stuart Street* as his second wife in 1863.

The eldest child of James and Mary Kinnear, George (1833–1915), wrote his *Recollections* for his children and the book was privately printed in 1900. He remembered being taken by his nurses across Doune Terrace in 1836 to look at a total eclipse of the sun through smoked glass. Aged about six, he was taken by his father to boarding school at The Grange, in Sunderland. When the headmaster offered the boy a glass of port or sherry, George replied, 'No thank you. I never drink anything but champagne or constantia!' The headmaster's butler was sent to fetch a glass of champagne. Edinburgh boys travelled to The Grange by coach from the Black Bull Hotel in Leith Street to Newcastle and then by rail – there was no railway from Edinburgh to Newcastle until 1847.

George later assumed the surname of Balfour-Kinnear. In 1848 he married a former neighbour, Agnes Gordon, whose mother was then living at 2 Clarendon Crescent, next door to George's mother. These were the first families to occupy houses on the far side of the Dean Bridge, on ground which had previously been used as market and fruit gardens. The Gordons had earlier lived at *2 Doune Terrace* from 1847–1853, after six years in *3 Moray Place.*

After 17 years of marriage, George bought *6 Doune Terrace* for £3000 and spent a further £1000 on improvements.

A third generation of the Balfour-Kinnear family continued the tradition of living in Doune Terrace when George's son James, another WS, moved in 1887 to *no. 3* after his marriage. In the space of sixty years, members of one family had lived in four of the ten houses in the Terrace.

The man who purchased no. 9 over James Kinnear's head in 1838 was James Mackenzie WS. He had previously lived at *22 Moray Place* for five years and then at *10 Ainslie Place* for one year before being able to buy his own home, to which he took his mother and his two unmarried sisters. James Mackenzie remained at no. 9 until 1870, and was still in practice as a solicitor when he was over 80.

The only clergyman to live in Doune Terrace in the nineteenth century was the Rev. Hamilton MacGill of the United Presbyterian Church. He and his wife lived at no. 9 from 1870. He served, successively, as Home Mission Secretary and Foreign Mission Secretary of the UP Church, after resigning from pastoral responsibilities in Glasgow. Earlier, he had originated and edited the *Juvenile Missionary Magazine* for many years, followed by the *Missionary Record*. He was said to be 'an eloquent and popular preacher who performed his secretarial duties with care and judgement' (DNB). He died in Paris in 1880, having gone to the south of France for the sake of his health.

The MacGills were succeeded at no. 9 in 1883 by another United Presbyterian family. Based in Edinburgh, Andrew Mitchell served as Interim Sheriff Substitute in a number of Scottish courts before moving to Stirling 23 years later, on appointment as Sheriff Substitute there. He served as a Liberal member of Edinburgh Town Council for eleven years and was active in the Young Men's Christian Association, the Navvy Mission, the Bible Society, Hellenic Society and Browning Society.

Andrew Mitchell believed in giving his daughters a good education, sending them to St George's School which was then in Melville Street. The third of his five daughters, Elizabeth, and probably her sisters, had first attended Miss Maughan's private school for boys and girls at *5 Randolph Cliff*.

Many years later, Elizabeth recalled in her autobiographical *The Plan That Pleased:* 'The Moray Place gardens were good in their way, lawns good for running about and playing French and English [a children's game], but far more interesting were the Doune Terrace gardens. For them, you went through an ordinary sort of gate and along an ordinary path round a corner, and then suddenly you found at your feet daisied slopes plunging down adventurously through sunshine and shadow to the dark river.

At the age of 21 Elizabeth Mitchell became the first St George's girl to go to Oxford University as 'a shy, stiff, Scotch fresher… embarrassed to arrive with a Sunday hat and a bicycle,' having temporarily lost her luggage.

From 1917 to 1951, Elizabeth was honorary secretary to the Council of St George's School in Edinburgh. From her home in Biggar, she unsuccessfully stood as Liberal candidate for Lanarkshire in 1924 and 1929 and was a town councillor in Biggar from 1935 to 1953.

She had long been interested in the creation of new towns to relieve the overcrowded conditions of Glasgow. She was the first secretary of the Scottish branch of the Town and Country Planning Association and for over twenty years was chairman of its executive committee. She was an active participant in the formation of East Kilbride New Town and in 1955 the TCPA recognised her great contribution to its work by presenting her with the Ebenezer Howard Medal. Elizabeth Mitchell died in 1980, on her hundredth birthday.

Number 10

The first resident in Doune Terrace was Miss Magdalene Erskine of Dun. The Post Office Directory gave her address in 1826 as 'north back of Moray Place' but a year later it was Doune Terrace, without a number. By 1828 it was number 10. The Erskines were an ancient family of Dun (a house now owned by the National Trust for Scotland), in Forfar. An ancestor, Robert Erskine, and two of his sisters were beheaded in 1613 for having practised witchcraft and for having poisoned two nephews, one of whom survived. Magdalene Erskine lived here for only three years, possibly with her widowed sister Anne Wauchope and her infant nephew and nieces David, Alice and Anne Wauchope, for whom she was trustee.

Dr Alice Ker, who spent only a short time in Doune Terrace, came to no. 10 in 1887, the year in which Dr Sophia Jex-Blake founded an Edinburgh School of Medicine for Women. Alice Ker was the thirteenth woman to be on the British Medical Register. Born in Banffshire in 1853, she was a niece of the redoubtable Stevenson sisters, Louisa and Flora, who lived at *13 Randolph Crescent.* While living with them in 1871–73, they encouraged her to attend University Classes for Ladies, where she particularly enjoyed the physiology lectures. She went on to become one of the first students at the London School of Medicine for Women, opened in 1874 by Sophia Jex-Blake.

After graduating in Dublin in 1879, she returned to Edinburgh and worked briefly as assistant to Dr Jex-Blake who, she said, was 'not an easy person to live with'. Like Sophia Jex-Blake, Alice Ker then graduated MD in Berne, Switzerland, and was the first woman

Dr Alice Ker

doctor to become a Licentiate of the Royal College of Physicians in Edinburgh in 1886.

In her *Beginnings of a Memoir*, Alice Ker wrote that 'Aunt Louie found a house for me. She described it as "a real lady's house" and I had not the courage to retort that it was not a doctor's house, for it was the basement – ground floor rather – of a block of flats, with no through ventilation, and the lavatory in a shaft. However, Aunt Louie was paying the rent, and I lived there for a year, without any harm, although sometimes feeling rather stuffy. In 1888 I moved to a healthier house *[no. 1]* in the same Doune Terrace.'

While living in Doune Terrace, Alice Ker's diaries recorded her daily life. She saw patients at dispensaries in Stockbridge and the Canongate as well as in her own home. She sometimes visited the Asylum and Lauriston Lane Home and also patients as far apart as Morningside and Leith. After moving to no. 1, she personally laid carpets, stained floors, painted furniture, sewed and hung curtains, and fixed finger plates to doors. She made some of her own clothes, embroidered handkerchiefs, knitted socks for a brother and made plum jam and damson jam. Every day friends called at her home, usually in the afternoon, and she visited her aunts at *13 Randolph Crescent* once or twice a day. She left Edinburgh when she married her cousin, Edward Ker, at the end of 1888.

Alice Ker had, in 1884, published *Infancy and Childhood, Girlhood* and *Womanhood*, price one penny each, all being her lectures to women at the Manchester Domestic Economy classes. After leaving Edinburgh, she published *Motherhood* in 1891, written when she was honorary medical officer to the Wirral Hospital for Sick Children and to the Birkenhead Lying-in Hospital. She gave very simple, useful, practical advice for women on health, hygiene, food and clothing (no stays!) from the moment of giving birth. She wrote 'I think this is the first time that so many directions for the healthy living of a woman's life have been brought together in one book.'

Doune Terrace Householders

1.
1830 Thomas Hutton esq.
1835 Richard Hunter esq.
1846 Robert Chambers, publisher
1861 Miss Martin; Miss Mitchell to 1863
1867 Charles Shirreff; Mrs Alexander G.
  Edington
1874 James Hunter
1879 E. J. W. Smith
1888 Alice J. S. Ker MD
1891 Frank Armitage Hardy
1894 A. G. Anderson, fishmonger

2.
1830 James Crawfurd, advocate
1835 Robert Mackenzie WS
1843 William Stothart esq. of Cargen
1847 Mrs Harry Gordon
1854 Robert Romanes
1857 Miss Somerville, boarding school
1862 Mrs Cheyne
1874 Charles Henderson SSC
1892 & Thomas Henderson WS
1895 James Kirkwood, printer
1902 Ewan F. Macpherson, advocate

3.
1832 David Smith WS
1847 Mrs Dunbar
1852 Misses Hutchison
1860 Mrs Elizabeth Shaw
1861 Mrs Macpherson
1882 Miss Violet C. Brown
1887 James Balfour-Kinnear WS

4.
1831 Lt. Col. Riddell, asst. QM
1851 George Falconer, landed proprietor
1852 Misses Turnbull
1862 John M. McCandlish WS
1885 John Hamilton Buchanan CA

5.
1828 John Cockburn, wine merchant

1886 Mrs Maconochie

6.
1831 Robert A. Harden esq.
1875 George T. Balfour-Kinnear WS

7.
1834 Mrs Macleay
1838 Thomas Grove esq. RN
1841 Francis Grove, Capt. RN
1849 Capt. James Wemyss of Wemyss Hall
1851 Lt. Col. George A. Underwood, EICS
1856 Jules Fleury, consul de France
1859 Misses Abercrombie

8.
1827 James Steuart WS
1832 Robert Hudspeth, bdg house for young
  gentlemen
1835 James Steuart WS
1871 & Charles Steuart WS
1891 Archibald Steuart WS; George B. Steuart
  WS

9.
1828 Archibald Davidson, advocate; David
  Davidson esq.
1834 James Kinnear WS; Thomas Balfour,
  advocate
1839 James Mackenzie WS
1870 Rev. H. M. MacGill DD; Foreign
  Mission Sec, UP Church
1878 & Misses Heugh to 1879
1883 Andrew Mitchell, advocate

10.
1829 Miss Armstrong
1851 Miss M. Wallace Ferrier
1870 John Kirkpatrick, junior advocate
1873 Miss Crawford
1878 Mrs Gregorson
1882 Miss Belfrage
1886 Alice J. S. Ker MD
1891 Miss Stevenson

Ainslie Place

In 1801 the tenth Earl of Moray married his second wife Margaret Jane Ainslie – daughter of Sir Philip Ainslie of Pilton – and he named this oval after her family.

The first houses to be occupied were *numbers 1 to 15*, on the north-west side, from 1826 to 1828, and also *number 17* on the south-west side. By 1832, all the houses were built and occupied except for *numbers 19 to 22*, which were completed between 1858 and 1860. All corner houses had a ground floor and basement, or garden floor. The upper floors were part of the houses in the adjacent streets.

Ainslie Place, 1829

Number 1

Above the doorway of number 1 are the words *Pax intrantibus: salus exeuntibus*. The house was first occupied in 1828 by J. A. Cheyne, WS and also an accountant. He remained for four years, and had his office at 23 Dundas Street, where he had previously lived.

The house had been unoccupied for five years when Mrs Gillespie Graham moved there in 1858 (see Introduction).

Number 2

William Horsman of Stirling and his son Edward (1807–1876), an advocate, spent five years at no. 2 from 1831. They both left their home here in 1836 when Edward was elected Liberal MP for Cockermouth, later serving as Chief Secretary for Ireland for two years from 1855. He subsequently maintained a more independent position, resisting Gladstone's Reform Bill in 1866. He was described by John Bright MP as 'retiring into his political cave of Adullam, to which he invited everyone who was in distress and everyone who was discontented.' His minority group then became known as 'the cave' or 'the Adullamites'.

for Smith, 1846 to 1858, see *2 Doune Terrace*

William Blackwood, son of William Blackwood (see *number 3*), lived at no. 2 from 1858–1867, with a country house at Gogar Mount. He was then head of the publishing firm of Blackwood, having retired from the Honourable East India Company Service as a major.

An advocate, R. Stanser McNair, came to no. 2 in 1900. His daughter became an international breeder of pugs from 'Twinkle of Ainslie'. Looking down into the basement area, passers-by could see a washing-basket, apparently full of oval bread rolls, in a doorway: closer inspection revealed it to be full of baby pugs!

Number 3

William Blackwood (1776–1834) spent the last three years of his life at no. 3, dying there in 1834. After having lived with his wife and their seven sons and two daughters in a large airy house at 2 Salisbury Road, he wrote to his son William in India about their new home: 'We have taken a capital house in Ainslie Place. It stands quite on top of the bank immediately above St Bernard's Well, and has a beautiful view over to Fife, the Forth and all the country betwixt.'

Born in 1776, William Blackwood was a bookseller before becoming a publisher. After a six-year apprenticeship with Bell and Bradfute, he spent a year as the Glasgow agent for Mundell and Company, Edinburgh bookseller and University printer. In 1804 he opened his own shop at 64 South Bridge, buying and selling rare books. In 1812 he published a highly-acclaimed catalogue of 15,000 classical and antiquarian books. After selling them, he removed to 17 Princes Street, where he had an elegant oval saloon in which 'young men of genius' could meet. His premises changed again in 1829, when he bought a house at 45 George Street for 3,500 guineas, which became the headquarters of Blackwood's publishing business for over 150 years.

Meanwhile, William Blackwood had launched and edited the *Edinburgh Monthly Magazine* from 1817, soon to become *Blackwood's Magazine* and later to be known as the *Maga* reaching a circulation of 10,000. Later in 1817 the Magazine included what appeared to be a copy of a long-lost biblical text. In fact, it was a spoof referring, for instance, to 'a man ... and his name was as it had been the colour of ebony, and his number was the number of a maiden when the days of the years of her virginity have expired.' One of the early major contributors was John Wilson ('Christopher North'), Professor of Moral Philosophy, who later took over the editorship. Thomas De Quincey and James Hogg ('The Ettrick Shepherd') were also regular contributors. The magazine continued to be published until 1980.

William Blackwood also published, as books, many of the contributions to his magazine, such as Susan Ferrier's *Marriage*. As publisher, he dared to criticise Walter Scott's anonymous novel *The Black Dwarf* and asked to have the 'lame and impotent' conclusion altered. Scott angrily replied that 'I am one of the Black Hussars of literature who neither give nor take criticism.'

Shortly before his death he completed his 18-volume *Edinburgh Encyclopaedia*. After his death, his widow and three of her sons lived at *18 Great Stuart Street* until 1845 and then at *3 Randolph Crescent*. That house became the home of her son John, editor of the *Maga* (see also *3 Randolph Crescent*).

for Drummond, 1835 to 1837, see *35 Moray Place*
for Maitland, from 1856, see *3 Randolph Cliff*

Number 4

Among the doctors who settled in Ainslie Place was John MacWhirter (1780–1853) who retired from the Indian Medical Service in 1825 and, two years later, moved into no. 4 with his family. He was President of the Royal College of Physicians of

Edinburgh for two years from 1831 and wrote to explain his inability to attend a meeting of the council in 1832: 'as being *bona fide* attending a Lady in Labour which they will all agree cannot be avoided by me.' He left Edinburgh in 1849 but returned in 1853, in which year he died at his new home at *50 Moray Place*. His son John Peach MacWhirter, another doctor, went to Delhi for medical advice at the time of the mutiny in 1854 and was never heard of again.

Number 5

Dugald Stewart, Professor of Moral Philosophy, died here in 1828 aged 75, while visiting a friend, Mrs Lindsay. An imposing memorial to him, designed by William Playfair, stands on Calton Hill. His second wife was Helen D'Arcy Cranstoun who was his devoted amanuensis, and sister of the judge Lord Corehouse.

for Fothringham, 1836 to 1841, see *23 Moray Place*
for Fletcher, 1845 to 1870, see *1 Randolph Crescent*

Henry Lancaster (1829–1875) and his wife and four very small children lived at no. 5 from 1870. He died there suddenly on Christmas Eve in 1875 from apoplexy. He had simultaneously obtained two honours degrees at Oxford in 1853, a first in greats (classics) and a third in law and modern history. In the same year, he won the William Arnold prize for his essay on *The benefits arising from the Union of England and Scotland in the Reign of Queen Anne.* After being called to the Scottish Bar he showed an active interest in the cause of education and was a member of the Royal Commission on Scottish Educational Establishments, which led to the Scottish Education Act 1872, providing for the formation of the Scotch (sic) Education Department and for compulsory education. As an advocate, he defended Edinburgh University in its refusal to admit Sophia Jex-Blake to its medical school. He was also an essayist, contributing to the *North British Review* and the *Edinburgh Review.*

Number 6

Sir Charles Bell (1778–1842) was appointed Professor of Surgery in Edinburgh University in 1836; he then returned to his native city from London, where he had been Professor of Anatomy and Surgery to the Royal College of Surgeons. His father was a clergyman in the

Scottish Episcopal Church and his maternal great-grandfather, Bishop White, had been Primus of Scotland.

Sir Charles and Lady Bell lived at 6 Ainslie Place until he died in 1842. He wrote to a friend: 'This is a capital house, with two spare rooms and all your friends within a gunshot.' His wife later reported, 'we came to Scotland at the right season and were welcomed by all whom we wished to welcome us. The garden was in terraces, down to the Water of Leith, and the walks there among the sweet-briar hedges made our home in Edinburgh very delightful.'

As a student, Charles Bell had the first of his many text books published – *A System of Dissections* – illustrated with his own drawings. He made advances in surgery: for example, he used a knife in the operation of lithotomy and could remove a stone from the bladder in two and a half minutes, eliminating the protracted suffering of a patient operated on with a gorget.

He early became an expert on gunshot wounds and treated many men after the Battle of Waterloo, 'brought from the field after lying many days on the ground; many dying, many in agony.' His extensive anatomical collection, of more than 2,000 specimens, was bought in 1825 for the museum of the Royal College of Surgeons of Edinburgh for £3,000, and can still be seen by those who are not faint-hearted. The collection was packed in 65 cases, arrived at Leith on board the smack *Robert Bruce*, and was conveyed to Surgeon's Square in spring wagons lent by the Artillery.

For some years Sir Charles had explored the functions of the nervous system, and in 1827 he wrote, 'I have made a greater discovery than ever was made by any one man in anatomy.' This was that there were two kinds of nerves, sensory and motor. The facial palsy known as Bell's palsy is named after him.

for Begbie, 1843 to 1844, see *16 Great Stuart Street*

Mark Napier (1798–1879) spent 35 years at no. 6 from 1844 until his death. Descended from the 1st Lord Napier (inventor of logarithms and Napier's Bones) he was an advocate and historical biographer. At his death, he was the oldest practising member of the Faculty of Advocates. He and his wife (his cousin Charlotte) and their two children had an ever-increasing household. The number of resident servants increased from seven in 1851 to twelve in 1871, by which time their daughter was there, with her own four children, the eldest being three years old.

In spite of being Sheriff of Dumfriesshire, Napier's reputation was literary rather than legal. He published many papers about Napier of Merchiston and about Montrose. 'His Jacobitism was of the old-fashioned fanatical type, and although in many cases his representations are substantially founded on fact, his exaggeration necessarily awakens distrust even when he has a good case' (DNB). *The Scotsman* was kinder in an obituary: 'Though a keen controversialist and most unsparing in epithets of abuse, Mark Napier was in person and address a genial polished gentleman of the old school – a really beautiful old man, worn to a shadow, but with a never-failing kindly smile, and a lively, pleasant, intellectual face, in which the pallid cheek of age was always relieved by a little trace of seemingly hectic or of youthful colour.'

for Moncreiff, from 1881, see *15 Great Stuart Street*

Francis Cadell (1883–1937), known as 'Bunty', one of the Scottish Colourists, lived in the bottom half of no. 6 from 1920 to 1927. (See his family at *no. 22*, where he was brought up.) Towards the end of his life he had difficulty in selling his paintings which now fetch high prices.

Number 7

The Hon. Mrs Ann Strange, daughter of the 1st Viscount Melville, and her second husband James Strange of the East India Company Service, came to this house in 1827. He died in 1840 and she in 1852. In 1841, the widowed Mrs Strange had no family living with her but had seven resident servants, five women and two men (Census). Ten years later, her daughter Louisa Trotter was there with four of her children (see *13 Randolph Crescent*) as well as a Dundas granddaughter with a governess and nine servants, all women except for a footman.

The Moray family returned to the estate in 1904 when Anna, Dowager Countess of Moray lived at no. 7 until her death in 1915. She was the widow of the 15th Earl, who had succeeded to the title in 1895 and died in 1901: he was a grandson of the 9th Earl. While at no. 7, the Countess broke her leg and had a brass handrail installed on the right-hand side of the staircase, the original banister remaining on the left. This house once had an extra door to the basement area, providing direct access to the garden.

Number 8

for MacFarlane, 1844 to 1848, see *6 Randolph Crescent*

John Duncan, MD, FRCSEd, FRSE, lived here with his wife and five children from 1873 until his death in 1899. In 1882 he was a candidate for the chair of surgery on the death of James Spence (see *no. 20*) and was upset when he was not elected. However, he soon became Senior Ordinary Surgeon to the Royal Infirmary, excelling in clinical teaching. He retired in 1895, after 20 years in charge of wards.

Number 9

James Ivory (1792–1866) brought his wife and children from Dundas Street to no. 9 in 1830. He was appointed a judge in the Court of the Exchequer in 1840 and a Lord of Justiciary, as Lord Ivory, in 1849. His son William, Sheriff of Inverness-shire, was householder from his father's death in 1866 until 1874. In April 1882, the sheriff took a force of sixty Glaswegian policemen against the crofters of Braes in Skye. They were conducting a rent strike against their landlord, Lord Macdonald, in protest at his removing a large area of common grazing. The sheriff and police were surrounded by stone-throwing crofters and their wives and had to escape to Portree. The 'Battle of the Braes' resulted in the dispatch of troops and warships to Skye, the appointment of a Royal Commission on Crofting, and major reforms in crofting tenure.

A month later William's brother Thomas, an advocate, threw himself over the Dean Bridge. *The Courant* reported that 'for some time past Mr Ivory had been observed by his friends to be affected by mental depression for which his circumstances offered no cause whatever. During the recent visit of Messrs Moody and Sankey he interested himself very deeply in their proceedings and it is feared that since then he suffered from the excitement thereby induced.' (Moody and Sankey were popular evangelical hymn writers from the United States of America).

for Brodie, 1875 to 1896, see *2 Randolph Crescent*

The undermentioned Houses are situate within the Boundaries of the

Page 14]

Civil Parish of	School Board District of	Parliamentary Burgh of	Royal Burgh of	Police Burgh of	Town of	Village or Hamlet of
St Cuthbert	Edinburgh	Edinburgh	Edinburgh	Edinburgh		

No. of Schedule	ROAD, STREET, &c., and No. or NAME of HOUSE	HOUSES Inhabited / Uninhabited or Building	NAME and Surname of each Person	RELATION to Head of Family	CONDITION as to Marriage	AGE (last Birthday) Male / Female	Rank, Profession, or OCCUPATION	WHERE BORN	Whether 1. Deaf-and-Dumb 2. Blind 3. Imbecile or Idiot 4. Lunatic
37	9 Ainslie Place							Midlothian, Leith	
38	10 Do	1							21
39	11 Do	1							22

Total of Males and Females ... Total of Windowed Rooms ...

Total of Houses ...

79

Copy of Census return for 11 Ainslie Place in 1881

Reproduced with the kind permission of the Registrar General for Scotland (RD 685 1/1881/55 p 14)

Number 10

The widow of Dr James Gregory was the first resident of Ainslie Place, in 1826, bringing her family of five sons and two daughters to no. 10 from Northumberland Street. Her husband had died at their home at 2 St Andrew Square five years earlier, as the result of a carriage accident. He is best remembered today for his invention of Gregory's Powder, a laxative made of rhubarb, magnesia and ginger. He was Professor of the Practice of Physic and used to wear his hat when lecturing to students, after apologising for doing so. He wrote a number of caustic pamphlets; one led to legal proceedings against the publisher of an anonymous book, *A Guide for Gentlemen Studying Medicine at the University of Edinburgh* which, in Gregory's opinion, was over-critical of some professors while lavish in its praise of Drs Hamilton (father and son) and their midwifery classes. Gregory was convinced that the Hamiltons were the authors of the book.

While the Gregory family lived in Ainslie Place, the eldest son John was an advocate; Donald was Secretary to the Society of Antiquaries and died in 1836; James was a doctor who died in 1832 of typhus fever passed on by one of his patients in the Royal Infirmary; Duncan was a mathematician; and William another doctor who later became Professor of Medicine. Shortly before his death, Donald Gregory's *History of the Western Highlands and Isles of Scotland, 1493–1625* was published.

for Mackenzie, 1837 to 1838, see *9 Doune Terrace*

Number 11

James Abercromby (1776–1858), later Baron Dunfermline, lived at no. 11 for two years from 1831. He was brought up in Edinburgh, the son of a distinguished general. As an English barrister he had been Member of Parliament for Calne in Wiltshire for eight years before being appointed, in 1830, Lord Chief Baron of the Exchequer in Scotland. Lord Cockburn considered that 'publicly he is thrown away here' as there was not enough work in the Exchequer. He had the welfare of Edinburgh citizens at heart for he had, in 1824 and 1826, brought motions for bills to amend the representation of the City of Edinburgh, which was then in the hands of a self-selected Council of 33 men; he was unsuccessful on both occasions.

From 1832–1839, in the first reformed Parliament, he was MP for

Edinburgh. For the last four of those years he was Speaker of the House of Commons. Opinions differed about his performance there. One commentator said, 'he proved inefficient and let the House get out of hand'; another described him as 'acting with great impartiality, while he possessed sufficient decision to quell any serious tendency to disorder.' Sydney Smith dubbed him 'Abercrusty'. In 1834 he was, briefly, a member of the Cabinet as Master of the Mint.

James Abercromby was created the first Baron Dunfermline in 1839. He was later one of the originators of the United Industrial School in Edinburgh, for the support and training of destitute children. Lord Dunfermline's nephew George, the third Baron Abercromby, married Louisa Forbes in 1832, one of the daughters of a neighbour, Lord Medwyn of *17 Ainslie Place*.

for Ramsay, 1833 to 1842, see *no. 23*

Admiral Sir William Edmonstone (1810–1888) had his town house at 11 Ainslie Place from 1875 until his death there in 1888. When he was nearly thirteen, and after a year at the Royal Naval College, he served as a volunteer on the 'Sybille', a ship of 48 guns. Three years later, in 1826, he was severely wounded in the face and arm in a desperate action against pirates off the island of Candia (Crete) in the Mediterranean.

He later married Mary Parsons, whose father was Resident of the island of Zante: they had eight daughters and one son. William Edmonstone was appointed as a naval ADC to Queen Victoria in 1856 while captain of a guardship at Devonport, continuing as ADC until 1869. He ended his active career as superintendent of Woolwich Dockyard for five years, retiring in 1871. In that year, he succeeded his half-brother as fourth baronet and lived at Duntreath, Stirlingshire. He was Conservative Member of Parliament for Stirlingshire from 1874 until 1880, a seat which his father had earlier held for many years.

In 1881 Sir William, his wife and four of their children had a governess for the two youngest children, as well as ten resident servants, the youngest being a fifteen year old page boy (Census).

After Sir William's death, the house was occupied by Sir John Don-Wauchope of Edmonstone (1816–1893), 8th baronet, with some of his family of four sons and four daughters. On succeeding Sir William Don as baronet in 1862, Sir John had resumed the additional surname of Don, which had been discontinued by his great-grandfather. Sir John was Chairman of the General Board of Commissioners in Lunacy for Scotland from 1863 and also, from 1872, Chairman of the Board of Education for Scotland. Four years later the family moved next door, to *no. 12*, where they remained into the next century.

for Blair, from 1892, see *15 Randolph Crescent*

Number 12

The judge Lord Corehouse (George Cranstoun, brother-in-law of Dugald Stewart – see *no. 5*) lived here from 1827 to 1840. He had a bloody background. Two ancestors of his, the 8th and 9th Earls of Argyll, were beheaded at the mercat cross of Edinburgh in the seventeenth century. His mother's uncle, William Boyd, 4th Earl of Kilmarnock, was a Jacobite, taken prisoner at Culloden and beheaded on Tower Hill in 1746 for his share in the Rebellion.

Lord Corehouse's niece Miss Maria Cuninghame of Lainshaw, moved from George Street to share his house. She succeeded to his estate of Corehouse in 1850 when he died unmarried.

Lord Corehouse was said by Lord Cockburn (*Memorials*) to have 'a rather featureless countenance (with) a pleasing and classical profile … his speaking was anxiously precise.' He had a keen sense of humour and was the author of a clever sketch 'The Diamond Beetle Case' in which he caricatured the manner and style of several of his fellow judges in delivering their opinions. An Edinburgh jeweller was depicted as suing a surgeon for defamation for calling his diamond beetle an Egyptian louse.

for Forbes, 1841 to 1843, see *no. 15*
for Don-Wauchope, from 1892, see *no. 11*

Number 13

Although the buildings in this prime residential area were designated by the Earl of Moray to be used solely as dwelling houses, parts of some houses were used as offices as well as homes.

Claud Russell, accountant, made his home here from 1827, also establishing it as the office of Russell and Mansfield, accountants. The house came on the market again in January 1830: it was advertised in the *Edinburgh Evening Courant* as having, '… on the second sunk floor, laundry with three other apartments, with good cellarage; an excellent kitchen and scullery and three other apartments on the kitchen floor; a large dining room and two other rooms on the entrance floor; two drawing rooms and one other room on the floor above; four excellent bedrooms with a dressing-room; ...in good order, being all painted and papered.'

for Agnew, 1849 to 1850, see *24 Moray Place*

Number 14

John Tod WS moved from 46 Charlotte Square to 14 Ainslie Place in 1827; his office of Tod & Romanes was at *1 Great Stuart Street*, moving to *7 Great Stuart Street* in 1838. He died in the 1850s, but his widow stayed on until 1874. The family had a good complement of domestic servants – nine in 1851 (including a butler, footman and two lady's maids), reducing to seven in 1871. Meanwhile, their three sons (Thomas, advocate, Alexander WS and John Robert WS) had moved out. John Robert Tod had married in 1844 and lived in *30 Moray Place* until 1857. His wife soon died, leaving him with two very small children.

Number 15

Professor James David Forbes (1809–1868), lived for four years in Ainslie Place. He was a nephew of Lord Medwyn at *no. 17*, and son of Sir William Forbes, baronet of Pitsligo. He came from Dean House and had two years at *no. 12* and then two at no. 15 on his marriage in 1843 to Alicia, daughter of George Wauchope of *8 Moray Place*. Alicia was much younger than her husband.

In 1832 he was a founder member of the British Association for the Advancement of Science. In the following year, at the age of 24, he was appointed Professor of Natural Philosophy at the University of Edinburgh, remaining in that post until he became Principal of St Salvator's and St Leonard's College, St Andrews, in 1860. Meanwhile he had also been Secretary of the Royal Society of Edinburgh for eleven years from 1840. His chief interests were physics and geology, and especially the study of the movements of glaciers. Among the many papers he published, one was on the climate of Edinburgh and another on the temperature of the earth's crust at various depths near Edinburgh.

His book *Travels Through the Alps of Savoy*, published in 1843, was described in the *Edinburgh Review* as 'pregnant with interest'. It recounted many daring and hazardous adventures and contained notices of occasional catastrophes that had befallen less fortunate explorers.

He was said by Knight (*Some Nineteenth Century Scotsmen*) to have been very cold as a lecturer, 'the academic counterpart of the Mer-de-glace at Chamonix.' However, his insistence on examinations, in addition to attendance at professors' lectures, was academically valuable.

for Moncreiff, 1873 to 1881, see *15 Great Stuart Street*

Great Stuart Street enters here

Number 16

William Wotherspoon SSC moved to no. 16 from George Street in 1829. He and his partner Alexander Mack WS both lived here and had their office in the house. Mack soon married Wotherspoon's wife's sister and moved elsewhere, but the Wotherspoon family with two sons and six daughters remained in the house until 1845 before moving to *18 Great Stuart Street* where they were until 1891. Towards the end of his life, William Wotherspoon was Commissioner of Supply for the county of Fife.

The house was a lodging-house for ten years from 1856, where Mrs William Reid, the wife of an upholsterer, had four women lodgers, all unmarried, as well as her own three children and three domestic servants.

Number 17

John Hay Forbes (1776–1854) moved to no. 17 from Shandwick Place in 1827, two years after becoming a Court of Session judge as Lord Medwyn. Each year, he spent the winter and early spring in Ainslie Place and the summer on his family estate at Medwyn, West Linton.

It was largely through his efforts (and those of the episcopal congregation of the Cowgate Chapel) that the chapel of St Paul's, York Place, was built in 1818. His eldest brother Sir William Forbes, baronet, of Pitsligo was closely involved with the building of St John's Episcopal Chapel, Princes Street, consecrated in 1818.

After his death in 1854, Lord Medwyn's eldest son William succeeded to the house in Ainslie Place, where he died in 1891. William, as an advocate, was Secretary to the Board of Lunacy. Lord Medwyn's second son Alexander (1817–1875) retired from the HEICS at the age of 23 because of ill-health. After graduating from Oxford he was ordained and became Bishop of Brechin from 1847. He moved the headquarters of the bishopric from Brechin to Dundee. Lord Medwyn's daughter Louisa married the third Baron Abercromby, nephew of Lord Dunfermline of *11 Ainslie Place*.

Number 18

for Stuart, 1832 to 1837, see *no. 23*

During the incumbency of Dean Ramsay (see *no. 23*) at St John's Church, one of his curates was the Rev. Berkeley Addison who was also a neighbour, first at 18 Ainslie Place from 1847 for six years and then for two years at *19 Great Stuart Street*. Berkeley Addison and his wife Eliza had a family of at least three daughters and three sons (as shown at the 1851 census) and also had, as boarders, a teacher of classics and (again at that census) nine boy pupils aged eight to eleven. The family was clearly not impecunious since they had a resident groom and six women domestic servants.

Berkeley Addison did missionary work among the poor and started the Episcopal Free School in Earl Grey Street, with services morning and evening on Sundays and also a Sunday school. There were 172 children on the roll by 1848. In 1852 Mr Addison asked St John's Vestry to take over the responsibility for the school. The Vestry refused but made a grant of £25 and, a year later, agreed to pay the rent. His request for a chapel was also refused.

Number 19

After three years at *50 Moray Place*, in 1860 Dr William Henderson (1810–1872) brought his family to the newly-built 19 Ainslie Place, where they lived until he died. After being physician to the fever hospital in Edinburgh and then pathologist to the Royal Infirmary, he was appointed Professor of General Pathology in 1842. He was one of the first doctors in Britain to make use of a microscope in pathological study. He remained in his post until 1869, in spite of having become a homeopathist in 1845. His colleagues tried, unsuccessfully, to remove him from his chair and then, also unsuccessfully, to remove pathology from the obligatory curriculum for medical students. The Royal College of Physicians told him he should resign or be expelled, but neither happened. He stuck his ground and made his arguments in favour of homeopathy with tact, acute reasoning, playful irony and good-natured banter, finally regaining the respect of his colleagues.

A story is told that when a colleague objected to a candidate (a native of Ceylon) for graduation on the ground of poor spelling, one of the examiners exclaimed, 'Why, he actually spelled "exceed" with one *e*'. To which Professor Henderson retorted: 'You should remember that he came from the land of the Singal-ese.' His joke saved the candidate.

Number 20 (originally 20A)

for Professor James Spence, 1860 to 1862, see *no. 21*

Miss Katharine Brown was in charge of a private boarding school of eleven girls at no. 20 (then 20A) from 1866 to 1871, with the help of two resident governesses and four servants.

Ainslie House (originally 20B) – see under *11 St Colme Street*
Number 21A – see under *14 Glenfinlas Street*

Number 21

George Burnett (1822–1890) moved from Walker Street in 1858 with his mother, Mrs Burnett of Kemnay to live at no. 21 for five years. He was an advocate, a historian, a heraldic author and a genealogist. He restored the office of Lord Lyon from an honorary and titular one to a working one: previously the work had been delegated to the Lyon Depute. He was promoted in 1866 from Lyon Depute to Lord Lyon King of Arms.

The Lyon Court is a court of law with heraldic responsibilities and with sole jurisdiction relating to armorial bearings in Scotland. The office of Lord Lyon was re-organised by Act of Parliament in 1867.

George Burnett was a very shy man. He went out of his way to avoid having to speak to people: he would walk along Rose Street instead of Princes Street to lessen the chances of meeting anyone he knew.

John Chiene (1843–1923), who lived at 21 Ainslie Place from 1874 for ten years, succeeded his neighbour James Spence (see *14 Glenfinlas Street*) in the chair of surgery. Professor Chiene used one quarter of the class fees he received to employ young men recently graduated, for teaching and research. He set up a laboratory which was probably the first teaching bacteriological laboratory in the UK. He travelled widely and was one of the first to popularise antiseptic surgery in the United States, where he was made an Honorary Fellow of the American Surgical Association. In 1897 he became President of the Royal College of Surgeons of Edinburgh and was later Surgeon Consultant to the Forces in South Africa and was in Mafeking immediately after its relief.

Number 22

The first householder here, in 1858, was William Mackenzie, a lodging-house keeper. At each of the two censuses in 1861 and 1871 he and his family had their own two or three resident servants and also from three to five lodgers, usually unmarried lawyers. The house was again used as lodgings from 1878 to 1882 by Neil Kerr who was also a butler. He had three lodgers, one of whom was an elderly woman with her own two servants.

Francis Cadell (1844–1909), another Fellow of the Royal College of Physicians of Edinburgh, and his family lived at no. 22 from 1889. He was an expert in the treatment of syphilis, and was convinced that much harm was done by treatment with mercury. His uncle, Colonel George Cadell, had retired from the Madras establishment of the East India Company's Service to *no. 5* in 1841 and five years later moved to *13 Randolph Crescent* for eleven years. George's son William, who had also served in the EICS in Madras, lived at *6 Randolph Cliff* for six years from 1851. The widow of another uncle of Francis, Anne (Mrs Robert) Cadell was at *27 Moray Place* at the 1851 census with eight of her nine daughters; her husband Robert had been a partner of Archibald Constable, publisher, and his first wife had been Constable's daughter Elizabeth. After Constable's bankruptcy in 1826, Robert Cadell became the sole publisher of Sir Walter Scott's works, enabling the novelist to make satisfactory arrangements with his creditors.

Two children of Francis Cadell were to become famous. One was a daughter, Jean, who was an actress remembered especially for her performance as the formidable mother in the film of *Whisky Galore*. The other was a son Francis ('Bunty'), one of the Scottish colourists who, many years later, lived at *6 Ainslie Place*.

Number 23

The Rev. Edward Bannerman Ramsay (1793–1872) and his mother Elizabeth, the Dowager Lady Ramsay of Balmain, moved from Shandwick Place to *7 Darnaway Street* in 1825 for one year, when he

Dean Edward Ramsay at the Lectern, St John's Episcopal Church, Princes Street

was curate of St George's Chapel (later, St Paul's) in York Place. They next had four years at *4 Darnaway Street* before returning to *no. 7* for three years after his marriage. In 1833 he and his wife were able to move to a larger house at *11 Ainslie Place* and in 1842 to 23 Ainslie Place, where he stayed until his death in 1872. The family surname had originally been Burnett and was changed to Ramsay on his father's succession to the estate of Balmain and Fasque in Kincardineshire in 1806.

Meanwhile Edward Ramsay had been successively in charge of Old St Paul's in Carrubber's Close and curate of St John's, Princes Street, where he became Rector in 1830. Edward was one of seven sons and seven daughters. He was a proficient flautist and, being particularly fond of Handel's music, he improved the music at St John's. As the congregation increased, a gallery was built at the west end of the church and extra seats were installed near the south-east door. His proposal in 1838 for a 'Singing Academy' for ten boys was rejected. Queen Victoria and Prince Albert attended a service at St John's in 1842, as did the Queen's mother, the Duchess of Kent, in 1850, walking to and from the church from Barry's Hotel in Queen Street.

Dr Ramsay was one of the originators in 1837 of the Scottish Episcopal Church Society which aimed to raise the stipends of poorer Episcopal clergy. He was appointed Dean of Edinburgh in 1841, while continuing as Rector of St John's (where his bronze and enamel monument, designed by Sir Gilbert Scott, can be seen) until his death. He had turned down offers of the bishoprics of New Brunswick and of Glasgow. The Rev. Dr Thomas Guthrie, one of the founders of the Free Church of Scotland in 1843, wrote of Dean Ramsay, 'He is one of the most saintly and at the same time the most courtly, Christian gentlemen it has ever been my fortune to meet.'

Edward Ramsay married Isabella Cochrane in 1829, having met her when she was on a visit from Nova Scotia. They had no children but gave a home to her Canadian nieces Lucy and Alice (twins) and Ella Cochrane (aged ten to eight) after their parents died in 1851. Tragically Lucy died at 23 Ainslie Place in 1866, fifteen hours after her dress had caught fire.

Dean Ramsay's popular *Reminiscences of Scottish Life and Character* was published in 1858 and ran to 23 editions. The book was written partly to refute Sydney Smith's charge of lack of humour in the Scots, when he said, 'it requires a surgical operation to get a joke well into a Scotch understanding.'

The Dean's brother Admiral Sir William Ramsay, who never married, also made his home at no. 23 until he died in 1871. He had taken part in the Battle of Navarino in 1827 and, when in command of the tender *Black Joke* in 1831, had captured a Spanish slave brig. The Ramsay household maintained a staff of four to six resident domestic servants.

After the Dean's death, no. 23 was let to Maj.Gen. Sir Hugh Douglas for four years while he was Commander of the Forces in Scotland. His father-in-law, the second Earl of Cathcart, had earlier held the same appointment, succeeding Maj.Gen. the Hon. Patrick Stuart who lived at *18 Ainslie Place* 1832 to 1837 and, in 1843, became Governor of Malta.

The two remaining nieces of Dean Ramsay returned to the house in 1880, Ella as house owner and Alice with her husband, Sir James Stewart-Richardson, baronet. He was Major Adjutant of Volunteers and secretary to the Order of the Thistle, and their family grew to three sons and six daughters.

John Rankine (1846–1922), advocate, lived at no. 23 from 1886. Two years later he was appointed Professor of Scots Law at Edinburgh University. Never marrying, he took a great interest in the promotion of social life among undergraduates and was a generous supporter of the Students' Union: he was knighted a year before his death. His niece presented a hall of residence, Rankine House, in his memory.

Number 24

The first occupier of this house was advocate Robert Clerk-Rattray (1795–1851) of Craighall, Rattray, near Blairgowrie. His father was James Clerk-Rattray, a Baron of the Exchequer, who married a granddaughter of the 1st Earl of Fife. Robert and his wife Christine Richardson had two sons and five daughters. James, who was born in 1832, served in the Crimea (including the siege and fall of Sebastopol) and in the Indian Mutiny (including the relief and defence of Lucknow). He rose to be a Lt. General in 1881 and was knighted in 1897.

Number 25

Professor James Robertson (1803–1860) lived at no. 25 from 1844 until his death. He came to Edinburgh from Aberdeenshire in 1844 as Professor of Divinity and Church History. He had been headmaster of Gordon's Hospital before being ordained and appointed to the church at Ellon, where he married the widow of his predecessor. In 1842 he was suspended as a member of the presbytery for holding communion with the deposed ministers of Strathbogie.

Meanwhile, he had become interested in chemistry and in 1841 he was the first man in Britain to adopt a suggestion that farmers should dissolve bones in sulphuric acid before applying them to the soil as manure.

In Ainslie Place, Professor Robertson used to invite his students to supper: they were impressed by his geniality and kindness. His four year course began with Abraham and ended with Luther. He worked long hours, dictating his lectures to an amanuensis until after midnight and rising again at four o'clock to continue his work.

Professor Robertson was convenor of the Church of Scotland committee for the endowment of Chapels of Ease. Since the Union of 1707, the population of Scotland had increased from 800,000 to three million, with no increase in the number of parishes. By the time of his death he had obtained half a million pounds for the endowment of 65 new parishes.

Jemima Blackburn, who was brought up in Heriot Row and married Hugh Blackburn, Professor of Mathematics at Glasgow University, was an accomplished artist whose work was admired by Ruskin, Landseer and Millais. Her brother George Wedderburn WS and their mother (Isabella Clerk of Penicuik) spent a few years at 25 Ainslie Place from 1861. Jemima and George's nephew Colin Mackenzie WS and Colin's brother and sisters then made their home here until 1898. Colin was Deputy Keeper of the Great Seal of Scotland.

In her published memoirs, (*Jemima*, edited by Robert Fairley, 1988), beautifully illustrated with her paintings, Jemima wrote that George did well enough as a WS to be able to keep a horse. Jemima used to 'jump him over the wooden things they set along the new part of the roads' while these were being tarmacadamised.

George Wedderburn suffered from tuberculosis for many years: in 1861 when he was seriously ill he was advised to spend the winter in a warmer climate. He had become an irascible and difficult man and refused to go to Egypt without his sister Jemima. Accordingly George, Jemima, her eleven year old son William and Colin Mackenzie all sailed to Egypt, returning several months later. George's health did not improve and he died in 1865, as did his mother.

Jemima gave a description of life in Heriot Row – presumably similar in houses of the Moray Feu – in the early 1820s, when she was a small girl. 'People did their cleanliness in clothes, not in their skins.' Men had two clean shirts a day, while girls wore washable caps under their bonnets and short petticoats and cotton trousers with frills.

POPULATION OF AINSLIE PLACE

The total number of residents rose rapidly to reach a peak of 292 at the 1861 census: that included 32 in the school boarding house at Ainslie House. At each of the next three censuses, there were always well over 200 residents. The number of children under sixteen steadily declined from 45 in 1851 and 1861 (in 15 households) to 18 in 1891 (spread over only six families).

The number of resident domestic servants rose from 67 in 1841 to 105 in 1851 (in both years, several houses were unbuilt or unoccupied) to 140 in 1861. Thereafter the number was about 125. Families with a large number of servants included the Hon. Mrs James Strange at *no. 7* with a widowed daughter and five grand-children. In 1851 she had ten servants including a footman, a kitchen maid and a scullery maid. Mark Napier, Sheriff of Dumfriesshire, had his daughter and four grandchildren in his house at *no. 6* in 1871, with twelve servants living-in, including two laundresses.

Fewer than half of all households had male servants. The greatest number was eleven in 1851, when John Tod WS at *no. 14* had both a butler and a footman and Mrs Sprot of Clapham at *no. 24* had a coachman and a footman. The smallest number of men servants was four in 1881, when John Hoyes, a retired merchant, at *no. 7*, had a footman as well as a groom.

Ainslie Place Householders

1.
1828 J. A. Cheyne WS
1832 Mrs Williams
1835 William Robertson, advocate
1840 James Brown esq.
1843 Miss Barbara Scott
1853 -
1858 Mrs Gillespie Graham; Miss Campbell
1868 Thomas Scougall
1876 William F. Hunter
1880 Thomas Barclay, advocate

2.
1827 Dr Spalding
1831 William Horseman esq.
1834 & Edward Horseman, advocate
1836 Mrs Brown, lodging keeper
1842 Mrs Campbell
1844 William Forbes, advocate
1846 David Smith WS
1858 Maj. William Blackwood
1867 George Miller Cunningham, civil
   engineer
1892 & George Cunningham, advocate
1900 R. Stanser McNair, advocate

3.
1831 William Blackwood
1835 Mrs Drummond, lodging keeper; George
   Hay Donaldson WS; Peter Wilson WS
1837 Mrs Margaret Roberts
1856 E. F. Maitland, advocate
1867 & John Maitland, advocate
1871 John Millar, advocate (later, Lord
   Craighill)
1889 J. H. Millar, advocate
1894 Miss Houldsworth

4.
1827 John Macwhirter PRCP, FRSE, MD
1849 John Cowan, advocate (later Lord
   Cowan)
1856 & Hugh Cowan, advocate
1861 & John Cowan WS
1874 Sir Francis B. Outram, Bart.
1881 Mrs Edward
1886 R. W. Rankine of Cunnoquhie, Fife
1891 & James Rankine CA

5.
1827 Mrs Lindsay
1834 Mrs Percival

1836 J. Scrymsoure Fotheringham esq. of
   Tealing
1839 & Mrs Gunson
1841 Col. George Cadell
1844 G. A. Stuart esq.
1845 Angus Fletcher, advocate
1870 H. H. Lancaster, advocate

6.
1830 Anthony Mactier esq.
1836 Prof. Sir Charles Bell
1843 James Begbie MD
1844 Mark Napier, advocate; & Mrs Ogilvy
1863–66
1880 Hon. J. W. Moncreiff WS

7.
1828 James Strange esq.
1854 Maj. Gen. Archibald Brown Dyce,
   HEICS
1856 John Hoyes
1862 R. C. Williamson
1868 John Hoyes
1887 W. M. Webb, Dep. Surgeon-General
1888 Mrs Hoyes
1892 R. Fitzroy Bell, advocate
1904 Anna, Dowager Countess of Moray

8.
1827 David Snodgrass Buchanan of
   Cunninghamhead
1834 J. Glassford esq. of Douglaston
1838 Charles S. Buchanan esq.
1844 David McFarlan esq HEICS
1848 Mrs Veitch to 1853
1850 Misses Charlotte & Margaret Pitcairn
1856 Mrs Col. Scott
1873 John Duncan MD, FRCSE
1900 Alexander Bruce MD

9.
1829 Anthony Mactier esq.
1831 James Ivory, advocate
1837 & Miss Lawrie to 1869
1855 & Thomas Ivory, advocate
1874 Sir William H. Gibson Carmichael Bart.
1875 Thomas Dawson Brodie WS
1903 Mrs Thomas Nelson

10.
1831 Donald Gregory; Duncan Gregory; John
   Gregory; Dr James Gregory

1837 James Mackenzie WS
1838 Mrs Gordon of Knockespock
1852 Richard Hunter
1893 James Mylne WS

11.
1830 George McKillop esq.
1833 Rev. E. B. Ramsay
1842 Miss Millar of Earnock
1866 Mrs Williams of Earnock
1875 Admiral Sir William Edmonstone, Bart
1888 Sir J. Don Wauchope; A. R. Don
Wauchope, advocate; P. H. Don Wauchope
WS
1891 Patrick Blair WS

12.
1827 Hon. Lord Corehouse; Miss Cunningham
of Lainshaw
1839 George Cranstoun esq.
1841 Prof. J. D. Forbes
1843 David Mure, advocate (later Lord Mure)
1874 & W. J. Mure, advocate
1892 Sir A Don Wauchope; P. H. Don
Wauchope WS; A. R. Don Wauchope,
advocate

13.
1831 Mrs Anderson
1848 Sir William Scott Bart.; & Lady Agnew
1849–50
1851 James Wright
1877 John Bruce
1896 William Murray, advocate
1900 Robert Harrower Guild

14.
1827 John Tod WS
1834 & Thomas Tod, advocate to 1837; &
Alexander Tod WS to 1839
1874 James Young MD
1892 & James Y. Simpson Young MB, CM
1893 & Richard G. Erskine Young MB CM
1895 & R. J. Young MD
1897 Mrs Crommelin Brown

15.
1827 Mrs Lamont of Lamont
1832 & Mrs Campbell of Ross to 1837
1840 Mrs Seaton of Preston
1841 David Mure, advocate
1846 Mrs Donaldson
1852 Lady Keith
1858 Anthony Murray of Crieff WS

1867 Mrs Fair
1873 Hon. Henry James Moncreiff, advocate
1881 Rev. George Macaulay
1882 Charles Matthew LDS Ed

16.
1829 W. Wotherspoon SSC
1845 Richard Gordon, accountant
1851 Mrs Mary Johnston
1852 Mrs Bruce
1856 Mrs Reid, lodging keeper
1868 Mrs Maj. Gen. Anderson
1883 J. Graham Brown MD, FRCPE
1895 John Girdwood LDS, DDS
1898 & R. A. Dickson, LDS, DDS; & E.
Robinson, LDS, DDS

17.
1827 Hon. Lord Medwyn
1831 & W. Forbes, advocate to 1843
1853 & J. H. Forbes
1898 Miss Absolon, nursing home

18.
1832 Maj. Gen. the Hon. P. Stuart
1838 Lady Marjoribanks
1847 Rev. Berkley Addison
1853 John Stewart WS; John Murray WS of
Murray's Hall
1858 William Cumming MD, FRCPE
1873 & James Cumming MD

19.
1860 Prof. William Henderson
1868 & A. E. Henderson, advocate
1874 Patrick Blair WS
1893 & Ninian J. Finlay WS; & Chilean
Consul

20.
1860 William Stirling
1866 Miss Brown, boarding school
1871 Arthur Allison
1874 John Ord Mackenzie WS

21.
1858 Mrs Burnett of Kemnay; George Burnett,
advocate; Charles Burnett
1863 James McEwen WS
1874 John Chiene, surgeon
1884 Arthur W. Hare MB, surgeon
1890 Miss Matthew, private school
1891 Alick C. Harkness, physician & surgeon
1893 Philip Francis Wood, advocate

22.
1858 William H. Thomson, advocate
1859 William C. Mackenzie, lodging keeper
1868 James Craik
1874 Mrs Edward Arbuthnot
1878 Neil Inglis Kerr
1882 John Donaldson, seed & oilcake
 merchant; Mrs Forrester
1889 Francis Cadell, MB, FRCSE

23.
1833 Mrs Drummond, lodgings; Peter Wilson
 WS; Robert Handyside, advocate
1835 D McPhail, lodging keeper; George
 Gillanders WS
1837 Graham Speirs, advocate
1842 Very Rev. E. B. Ramsay
1870 & Admiral Sir William Ramsay
1873 Sir John Douglas KCB
1877 Mrs G. R. Campbell

1880 Maj. Stewart-Richardson; Miss Cochrane
1884 Dowager Lady Torphichen
1886 John Rankine, advocate; C. S. Rankine
 Simson, WS

24.
1830 Robert Clerk Rattray, advocate
1833 Col. Robert Ross
1838 John Murray esq.
1851 Mrs Sprot
1854 William F. Burnley

25.
1832 James Gillespie Davidson WS
1836 Gideon W. Bell WS; W. M. Boyd WS
1840 Capt. Arrow RN
1849 Rev. Prof. James Robertson
1861 George Wedderburn WS; Colin
 Mackenzie WS
1899 James S. Dalziel WS; John Dalziel CA

Great Stuart Street

This street was called after James Stuart, 1st Earl of Moray (1531–1590), who was a son of James V of Scotland and a half-brother of Mary Queen of Scots: he was Regent of Scotland. The first intention was to use the name Stuart Street, but 'Great' was added for comparison with Great King Street.

The street is in two parts: *numbers 1 to 6* to link Moray Place to Ainslie Place, and *numbers 7 to 20* to link Ainslie Place to Randolph Crescent. In both parts the odd numbers are on the north-west side and the even on the south-east. The corner houses, *1* and *2, 5* and *6, 7* and *8, 19* and *20*, were each built as flats with a common stair.

The reader can explore the short section first, down one side and up the other, followed by the longer section in the same manner.

Number 1

John Tod WS was the first to take advantage of the new buildings by moving his office (Tod and Romanes WS) in 1827 from 46 Charlotte Square to 1 Great Stuart Street, re-siting it at *no. 7* from 1842 to 1856 (see also *14 Ainslie Place*).

In three generations, a son succeeded his father in the chair of Anatomy and Practical Surgery for 126 years, all called Alexander Monro. The third and last (1773–1859) lived at 1 Great Stuart Street for two years from 1832, coming from 121 George Street. He had held the chair jointly with his father from 1798 and was the sole holder from 1808 to 1846, being succeeded by John Goodsir (see *37 Moray Place*).

Professor Alexander Monro tertius did not maintain the standards set by his father and grandfather, and was an uninspiring lecturer. Sir Robert Christison said: 'he lacked neither ability nor accomplishment. But apathy in a teacher cannot stir up enthusiasm in the student.' Sometimes he read lectures written a century earlier by his grandfather, even including contemporary detail such as 'next Tuesday there will be no lecture because ...' He provoked wit and sarcasm in his students, two-thirds of whom deserted his lectures. Like his father, he resisted the establishment of a separate chair of surgery. However, he had talent and wrote some valuable text books on anatomy. He also spoke Latin well and enjoyed gardening at his mansionhouse at Craiglockhart.

John Kieser (1809–1860), at no. 1 for a year from 1844 (and briefly at *1 Moray Place* in 1851) was a piano teacher. He was also organist at St Peter's Episcopal Church, Roxburgh Place, for 30 years and a composer. He edited the *National Melodist* in the middle 1850s. His father had been a good horn player, playing for over 30 years at the Theatre Royal, while his daughter Eleanor was 'an esteemed teacher of music in Edinburgh.'

Another professional musician at no. 1 was Bernhard Kreutzer, from 1851 for four years. He was Director of Music to HRH the Grand Duke of Baden.

The Rev. Richard Hibbs, at *1 Randolph Place* in 1852 for three years and then at 1 Great Stuart Street to 1861, was a controversial clergyman. From 1852 he was assistant minister at St John's Episcopal Church, but two years later his employment was suddenly terminated after a bitter controversy with the Rector, Edward Ramsay (of *23 Ainslie Place*). He then established the New Church of England Chapel in St Vincent Street. Some hint of his differences with Dean Ramsay is given in the title of a work he published in 1856: *Scottish Episcopal Romanism, or Popery Without a Pope.*

He also published anonymously, in 1854, a tract entitled *Remarks on The Italian Opera* in which he said he had once 'confidently entertained the hope that the Italian Opera, if ever introduced into Edinburgh, would scarcely be tolerated and certainly never become popular.' He then found that Edinburgh people were paying to see opera and, in particular, *Don Giovanni*, of which he considered the words and acting to be immoral, although the music was exquisite. Money would be better spent, he said, in maintaining Apprentice Asylums and the Apprentice School Association.

for Fettes Douglas, 1868 to 1871, see *4 Wemyss Place*

Number 3

John Christison, advocate (1788–1862), lived at no. 3 from 1829 until his death. His brother, Professor Sir Robert Christison, also lived there for the first six years before removing to *5 Randolph Crescent* and then *40 Moray Place*. John Christison married Charlotte, widow of Miles Angus Fletcher who died in 1831 aged 29. Her grandson, another Miles Angus Fletcher, was briefly married to Martha

Maitland-Makgill-Crichton of *28 Moray Place* in 1871.

As Sheriff of Ayrshire, John Christison was concerned that excursion trains and steamers used to bring reinforcements of Irish Catholic rioters from Glasgow to Ayrshire for their annual encounters with the Protestant Orangemen on 24 July. He put a stop to this practice in the late 1850s by using the militia to prevent the entry of Glaswegians from boats or trains.

Alexander Shand (1828–1904) and his wife spent eight years at no. 3 from 1864: they had no children. He was raised to the bench in 1872 and in 1890 went to London, where he was a Lord of Appeal as Baron Shand until his death. He was of unusually small stature and had a habit of walking about while counsel were speaking. George Young (see *28 Moray Place*) once stopped in the middle of a speech to complain: 'My Lord, I really cannot address a moving object', whereupon Lord Shand meekly sat down.

The first holder of Edinburgh University's chair of engineering in 1868 (endowed by Sir David Baxter of *5 Moray Place*) was Fleeming Jenkin, who left a similar chair in University College, London. He and his family lived at 3 Great Stuart Street from 1874 until he died from blood poisoning, following a minor surgical operation on his foot.

Jenkin wrote to his wife, Anne Austin, before their marriage in 1859, 'I find the study of electricity so entertaining that I am apt to neglect my other work.' He then began work on the transmission of electric signals through underwater cables, and he was involved in the manufacture of the first transatlantic telegraphic cable, the Red Sea cable and others.

In Edinburgh, Professor Jenkin became interested in sanitation and was responsible for the formation of Sanitary Protection Associations in Edinburgh and other cities. He wrote a helpful booklet entitled *Healthy Houses*.

From 1876, Jenkin was fascinated by Edison's phonograph, a new scientific marvel. He and his close friend, former pupil and eventual biographer, Robert Louis Stevenson, made one, following a description given in *The Times* newspaper. Together, they gave demonstrations at a charity bazaar.

Next, in 1882, he worked out a system of electrical transport which he called telpherage, a means of transporting goods and passengers by electric panniers supported on a wire which supplied electricity.

Professor and Mrs Jenkin were keen amateur actors and had a

stage in their house in Great Stuart Street, where Robert Louis Stevenson often performed in Shakespearean plays.

The Jenkins' son, Charles Frewen Jenkin, who became the first professor of engineering science at Oxford University, married a neighbour, Mary, youngest daughter of Lord Mackenzie of *12 Great Stuart Street.*

Professor Fleeming Jenkin

Cossar Ewart (1851–1933) lived at no. 3 for three years from 1886, soon after being appointed to the chair of Natural History at Edinburgh University. He had previously held a similar appointment in Aberdeen, where he established the first marine zoological station in Britain. He had earlier been Conservator of the anatomical and zoological museum at University College, London, where he reorganised and expanded the whole museum.

Professor Cossaar Ewart

In Edinburgh, Professor Ewart was a popular lecturer. He inspired many students to work harder by arousing their interest in his subject. Nearly all the students of medicine attended his practical class. As a scientific member of the Fishery Board for Scotland, he started important studies of marine life, especially the feeding habits of fish. In the late 1890s he carried out experiments by crossing the zebra with the horse, both ways. Later, when penguins were reared at Edinburgh Zoo, he studied the origins and history of feathers and the relationship between feathers and scales.

for Blackburn, 1891 to 1897, see *no. 9*

Number 5

The first girls' school to come to Great Stuart Street was at no. 5, where Mrs W. W. Brown had a boarding and day school for 'young ladies' from 1827 to 1831, having previously been in Saxe-Coburg Place.

Number 6

A family of three artists lived for five years at no. 6 from 1832. Anna Andrews had spent the previous year at *no. 5*. She was a portrait miniaturist who exhibited annually at the Royal Scottish Academy during her time in Great Stuart Street. D. A. Andrews who lived in Dundee before and after his sojourn in Edinburgh, was an oil painter of portraits, historical subjects and still life. He became the first drawing master at Dundee Seminaries (later, Dundee High School). Miss M. Andrews was a teacher of painting and drawing.

Signor Joseph Rampini (c.1805–1863) taught Italian for several years at the Scottish Naval and Military Academy, founded in 1825. He lived for five years at 6 Great Stuart Street from 1832, and then for two years at *no. 2*. He also taught privately at 45 and 121 George Street. At the latter address, he and a colleague, Monsieur Dubuc, advertised a 'complete and connected course' in Italian and French 'whereby a competent knowledge of both will be acquired with a great saving of time and expense.' He later taught at the Scottish Institution at *9 Moray Place* where Jessie Carrick (see *11 St Colme Street*) described him as 'the most eccentric and most particular man I ever set eyes on.'

Joseph Rampini had a son Charles, a sheriff-substitute of Zetland

and of Inverness, and a son Robert who was Chief Justice of Bengal in 1907. Robert changed his surname in 1908 to his middle name of Fulton, and was knighted in that year.

Barclay Dun, at no. 6 from 1841 for three years, came from a family of teachers: he taught dancing. His son Finlay taught singing at the Atholl Crescent school. The Dun family was also responsible for Edinburgh's two Lancastrian schools, the first of which was a long, low, wood and brick erection on the top of Calton Hill in 1807. Joseph Lancaster's monitorial system provided schools for poor children, in which children aged 12 or more acted as monitors and helped the younger children to learn. Two tickets for good work could be exchanged for a paper kite and three for a ball.

John Blake Macdonald RSA (1829–1901) lived here from 1861 to 1876. He came to Edinburgh in 1852, having earlier 'followed the plough'. He soon entered the RSA life school and in 1862 carried off the first prize for painting from life. He is best known for his paintings of incidents during the Jacobite rebellions and of other historical scenes.

Living on the same common stair as Macdonald were James Hogg and his family from 1866 to 1872. He was a brassfounder, gas engineer and plumber, employing 25 men and 30 boys at 25 Lothian Road and later also at 1 Haymarket Terrace. The works were in King's Stables Road and Spittal Street. The firm imported French bronzes, Parian [from the island of Paros] and Bohemian glass, and supplied the newest designs for drawing room, dining room and bedroom use.

Dr and Mme Adolph Schulz lived at no. 6, from 1883 to 1887. He was a lecturer, translator and teacher of German and Italian. He taught at the Ladies' College, 70 Queen Street, the Misses Forbes' School in Rothesay Place and several other private schools. He and his wife (a teacher of French and Italian) advertised 'select day classes for ladies and evening classes for gentlemen' in their home. They also offered private lessons in families.

Number 4

for Murray, 1830 to 1837, see *24 Moray Place*

Another boarding school was at no. 4 for eight years from 1840, in the charge of Miss Frances Home, who had five resident girl pupils.

for Handyside, 1848 to 1854, see *10 Moray Place*

Number 2

The Misses Laidlaw moved their boarding school to no. 2 from Northumberland Street in 1828, remaining for only two years.

Several teachers of music came to live in Great Stuart Street. First was Signor Theophilus Bucher (c.1802–1871), at no. 2 from 1836 to 1866 and then at *no. 19* until 1872. He described himself as professor of singing and was singing master at a school in Atholl Crescent and then at the Scottish Institution, where he taught Jessie Carrick (see *11 St Colme Street*). She wrote to Frank Forbes in 1858: 'My singing is a little better than it used to be, owing to my having had lessons from Signor Bucher. (He) is very nice and always makes my lesson last two hours instead of one only.'

In 1837, Signor Bucher gave a violin performance, attended by over 600 people, at the Assembly Rooms. Baptie described him as a celebrated teacher of voice-training and composing and a flautist. He 'published a set of excellent vocal exercises and several highly artistic songs.' He never married.

John Brunton, who lived at no. 2 from 1844 to 1862, employed six men and two apprentices at his tailor's and clothier's shop at 82 and then at 95 Princes Street.

George Lichtenstein (no. 2, from 1864 to his death in 1893) was a pianist, teacher and composer. A refugee from Hungary in 1851, he went to London with an introduction to the soprano Jenny Lind. He taught there, chiefly the piano, for four years before going to Edinburgh to continue his teaching. From 1864 he was one of the Directors of the Edinburgh Collegiate School in Charlotte Square. Lucy Colquhoun and her sisters, of Royal Terrace, were taught at home by Lichtenstein but always with their mother or another adult in the room: 'he was altogether too personable, too agreeable.' His two nieces, Clara and Georgette Lichtenstein, who lived with him at the 1881 census, also taught at the School. Clara was a brilliant soprano and also gave piano recitals, while Georgette was an accomplished artist.

Marianne Kay, a piano teacher, lived at no. 2 from 1891 with her sister Harriet, a miniature painter in oil who exhibited at both the Royal Academy and the Royal Scottish Academy.

moving to the longer stretch of Great Stuart Street

Number 7

The Misses Ann, Margaret and Charlotte Moir had a small residential school, first at no. 7 from 1849 to 1857 and then at *no. 8* until 1874. Ann taught music and singing while her sisters were governesses. In 1851 they had five girl boarders aged 12 to 19; in 1861, again five, aged 5 to 13. By 1871 they were no longer teaching but had two sisters in their 20s as boarders, one of whom was a vocalist, Elinor Winsberg.

Thomas Kay, who was here from 1858 for four years, was an upholsterer and undertaker, employing fifteen men, two women and one girl at 89 George Street. He had seven children of whom the eldest was a cabinet maker's apprentice by the age of 14.

for Moncreiff, 1870 to 1880, see *no. 15*

James Gillies, at no. 7 from 1873 to the turn of the century, was a linen and silk merchant at 32 and 34 George Street. Andrew Hogg, at no. 7 from 1889 to 1897, was a tailor and clothier with his business at 94 George Street.

Number 9

Robert Blackburn, brother-in-law of Jemima (see *25 Ainslie Place*) spent 30 years in the Moray Feu. He came to 9 Great Stuart Street on his marriage to Frances Dewing in 1847, staying until 1863; and at *2 Moray Place* from 1867 for ten years. He was an advocate, and Sheriff of Stirling from 1868 for ten years. He and his wife Frances had five daughters and four sons, of whom one, another Robert, lived at *3 Great Stuart Street* from 1891 to 1897. In 1893, that son married – while he was in Great Stuart Street – Lady Constance Bowes-Lyon, daughter of the 13th Earl of Strathmore and aunt of Queen Elizabeth the Queen Mother. In 1918 he was elevated to the Bench, with the title of Lord Blackburn.

Number 11

for Playfair, 1830 to 1831, see *no. 17*

John Murray (1777–1859) lived at no. 11 from 1840, the year after becoming a judge as Lord Murray, until his death. He had been elected unopposed as Whig Member of Parliament for the newly created parliamentary district of Leith in 1832. He was re-elected in 1835, when the election was fought on the question of whether he was a fit person to represent his constituents, having played backgammon on the Sabbath on a steamboat journey from London to Leith. Meanwhile, he had been appointed Lord Advocate in 1834, succeeding Lord Jeffrey. He remained in office until 1839.

English MPs usually paid little attention to Scottish legislation, but Murray succeeded in 1839 in increasing the salaries of Scottish judges to £3,000 although they were said to sit, on average, for an hour and a half on each day. His measure was sparked by the report that the Lord President of the Court of Session had to drive to court in a hackney coach because he could not afford a carriage.

Lord and Lady Murray frequently gave select dinner parties, well-known for the excellence of the food and the rarity of the wine. He was a gourmet who knew exactly what ingredients went into each dish, and he often made special sauces himself. Perhaps his nine servants had vacated the kitchen when, after a party, he sometimes took three or four male guests to the kitchen where he prepared fresh woodcock or snipe for them. He then mixed together the brains of the birds, put them on one piece of toast and handed the morsel around his guests. Invariably they all refused it, leaving him to enjoy his own special treat. He and his wife also gave large weekly evening parties, at which Lady Murray played the piano, for which she had a fanatical love: she also persuaded other distinguished players to perform on the flute, harp or violin.

Lord Cockburn considered that Lord Murray was too fat for hard work, always being afraid that his good living would bring on an attack of gout.

Sir John Maxwell of Pollok, 9th baronet, had an Edinburgh home at 11 Great Stuart Street for four years from 1862. The Pollok estate in Glasgow was given to the City of Glasgow in 1966 by the Maxwell family, who had owned it since 1270. The present Pollok House dates from the late 1740s and the Burrell Collection Museum stands in its grounds.

Sir John had been MP for Renfrewshire 1818 to 1830 (standing latterly as a Reformer) and for Lanarkshire 1832 to 1837. Both in and out of Parliament, he worked to alleviate the sufferings of handloom weavers, many of whom had become unemployed. His wife Matilda, daughter of Thomas, Earl of Elgin, died childless in 1857. In that year, Sir John was instrumental in founding the Industrial School of

Pollokshaws, with over 300 pupils. Boys were taught carpentry, tailoring and shoemaking whilst girls were taught sewing and knitting and took part in the washing, baking and cooking of the establishment. Free board and lodging was supplied for a limited number, with cheap food and clothing for all pupils. In 1862, Sir John paid for the building of a new church of Pollok at Eastwood.

Number 13

for Baillie, 1836 to 1844, see *14 Randolph Crescent*

William Fox Talbot (1800–1877) came to no. 13 in 1864, remaining there for eight years. He is famed for his experimental work in photography, but he also had a varied and distinguished career in other fields. He had been briefly at *11 Moray Place* at the time of the 1861 census. In both houses he and his wife had eight resident servants.

Fox Talbot was Liberal MP for Chichester in the first reformed Parliament of 1832, but did not retain his interest in politics. As a wealthy country gentleman, of Lacock Abbey in Wiltshire, he was interested in photography from 1833. When sketching on the shores of Lake Como with the aid of a camera lucida and a camera obscura, he experimented with the possibility of making permanent the pictures which the camera lens threw onto his paper. He sensitised the paper with iodide of silver and nitrate of silver. He produced calotypes, later called talbotypes, which led to photography as we know it today. At the same time, daguerrotypes were being produced in France, on silvered copper plate.

Between 1844 and 1846, Fox Talbot published (in parts) *The Pencil of Nature*, the first book ever to be illustrated with photographs. He also published *Sun Pictures in Scotland* in 1845.

Number 15

for Scottish Institution, 1835 to 1841, see *9 Moray Place*

James Moncreiff (1811–1895) (whose father and brothers were described at *47 Moray Place*, where he was brought up) spent most of his life at 15 Great Stuart Street. He married Isabella, daughter of Robert Bell, in 1835 and they all three lived at 20 St Andrew Square. They all moved to *3 Moray Place*, together with Benjamin Bell,

James's friend and colleague and Isabella's brother in 1838, and to 15 Great Stuart Street in 1842. Benjamin soon left them, but Robert Bell lived there until he died in 1861. He was Sheriff of Berwickshire and Procurator of the Church of Scotland.

James Moncreiff and some friends founded the Classical Society in 1827, with debates in Latin, but the speeches were 'undeniably dull, seldom fluent and sometimes obscure'. His first client in his Bar practice was a Highlander accused of stealing money. On acquittal, without a word of thanks to his counsel, he threw his plaid over his shoulder, rushed from the court-house and 'was out of Inverness and away to Benbecula before the clerk had recorded the verdict', according to Moncreiff. Lord Cockburn wrote of James Moncreiff

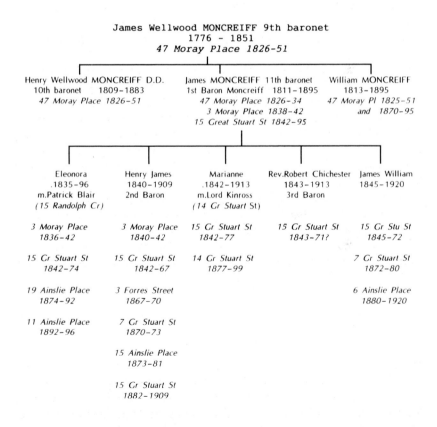

Some members of the Moncrieff family, who lived in many houses in the Moray feu

that he 'prolongs the hereditary talent of the family, is a good lawyer, a pleasing and forcible speaker, a most agreeable writer, judicious, honourable and friendly.'

He rose to be Lord Advocate in 1851 and MP for Leith and, in 1859, for Edinburgh City. For nearly twenty years he travelled frequently and cheerfully on the night express between Edinburgh Waverley and King's Cross. As Lord Advocate, he made six unsuccessful attempts to provide a national system of education and to establish a Board of Education for Scotland. He introduced and carried measures to abolish religious tests in Scottish universities and to reduce the number of Sheriffs. He guided the passing of over 100 Acts of Parliament and was associated with reform of legal procedure. He became Lord Justice Clerk in 1868, a judge in the following year, and a baronet in 1871. He was raised to the peerage, as Lord Moncreiff, in 1874 and also succeeded his brother Henry as the 11th baronet in 1883.

James and Isabella Moncreiff raised a family of five sons and two daughters. The daughters both married neighbours: Patrick Blair of *15 Randolph Crescent* and (as his second wife) John Balfour (later Lord Kinross) of *14 Great Stuart Street.*

One of Lord Moncreiff's sons, Henry James Moncreiff (1840–1909) also became a judge, as Lord Wellwood, later succeeding to his father's barony. He was a prolific writer, with a keen sense of humour. He contributed stories and articles to *Blackwoods, Cornhill* and other magazines. He wrote 'General Remarks on the Game of Golf' for the volume on golf in the Badminton Library. As a widower, he lived for three years at *7 Great Stuart Street* with his brother James William Moncreiff; then, on his remarriage, at *15 Ainslie Place* from 1873 until his second wife died in 1881, when he returned to his parents' home at 15 Great Stuart Street (until his own death) and his brother moved to *6 Ainslie Place.*

Number 17

After a year at *no. 11*, William Playfair (1789–1857) lived at no. 17 from 1831 until his death. He had come from London to Edinburgh in 1794 to live with his uncle, John Playfair, professor of mathematics, and later to follow his father's profession as an architect. He built up an extensive private practice, designing numerous country houses and he was responsible for many buildings in Edinburgh. After the insistence of the architect William Stark of the importance of following the natural contours of Calton Hill, his pupil William Playfair was commissioned to produce a plan for a 'proposed New Town between Edinburgh and Leith'. This led to the design for Regent, Royal and Carlton Terraces in 1819. Playfair also designed the Observatory on Calton Hill, the Royal Institution (later, the Royal Scottish Academy), the College of Surgeons and St Stephen's Church. Donaldson's Hospital is often considered to be his best work, and was much admired by Queen Victoria. He never married and he died after a long illness.

In September 1847, Playfair outlined the duties of two domestic servants. One was said to be a plain, tolerable cook, good-tempered, sober and honest. The other was a housemaid and tablemaid, good-humoured and clean. As well as marketing and cooking, the cook cleaned his business rooms, the clerk's office and the kitchen department; the housemaid cleaned the dining room, drawing room and bedrooms and answered the door. They both washed sheets, towels, stockings and flannels at home. But all his other washing was sent out. No followers (male admirers) were allowed, but the servants could go out on alternate Sundays. The cook's wages were twelve guineas a year, and the housemaid's ten guineas.

Andrew Rutherford Clark (1828–1899) had already lived at no. 17 for ten years when he married Margaret Rutherford in 1869. As a junior counsel he once wanted to put in a minute against the judge's wish. He persisted and won his point when the judge gave in and said, 'In God's name, Mr Clark, put it in.' 'No, my Lord, I'll put it in in the name of the pursuer.' He loved the life of a busy advocate but was said to be working himself to death before he was elevated to the bench in 1875. He jocularly suggested that he would take the title of Lord Backgreen, since that was the only land attached to his house, but settled for Lord Clark.

A great sportsman, Lord Clark was possibly the last golfer to play in a tall hat at Musselburgh.

Number 19

A coach and harness maker, James Thomson, lived at no. 19 from 1834 for three years, with his workplace in Melville Street nearby.

Joseph Moule (1797–1855) came here in 1848, leaving again five years later. He was Superintending President of the General Post

Office, Edinburgh from 1822 until his death. He was also, latterly, one of eight serjeants-at-arms in Her Majesty's household. This was a ceremonial appointment, involving attendance at levées and state balls.

for Steell, 1848 to 1855, see *1 Randolph Place*
for Addison, 1853 to 1855, see *18 Ainslie Place*

W. R. Montignani, at no. 19 from 1858 to 1864, was the senior partner of Wood and Co., music sellers of 49 George Street and 18 Waterloo Place. He was much respected by his customers for his abilities and intelligence. Italian by birth, he published *Gems of Scottish Melody* in 1844.

for Bucher, 1866 to 1872, see *no. 2*

Number 20

A distinguished map engraver, Alexander Keith Johnston (1804–1871), lived at no. 20 for three years from 1841 with his wife and some of their eleven children. They must have been a lively young family in one flat.

Johnston was apprenticed in 1820 to a copper-plate engraver, Kirkwood, who produced large-scale maps of Edinburgh in 1817, 1819 and 1821. Johnston joined his brother William's printing business in 1826. William was Lord Provost of Edinburgh from 1842 to 1851.

In 1830, a few years before his marriage, Johnston went on a walking tour with some friends in the west Highlands, and found so many inaccuracies in the best available maps that he decided to produce better ones himself. His first large work was *The National Atlas*, published in 1843 for ten guineas. Other editions followed. By the time of his death 2,500 copies of his *Physical Atlas of Natural Phenomena* had been sold. He also produced maps for sixpence each, so that poorer people could learn from them. It was said that he did more for popularising geography in this country than any other contemporary geographer.

The firm of W. & A. K. Johnston acquired the business of W. H. Lizars in 1862, including the engraving of bank notes. They began to use colour printing by lithography from about 1865: previously, colours had been added by hand. A. K. Johnston is credited with introducing the convention of colouring water (sea, lakes, rivers) in blue on the firm's maps and atlases.

Duncan Mackinlay, a woollen draper and outfitter in Bank Street, lived at no. 20 from 1860 to 1866.

for Readman, 1872 to 1881, see *9 Moray Place*

Number 18

for Blackwood, 1834 to 1845, see *3 Ainslie Place*
for Wotherspoon, 1845 to 1891, see *16 Ainslie Place*

Number 16

William Edmonstoune Aytoun (1813–1865) and his wife Emily moved from Inverleith Terrace to 16 Great Stuart Street in 1853. It

Professor W. E. Aytoun

was obviously a grander house, for he wrote: 'Last week I purchased a house in Great Stuart Street, big enough to lodge a patriarch. I am not frightened at what I have done: I am simply stupefied. There will be plumbers, and the gas fitters, and the painters; hum of upholstery work, and the slave that vendeth carpets, with all manner of minor harpies upon me at once.' Their former home had been so damp that they could not use the top floor, and his wife's wedding dress, 'hanging peacefully on a peg', became spotted with mildew.

Already an advocate, Aytoun held the chair of Rhetoric and Belles Lettres from 1845. Four years later he proposed to Emily, daughter of Professor Wilson, who was better known as an author under the name Christopher North. Emily sought her father's approval of the marriage and, writing against time, he pinned on her breast a piece of paper reading 'with the compliments of the author' and sent her back to Aytoun.

Professor Aytoun had made a career in law because he could not afford to pursue his literary interests. He continued his practice at the Bar after becoming Professor and became Sheriff and Vice-Admiral of Orkney and Shetland in 1852, involving a visit each autumn, when he took his rod and his gun. His writing career, meanwhile, had become successful. He was on the staff of *Blackwood's Magazine* from 1844 and succeeded his father-in-law as editor, and contributed to it until his death. His ballads, *Lays of the Cavaliers*, ran into many editions, and he also wrote humorous articles about railways, exposing the folly of railway mania in 1845.

He was a popular teacher, causing an increase in the number of students of rhetoric from 30 to 150 in twenty years. In 1853 he was a founder member of The National Association for the Vindication of Scottish Rights. The Association insisted that Scotland was inadequately represented at Westminster, and urged the appointment of a Secretary of State for Scotland, which object was not achieved until 1926.

Sadly, Emily died childless in 1859, after some years as an invalid, and Aytoun was then intolerably lonely. He remarried in 1863, his second wife being Fearne Kinnear (a sister of George Balfour-Kinnear of 9 *Doune Terrace*) but he died only two years later.

Dr James Warburton Begbie (1826–1876) made his home at no. 16 from 1866. He was a family practitioner in Edinburgh who, in 1854, was physician to the temporary cholera hospital. From 1868 he limited his work to consultancy, involving many tiring railway journeys. He was said to be the most popular and highly esteemed physician in Scotland, gentle and kind. When he entered a ward, a new light seemed to shine in the faces of the sick. He taught his students to be courteous to the poor.

In the year of his death, his *Book of Medical Information and Advice* was published, written for the lay reader. He provided an alphabetical directory of the more common ailments and their treatment; hints to be followed in cases of emergency (again, alphabetical); and advice on the preservation of health – diet, exercise, sleep, and the recommendation to have a daily cold bath. This valuable book ran into several editions.

Number 14

John Blair Balfour (1837–1905) brought his first wife, Lillias Mackenzie, to live at no. 14 in 1869, next-door to her father, Lord Mackenzie, a judge. Balfour had a distinguished career as a student at Edinburgh University but did not graduate. After twenty years at the Bar he was elected Liberal MP for Clackmannan and was also Lord Advocate for most of the years from 1881 to 1895, when he remained MP until being appointed Lord President of the Court of Session in 1899 and Baron Kinross in 1902. On his appointment as Lord President, Lord Rosebery said: 'I have never in my life known an appointment which gave such universal pleasure.'

His wife died in 1872 and five years later he married Marianne Moncreiff who had lived opposite to him at *no. 15* with her father Lord Moncreiff. Thus the families at numbers *12, 14* and *15* were inter-related.

Number 12

Donald Mackenzie (1818–1875), at *9 Randolph Crescent* 1853–1856 and then at 12 Great Stuart Street until his death, qualified as a doctor, becoming FRCS, and was in practice at Lasswade. He soon switched to the law, and was called to the Bar. As Advocate Depute, in 1857 he prepared the indictment against Madeleine Smith for murdering her French lover in Glasgow. He was raised to the bench, as Lord Mackenzie, as 1870.

Of Lord Mackenzie's five sons and five daughters, one son, Robert, became Rector of Edinburgh Academy in 1888 at the age of

31, resigning in 1901 for reasons of ill-health. He died ten years later, unmarried. Robert Mackenzie's major accomplishments have been set out by Magnus Magnusson in *The Clacken and the Slate*. They include launching the preparatory school, building a science laboratory and making science a compulsory subject, enforcing the system of promotion on merit (instead of automatically), starting Academy boarding houses, making sport compulsory, introducing a system of prefects (called Ephors) and starting a school choir and orchestra.

Lord Mackenzie's youngest son, Kenneth, became Bishop of Argyll and the Isles from 1907 for 35 years.

Number 10

for Adam, 1870 to 1882, see *34 Moray Place*

Number 8

David Bryce (1807–1876) lived at no. 8 for six years from 1831. He trained under, and became a partner in 1841 of, the architect William Burn. He went on to design Fettes College, the Royal Infirmary of Edinburgh and the Bank of Scotland building at the top of the Mound. He designed the Assembly Hall (opened in 1850), for which the ladies of the Free Church of Scotland collected £7,000; and St George's Free Church in Shandwick Place (1869). Bryce was also a painter in water colours. He exhibited at the Royal Scottish Academy throughout his adult life, not only architectural designs but also precisely drawn topographical subjects. He was the founder of the short-lived Architectural Institute of Scotland. He never married.

David Mackenzie, who lived at no. 8 for four years from 1836, painted landscapes in oils. In 1826 he exhibited at the Institution for the Encouragement of the Fine Arts, in Waterloo Place, of which he was a founder member. After the founding of the Scottish Academy in 1827, he exhibited there for four years and was elected RSA. However he forfeited his membership in 1832, the ostensible reason being that he had failed to satisfy the Council with his diploma submissions. It was generally believed that unseemly behaviour had led to his downfall, since many artists failed to submit works without losing their membership status.

Robert Hodgetts, engraver of landscapes and portraits, spent one year at no. 8 in 1839. He exhibited at the new Scottish Academy in 1827 (in Waterloo Place), and again from 1837–38, by which time William Playfair's building for the RSA, at the foot of the Mound, was in use. Robert Hodgetts had previously lived in Canonmills Cottage with his father, also a historical and portrait engraver.

A number of shopkeepers and tradesmen lived in the flats at no. 8. John Nicholson, a tailor and clothier of 25 Frederick Street was here for six years from 1841. Andrew Bryce (1862 for two years) was a plumber, employing three men and two boys in South Melville Place. David and George Glen (1880 for two years) were brothers who were cabinet makers, upholsterers and furniture dealers at 24A Frederick Street. John Armstrong (1864 to 1872) had a general drapery warehouse at 12 Charlotte Place. There, with one male and nine female employees, he provided millinery, dressmaking, outfitting and family mourning.

A printseller, John Mundell, spent eight years here from 1842. He was secretary of the New Association for Promoting Fine Arts in Scotland. His business premises were at 60 Princes Street, where he was an artists' colourman, printseller, picture frame-maker and fancy stationer.

Leitch Ritchie (1801–1865) spent two years here from 1856. From an early age he devoted his life to writing and editing. He travelled a great deal and wrote many books of travel. In 1840 he became the first editor of *Indian News and Chronicle of Eastern Affairs*. A native of Greenock, he came to Edinburgh and edited *Chambers Journal* for many years. Elizabeth Grant of Rothiemurcus (see *The Highland Lady in Ireland*) found him very appreciative of the many pieces she wrote for Chambers. He retired to London three years before his death (see also *9 Randolph Cliff*).

for Moir, 1857 to 1874, see *no. 7*

Several music teachers lived at no. 8: Alfred Huxtable (1874 to 1881), Otto Schweitzer, born in Zurich (1882 to 1890), and H. B. Fabiani (1881 to 1895).

The Rev. David Milne was appointed minister of St Luke's Church in Young Street in 1893, and made his home at no. 8 for a year or two. From the mid 1850s, the congregation had come largely from Charlotte Square, Moray Place, Ainslie Place and the surrounding streets. Mr Milne found a depleted congregation because private houses had given way to offices. He saw no future for a church in

Young Street and, largely through his efforts, a new church was opened in 1908 in East Fettes Avenue.

Great Stuart Street Householders

1.
1832–38 Prof. Alexander Monro
1832–34 Mrs Capt. A. McLean
1832–70 Robert Morris, stationer; James S. Morris, wine merchant
1834–41 Major Hope
1841–47 Mrs Dr Cundell
1844–45 John C. Kieser, pianoforte teacher
1846–48 Mrs Col. Craster
1847–51 Miss Keir
1848–59 Miss Dewar
1851–55 Bernhard Kreutzer
1855–61 Rev. Richard Hibbs MA
1861–   Miss Johnston
1861–63 Miss Mary McGregor
1863–66 F. Lindesay
1868–71 William Fettes Douglas RSA
1870–79 Henry Inglis WS; William Inglis, advocate
1871–80 Miss Campbell
1879–   Miss Rogers
1880–83 John Galloway
1883–   Miss R. Young
1889–90 Mrs E. John
1895–   Miss A. M. & Mrs Gordon

3.
1829 Prof. Robert Christison; John Christison, advocate
1864 A. Burns Shand, advocate
1874 Prof. F. Jenkin
1886 Prof. Cossar Ewart
1889 Mrs Corbett
1891 George Dunlop WS; Robert L. Blackburn, advocate
1897 Misses Mylne

5.
1827   Mrs W. W. Brown
1831–64 Misses Fraser
1832–38 Miss Maxwell
1835–38 Mrs Dr Deans
1838–41 Mrs Dr Anderson
1838–40 John Thomson, clerk of police
1841–42 Mrs Turner

1842–44 Miss Rutherford
1842–43 Mrs M. E. Pearce
1844–52 Miss Irvine
1844–49 Sir James Wemyss, bart, WS
1849–80 Mrs Edmonstoune
1856–95 Miss Hunter
1864–67 Mrs Henrietta Louise White
1868–90 Miss Simson
1879–80 Miss Bruce
1880–87 Miss Jane Whyte Balfour
1887–91 James Francis Bradbury CS
1890–95 George J. Brodie WS
1895–1902 Mrs Corbett
1895–   Mrs W. D. Thorburn
1899–   John Reid, upholsterer

7.
1832–37 William Lang WS, asst. Clerk of Session; Mrs George Stuart; George T. Chiene, accountant
1837–43 George Ross, advocate
1837–40 John Jobson Dickson, accountant
1837–43 Mrs Veitch
1837–39 John Chisholm, lodging keeper
1838–56 Tod & Romanes WS
1839–41 John Macdonald, lodging keeper
1841–44 Miss Dunlop, lodging keeper
1841–44 Miss Pattullo
1843–44 Robert Climie, civil engineer
1844–48 Edward McCallum, merchant
1848–49 Murray & Beith WS
1849–58 Misses Moir
1849–53 Mrs Borthwick
1853–60 Andrew Jamieson, writer
1858–70 John Hamilton WS
1858–62 Thomas Kay, upholsterer & undertaker
1860–66 Miss Cormack
1862–69 Rev. John Donaldson
1864–72 Mrs Clark
1869–73 Mrs Lindsay
1872–73 & Rev. T. M. Lindsay
1873–   James Gillies
1870–73 Henry J. Moncreiff
1872–80 Hon. James W. Moncreiff WS

1873–76 Miss Rollo
1876–89 Mrs Boyle
1876–79 Arthur Makgill, advocate
1880–87 James Keir, advocate
1882–83 James K. Donaldson
1886–88 Robert Younger, advocate
1887–90 Miss Ducat
1889–97 Andrew Hogg, clothier
1890–91 Thomas S. Esson
1891–93 Charles Hanson
1893–95 Mrs Wright
1897–99 Miss S. E. Hardie
1897–99 Capt. S. D. Foster, ASC
1899–   Miss Myrtle
1899–   Miss Wilson

9.
1834 John Walker of Crawfordton
1836 also Robert Brown(e)
1837 Alexander Campbell esq.
1840 Miss Hamilton of Kildonan, James
Hamilton esq.
1843 Lady Elliot of Stobs
1848 R. B. Blackburn, advocate
1863 Robert Kerr
1890 Mrs Robert Kerr

11.
1830 William H. Playfair architect
1834 William John Sands
1837 Sir Alexander Wood, bart
1840 Lord Murray
1862 Sir John Maxwell of Pollok
1866 Frederick Pitman WS & NP
1882 & A. R. C. Pitman WS & NP

13.
1831 Alexander Earle Monteith, advocate; M.
P. Brown, advocate
1836 Charles Baillie, advocate
1844 Mrs Gunson
1846 Maj. Gen. Thomas R. Swinburne,
Marcus Lodge
1864 Henry Fox Talbot. photographer
1872 James Campbell Tait WS; John Tait,
advocate
1881 Col. Hare of Calderhall
1883 George Dunlop WS
1887 James Graham Watson
1890 George Dunlop WS
1891 J. C. Pitman, advocate

15.
1835   Scottish Institution

1842–47 B. R. Bell, advocate
1842–61 R. Bell, sheriff of Berwickshire
1842   James Moncreiff, advocate

17.
1831 William H. Playfair, architect
1859 Andrew Rutherford Clark, QC

19.
1831–33 F. G. Smith, Sec., Scot. Union
Insurance
1833–42 John K. Smith WS
1833–44 Mrs Liddle
1834–37 James Thomson, coachmaker
1837–38 Thomas Murray
1840–46 P. S. Fraser, bookseller
1844–46 Misses Wallace Browne
1846–47 James Reid, silk mercer
1847–48 Archibald Christie, writer
1848–53 Joseph Moule, President of GPO
1848–55 John Steell RSA
1850–53 George Augustus Thomson,
accountant & actuary
1853–55 Rev. B. Addison
1853–55 Miss Keir
1855–75 Mrs Borthwick
1855–58 Charles Robertson, advocate
1855–58 James Elder WS
1858–64 W. R. Montignani, music-seller
1862–64 Miss Berry
1864–66 Dr Dubuc
1866–72 Signor Bucher
1872–75 Miss Thomson
1872–75 John Hall SSC
1873–75 Miss M. G. Roxburgh
1875–98 Louis Rothfield, prof. of music
1875–   Miss Macpherson
1876–   Mrs Rowe
1898–   Madame Middleton (= Mrs Hewat),
vocalist

20.
1836–41 Robert Sinclair, writer
1836–39 Misses Cameron
1836–48 Mr Robert Scott, commercial
traveller
1839–50 W. Turnbull esq., Royal Bank
1841–44 A. K. Johnstone, engraver
1844–55 Thomas Hudson, agent
1848–59 Mrs Boyce
1850–56 James Craig, manager, Sunbury
Distillery
1855–57 J. M. Baillie, accountant
1856–57 Edward W. Nightingale, clothier

1857–59 William Adamson Dewar
1858–61 A. Cockburn MD
1859–61 Mrs James Hogg
1860–66 Duncan Mackinlay
1861–64 James Wood
1862–68 Mrs Duncan
1864–80 Mrs Davie
1866–71 Mrs Oldham
1866–71 Mrs Goodshaw
1868–70 Miss Shannon
1871–81 Miss Alexander
1871–76 Mrs Macandrew
1872–81 George Readman, advocate
1876–90 Miss Hill
1882–90 Miss Brock
1883–84 A. Fulton
1885–88 John F. McLennan, advocate
1889–94 Miss Boswell
1892–   Miss Findlay
1892–   Miss Mitchell
1896–97 James Chisholm

18.
1836 Alexander & R. Blackwood
1841 & James Blackwood WS
1845 W. Wotherspoon SSC
1859–61 & W. Morison
1891 William Younger

16.
1837 George Dickson esq.
1839 William Smythe esq., advocate
1853 William Edmonstoune Aytoun, advocate
1866 J Warburton Begbie MD
1881 William Lang Todd, advocate
1892 M. R. Greenlees, advocate

14.
1856 R. B. Maconochie
1864 Maj. Gen. Christie
1870 J. B. Balfour, advocate
1889 Andrew Rutherford WS; James H. Rutherford WS

12.
1856 Donald Mackenzie, advocate

10.
1856 D. Robertson Souter, accountant; Henry Callender CA to 1857
1872 James Adam, advocate
1885 M. T. Stormonth Darling, advocate

8.
1831–36 David Bryce, architect
1831–36 William Robertson, advocate
1833–34 Mrs Robert Harper
1834–50 W. M. Boyd, advocate; G. M. Boyd WS
1836–40 David Mackenzie, artist
1837–40 Alexander K. Fraser WS
1837–38 A. Davidson, portrait painter
1839–40 R. M. Hodgetts
1840–42 Mrs Kerr
1842–47 John Nicholson, clothier
1842–43 Mrs Geddes
1842–50 John Mundell, printseller
1844–47 James Annan, plasterer
1848–70 William Innes, Union Bank
1848–50 Miss Rose
1850–52 Mrs Craigie
1851–52 Mrs William Lock
1851–55 Robert M. Stark
1852–55 John Campbell MD
1854–56 Miss Fuller
1855–64 A. Dingwall, advocate
1856–57 Leitch Ritchie
1856–62 Andrew McLure
1862–64 Andrew Bryce
1864–76 M. Rettie, advocate
1864–67 John Armstrong
1870–81 John Robertson FEIS
1874–78 George Duthie
1874–81 Alfred Huxtable
1876–78 Mrs C. Head
1878–79 Miss Urquhart
1878–88 Mrs John Menzies
1880–82 Mrs Glen
1881–   Miss Agnes W. Kilpatrick
1882–85 H. B. Fabiani, prof. of singing
1882–90 Otto Schweizer, music teacher
1885–89 Miss Lucy Smellie
1889–   Mrs Aikenhead
1890–94 A. Handley, commercial traveller
1891–   Mrs MacInnes
1894–95 Rev. David M. Milne
1894–97 Jonathan Davidson
1897–98 Miss C. Dunlop
1897–   James H. Brown, heraldic stationer
1898–   Miss E. B. Thomson

6.
1832–37 Signor Rampini
1832–55 Miss Cay; Robert Dundas Cay WS; Albert Cay, wine merchant
1836–37 Mr D. R. Andrews, portrait painter; Miss Andrews, miniature painter; Miss M.

Andrews, teacher of painting
1836–67 James Finlay, writer; Charles Finlay, writer
1837–41 E. Ricateau, teacher of French
1838–47 Gustaf Kombst, teacher of German
1841–44 Barclay Dun, teacher
1841–44 Miss Stanfield
1848–51 Thomas Macfarlane, writer
1848–49 Walter Black
1851–52 Miss Douglas Fyffe
1852–56 David Richardson, architect
1855–56 John Jameson
1856–61 Mrs Johnstone
1859–64 John C. Keiser
1861–62 Mrs Ballantyne
1861–76 J. B. McDonald, artist
1862–64 Mrs McNair
1864–66 Kenneth Bain
1866–67 Mrs M. E. Beveridge
1866–78 George Hogg & James A. Hogg
1867–80 Miss Jamieson
1869–77 P. Alexander Spiers, advocate
1876–83 Mrs W. C. Mackenzie
1878–79 Mrs Paterson
1879–82 John J. Reid, advocate
1880– Mrs Monteith
1882–84 John Little Mounsey
1882– Miss C. Dunlop
1883–85 Dr Adolph Schulz, teacher
1892–94 John H. Laidlaw
1894– James H. Brown

4.
1832 Sir Patrick Murray of Auchtertyre, Bt
1832 Signor Rampini
1836 Lady Dundas, Beechwood
1838 James Macinroy esq. of Lude

1840 Miss Home, boarding school
1848 Robert Handyside, advocate
1855 William Drummond Mercer
1864 A. Peddie Waddell WS
1874 –

2.
1829–30 William Robertson, advocate
1830–31 David Bryce, architect
1830–36 Miss Macaskill
1830–36 Andrew Grieve WS
1831–36 William Rae, accountant
1836–64 Signor Bucher, prof. of music
1837–39 Signor Rampini, Italian master
1837–38 Mr John Davidson, tea merchant
1839–42 Miss A. M. Clapperton
1840–45 Mrs Col. Craster
1842–43 Capt. James McDonald
1844–62 John Brunton, tailor
1845–48 Miss Dewar
1850–54 Mrs Skipton
1863–64 John Forman
1864–92 George Lichtenstein, prof. of music
1864–67 Rev. J. E. Dovey
1870–71 John Christie Deans SSC
1872–73 Mrs Petrie
1873–80 Mrs Messieux
1877–79 J. Guy Hamilton, advocate
1879–98 Capt. Charles Douglas
1880–84 Alexander & William Ramsay
1885–87 Miss H. S. Lang
1887–90 W. B. Rainnie SSC
1891– Miss H. Kay
1894–98 Thomas D. Kerr
1897–99 Capt. H. W. A. Christie RA
1899– Alfred Heys Thomson

Randolph Crescent
Randolph Cliff
Randolph Place

These three streets commemorate the name of Thomas Randolph who was created Earl of Moray by his uncle, King Robert the Bruce in 1312. In the following year, Thomas Randolph led the raiding party which captured Edinburgh Castle from the English by using a precipitous secret pathway on the north side, previously used by a soldier to visit a girl. The earldom subsequently reverted several times to the Crown, before being revived in 1562.

Randolph Crescent

This neat crescent of seventeen houses, bisected by Great Stuart Street, was built round the site of Drumsheugh House, sometimes known as Moray House, and shown on Kirkwood's map of 1817. After having the house pulled down in 1822, to make way for the feuing of the Moray Estate, the 10th Earl of Moray considered building himself a new house in the gardens in the middle of Randolph Crescent, but decided instead to build in Moray Place. A gatehouse on the Queensferry Road diameter of Randolph Crescent, also shown on Kirkwood's map, was demolished too. There is no evidence for the story that the Randolph Crescent garden is on the site of a plague cemetery.

Grant's *Old and New Edinburgh* (1882) states that Drumsheugh House 'of which nothing now remains but its ancient rookery in Randolph Crescent', was 'removed recently'. However the Ordnance Survey map of 1852 shows another Drumsheugh House on the west side of Queensferry Road: this was pulled down in 1872 or 1873.

The houses were gradually occupied between 1830 (*no. 1*, at the south end) and 1853 (*nos. 10 and 15*).

Number 1

Randolph Crescent houses, like those in Moray Place and Ainslie Place, were attractive to advocates, five of whom made their home there in the 1840s.

One of them, Angus Fletcher (1805–1875) of Dunans in Argyllshire spent two years at *1 Darnaway Street* from 1828. He was distantly related to Miles Angus Fletcher who married Martha Maitland-Makgill-Crichton of *28 and 29 Moray Place*. He returned to Edinburgh in 1840 to live at 1 Randolph Crescent. Five years later, on his marriage to Harriet Callanan of Lisbon he moved to *5 Ainslie Place*. In 1851, by which time he was Comptroller-General of Inland Revenue in Scotland, his wife died leaving him with two infant daughters, one of whom soon died also. He remained in his Ainslie Place house until 1870 and returned to Randolph Crescent, spending the last five years of his life at *no. 8*.

Number 2

Murdoch Maclaine, of Lochbuie on the Isle of Mull, had a family of five sons and five daughters, most of whom were grown up and possibly did not live at 2 Randolph Crescent during the three years of their father's occupancy from 1836.

The third householder at no. 2 was John Clerk Brodie WS (1811–1888) who came in 1841. After being widowed, he remarried in 1848 and removed to *26 Moray Place*. By his second marriage he had at least seven children who were educated at home by a governess. He was Crown Agent – the principal legal officer in the Lord Advocate's office – by 1851. Ten years later he was Principal Keeper of the Register of Sasines (records of purchase of property).

John Brodie's son Thomas by his first marriage was also a Writer to the Signet: he and his second wife lived at *9 Ainslie Place* for the final quarter of the century. Both they and Thomas's parents had half a dozen resident servants.

Thomas Brodie (1832–1896) was created a baronet in 1892 but he had no children by either wife and the title became extinct on his death four years later.

Another advocate in Randolph Crescent was Edward Gordon (1814–1879), who brought his bride, Agnes McInnes, to no. 2 in 1847, remaining there until his death. His widow continued to live there until she died too in 1895. They had five sons and three daughters.

Edward Gordon was twice Lord Advocate, from 1867–68 and 1874–76. He was keen to unite the established Church of Scotland and the Free Church of Scotland, which could not be done unless the people were free to choose their own ministers: he achieved the abolishment of patronage in 1874. He was MP for the Universities of Glasgow and Aberdeen 1869–76. Then, in failing health, he was appointed a Lord of Appeal and created Baron Gordon, dying three years later in Brussels, when his life peerage became extinct. Among Lord Gordon's sons, John became MP for Elgin and Nairn, Arthur became Chaplain of the Royal Company of Archers (the Sovereign's bodyguard for Scotland) and Frederick had a distinguished military career finishing as a Major General, KCB.

Number 3

John Blackwood (1818–1879), son of William (see *3 Ainslie Place*), succeeded to the editorship of *Blackwood's Magazine* on the death of his brother Alexander in 1845. John, with his mother and some of his siblings then moved from *18 Great Stuart Street* to 3 Randolph

Blackwood's Saloon

Crescent, a house which remained in his family after his death in 1879, passing to his widow and then to their daughter Mary, who married Gerald Porter in 1884.

Suffering poor health as a boy, John Blackwood showed his literary talent from an early age, being dubbed 'the little editor' by his family. He was described by his father as 'a very quick and thoughtless creature' and by his brother Alexander as 'a very idle scholar' who, nevertheless, 'read history from morning to night.'

As editor of the *Maga*, John published many new writers at the start of their careers, including George Eliot whom he was astonished to discover was a delicate-looking lady. Her 'Scenes of Clerical Life' had been sent to him anonymously. He started the practice of discussion of military topics in the *Maga*, including descriptions of current military campaigns. He considered that 'soldiers are the cleverest fellows we have' and it was said in *The Times* that articles in the magazine led to important reforms in the French army.

Blackwood's saloon at 45 George Street was a favourite meeting place of the literati of the time. The room was hung with portraits of contributors to the magazine; De Quincey and Thackeray were frequent visitors.

John Blackwood's country home was Strathtyrum, St Andrews, where he was captain of the Royal and Ancient Golf Club.

Number 4

for Orr, 1840 to 1849, see *3 Darnaway Street*
for Pringle, 1849 to 1854, see *2 Randolph Cliff*
for Sprot, 1859 to 1859, see *33 Moray Place*

Number 5

for Christison, 1835 to 1847, see *40 Moray Place*

In 1847, John Marshall (1792–1868), advocate, came to no. 5 with his second wife and six children. The five youngest children were all taught at home by a resident governess. The family moved to *11 Wemyss Place* in 1856 for five years. As a young man, John Marshall had walked from his home in Wigtownshire to study at Edinburgh University. After a long and successful forensic career, Marshall became Dean of the Faculty of Advocates in 1852 but, a few months later, was elevated to the bench as Lord Curriehill. His son John (by his first wife) was later on the bench, also as Lord Curriehill and lived at *6 Randolph Crescent*. The father was said to be no orator; 'his look, air and manner are dry, if not grim.'

Number 6

Miss Elizabeth Milne took in boarders at no. 6 from 1840 to 1847. In 1841 she had five women boarders and three young girls aged nine, ten and fourteen: none appeared to be related to any other. Four resident female servants looked after the household.

David MacFarlane retired from the Bengal Civil Service as the Chief Magistrate of Calcutta. With his wife and family he moved to no. 6 in 1848, after four years at *8 Ainslie Place*, but he died in 1855. His widow maintained her home here for a further twenty years: at the 1871 census she had young company in the form of a niece, a granddaughter and a grandson and their nurse.

for John Marshall (son), 1874 to 1882, see *no. 5*

Number 7

Miss Hill and her brother moved here in 1831 from Melville Street, staying for six years. Mr P. Hill was a collector of cess, or a tax collector.

Robert Horn (1810–1878), another advocate, lived at *50 Moray Place* for ten years from 1837. Then, on his marriage, he moved to 7 Randolph Crescent, remaining there until his death. For the last two years of his life he was Dean of the Faculty of Advocates. The Horns had five daughters and two sons, one of whom, William, returned to live in the family home for a few years before and after his father's death, eventually leaving his mother there with most of her other children.

Number 8

for Fletcher, 1870 to 1875, see *no. 1*

James Muirhead (1831–1889) lived here four years from 1875. First an advocate, he was Professor of Civil Law from 1862 until his death. He moved house several times, coming here from Northumberland

Street, and later had one year at *1 Albyn Place* before finally settling in Drumsheugh Gardens. He had a mercantile training and did not take a degree. He had three or four years working on the *Edinburgh Advertiser*, his father being the proprietor and publisher.

Number 9

The Rev. Robert Candlish (1806–1873) lived at no. 9 for only one year from 1840. He was then minister of St George's Church, but he left the Scottish Kirk in 1843 as a leader of the new Free Church of Scotland. Thereafter he was minister of the newly-built St George's Free Church, in what is now Rutland Street, until his death. His name is commemorated in the Candlish Room in St George's West Church, Shandwick Place.

The Home Secretary nominated Robert Candlish for the new Chair of Biblical Criticism at Edinburgh University in 1841, but then

The Rev. Dr Robert Candlish

cancelled the appointment because of the comment by the Earl of Aberdeen (who later became Prime Minister): 'This man has very recently committed a very flagrant violation of the law. This reverend gentleman, if dealt with by the court in the same way as any other person, should have been sent to prison, where he might find leisure to compose his first syllabus of lectures.'

This censure was because Candlish had moved the delicate and important resolution to the General Assembly to suspend the seven Strathbogie ministers for 'setting at naught the authority of the Assembly.' However, Candlish became Moderator of the General Assembly of the Free Church of Scotland in 1861 and Principal of New College in 1862. Edinburgh University honoured him with an honorary degree of Doctor of Divinity in 1865. Dr Candlish was a brilliant conversationalist. Eight days before his death he boasted of the soundness of his lungs in contrast to the feebleness of his limbs, saying, 'if you were to set me up in the pulpit, I still could make you all hear on the deafest side of your heads.'

for Mackenzie, 1853 to 1856, see *12 Great Stuart Street*

Number 10

Mrs Louisa Trotter moved to 10 Randolph Crescent in 1880 from Melville Street. She was the widow of Archibald Trotter, who died young after travelling around Europe with introductions to embassies and princes. She had lived at *6 Forres Street* at the 1841 census, with five very young children and two resident servants. As a widow aged 43, she lived with her mother, the Hon. Mrs Ann Strange, at *7 Ainslie Place* at the 1851 census.

Mrs Trotter's son, Coutts, and his wife Harriet Keatinge, divided their time between Scotland, the south of England and various spas in Europe for him to 'take the waters' for his health. On visits to Edinburgh they stayed at Trotter family homes or in hotels in the west end of Edinburgh. In 1876, their daughter (Louisa) Kathleen went briefly to Madame Froebel's school in *Moray Place* which she later described as 'as far as was possible at that date for a school for girls to be fashionable, the most fashionable in Edinburgh.'

When Mrs Trotter went to live in Randolph Crescent, Coutts and his wife and Kathleen lived at Gunn's Hotel which included *1 and 2 St Colme Street* and *2 Forres Street*. His sister, Ann Buck, with her daughter Lillias was there also, as well as a lady's maid from

Montreal. Kathleen, then aged 17, recalled visiting the house in Randolph Crescent in her autobiography, *Friends and Kindred*.

> I thought it a most romantic house after my father had taken me down into the basement, four storeys below the front of the house at street level, where there was a cavern–like place, with stalactites hanging from the roof, and in the middle of the stone floor a mysterious–looking trap–door. My father grabbed me when I was going to jump on it, and explained that it covered a well.

Her father arranged for a regular inspection of the trap-door by a man who 'always let down a jug with a string tied to the handle, and drank the contents, saying it "kept him right for a year".' From personal experience, I can say that the water still tasted good in 1996!

When Mrs Louisa Trotter died in 1895, Coutts and his wife lived at 10 Randolph Crescent. Kathleen later married J. S. Haldane CH, FRS, the distinguished scientist. Their children were J. B. S. Haldane, another eminent scientist, and Naomi Mitchison – a prolific author and Tribal Mother to Bakgatla, Botswana – who celebrated her 100th birthday in 1997.

Number 11

Erskine Sandford, advocate, lived here from 1835 to 1861. He and his wife had five children, a sister-in-law and eight servants resident here at the time of the 1841 census. Ten years later, only one child, a daughter, remained at home and there were seven servants including a butler and a page.

The next occupier was Sir David Baxter, for one year only (see *5 Moray Place*).

Number 12

Number 12 had three occupiers in as many years from 1840, but the third, Alexander Morrison, of Bognie in Aberdeenshire, remained until his death in 1874, following which his widow was in the house for a further ten years. He was a landed proprietor, who maintained a staff of six to eight resident servants. In 1851, he and his wife had a butler, footman, coachman and five women servants. Ten years later the same butler was there, with a different footman and, again, five women servants: the housekeeper had been promoted to lady's maid, while some others also served the family for more than ten years.

for Campbell, from 1896, see *4 Darnaway Street*

Number 13

Sir John Robison (1778–1843), at no. 13 from 1839 to 1843, had been in the service of the Nizam of Hyderabad, as contractor for the establishment and maintenance of the artillery service. He returned to Scotland in 1815 a wealthy man, and later settled in Edinburgh. From 1828 to 1840 he was general secretary of the Royal Society of Edinburgh, a position which his father had earlier held. He was knighted in 1838, by which time he had been twice widowed. One of his two daughters lived with him.

Sir John was an inventor, and was particularly interested in the use of hot air to warm houses and in the use of gas for heating, cooking and lighting. His neighbour at *15 Ainslie Place*, Professor James Forbes, wrote: 'From boring a cannon to drilling a needle's eye, nothing was strange to him. His house in Randolph Crescent was built entirely from his own plans and nothing, from the cellar to the roof, in construction or in furniture but bore testimony to his minute and elaborate inventions.' Sir John even designed door handles, chair castors and coal tongs. The house was always open to distinguished visitors.

James Stevenson made his family home at 13 Randolph Crescent from 1859, five years after he had retired to Edinburgh from being senior partner in Jarrow Chemical Company, South Shields. He was a widower, and four of his six daughters and one of his five sons helped to fill the house in Randolph Crescent. Ann Pollock (given the courtesy title of Mrs) came with the family, after being nurse to the children since their early days. She died aged 94, having been given one of the best rooms in the house for her final six years.

These four daughters, all unmarried, lived there for the rest of their lives. Elisa was one of the earliest members of the National Society for Women's Franchise. Two others were remarkable women, whose lives are remembered in *Recollections of the Public Work and Home Life of Louisa and Flora Stevenson*.

Louisa Stevenson (1835–1908) was particularly concerned with obtaining university education for women, and she arranged classes with university teachers in George Street and then Shandwick Place.

She was one of the band of pioneers who finally accomplished the opening of the Scottish Universities to women in 1894. She worked alongside Dr Sophia Jex–Blake to obtain medical education for women.

As 'Guardian of the Poor', Louisa was very concerned with nursing arrangements in the Poorhouse, where she used to pay surprise visits late in the evening, to see whether the inmates were comfortable in their beds. She convinced the Parochial Board that the key of the wine cellar should be removed from the Governor and given to the doctor. The evening before the change over, she interrupted a carousal which led to the dismissal of the Governor.

Louisa was on the Board of Managers of Edinburgh Royal Infirmary and was re-elected six times. A man who had been opposed to having women on the Board later said that Louisa was the most useful member of the Board during his twenty years as a Manager. She was a founder of the Edinburgh School of Cookery and Domestic Economy in 1875, originally in Chambers Street and later in Atholl Crescent (and now Queen Margaret College).

Louisa and Flora Stevenson

Unfortunately, Louisa had to give up her public work during the last five years of her life because of illness. She was awarded an honorary LLD by Edinburgh University in 1906.

Flora Stevenson (1839–1905) was also a promoter of education for women. As a young girl, she held classes in her own home for 'little message girls'. She later devised a scheme for feeding and clothing destitute children. Following the Education Act of 1872, she was elected a member of the first Edinburgh School Board in 1873. She was a member until her death and was chairman from 1900. She represented the Board as one of the governors of George Heriot's Trust. She was a member of many committees, an honorary Fellow of the Educational Institute of Scotland, and a vice-president of the Women's Liberal Unionist Association. A new school at Comely Bank in Edinburgh was named after her in 1899. In 1903 she was awarded an honorary LLD by the University of Edinburgh and was given the Freedom of the City of Edinburgh.

After Flora's death, an article in *The Scottish Review* said: 'What Miss Stevenson did not know about education was not worth knowing.'

Number 14

After four years at *1 Moray Place* (from 1832), followed by eight at *13 Great Stuart Street*, Charles Baillie (1804–1879) lived at 14 Randolph Crescent from 1844 to 1866 as the first occupier of the house. He briefly became Solicitor General and then Lord Advocate in 1858 and a Lord of Session (as Lord Jerviswoode) in the following year, after one month as MP for Linlithgowshire. He was descended from Baillie of Jerviswoode who was executed as a traitor in 1683 for his allegiance to the Dukes of Monmouth and Argyll. After fifty years of marriage, he and his wife died within a year of each other, at their home of Dryburgh House in Roxburghshire. A brother of the 10th Earl of Haddington, he had great charm but he was very shy and retiring, with delicate features.

Number 15

The first occupier of 15 Randolph Crescent was Hugh Blair WS, who lived there from 1853 until his death in 1880, his widow remaining there until their youngest son Hugh, CA, became the householder.

The eldest son, Alexander, was an advocate who later became Sheriff of Stirling and Dumbarton. He lived with his parents until his marriage in 1870. He and his wife Fairley, with three sons and three daughters, lived at *35 Moray Place* from 1877 for many years. They had six resident servants and, by 1881, a resident governess from Germany.

The middle son, Patrick WS, lived with his parents until his marriage in 1874 to a neighbour, Eleonora, daughter of Lord Moncrieff. She had spent her nursery years at *3 Moray Place* until moving with her parents to *15 Great Stuart Street*. After marrying, Patrick and Eleonora lived at *19 Ainslie Place* which later became his office (first, Blair and Finlay WS and then Blair and Cadell). Patrick then made his home at *11 Ainslie Place* in 1892.

The youngest son, Hugh, married a former neighbour, Margaret Bell, whose father was Sheriff Benjamin Bell; and she was a second cousin of Eleonora Moncrieff, sharing a grandfather in Sheriff Robert Bell. Hugh became President of the Society of Accountants in Edinburgh.

Number 16

for Crowe, 1852 to 1854, see *2 Darnaway Street*

First occupied in 1852, this house had no one else of note living in it; from 1882 to 1897, it appears to have been lodgings kept by a Miss Borrie. She had an advocate, William Francis Wood, living there; and then another advocate Hugh J. E. Fraser.

Number 17

The Rev. Daniel Fox Sandford (1821–1906), the grandson of Bishop Daniel Sandford (who died in 1830) was curate of St John's Episcopal Church in Princes Street from 1855. He lived at 17 Randolph Crescent for only one year from 1861, before moving over the Dean Bridge to Oxford Terrace. After 18 years as curate he was appointed Rector of his church, a post he held for a further ten years, and was appointed a canon in 1878. In 1883 he went to Tasmania as bishop there for six years, before returning to Britain to be Bishop of Durham in 1889.

In 1866, Dr Sandford generously offered to forego his stipend, in order to find extra help for Dean Ramsay, the former Rector of St

John's, who was in poor health at his home at *23 Ainslie Place*. However, his offer was refused.

For the last six years of his Rectorship, Dr Sandford moved house to one more conveniently situated for his church – St John's established its first official rectory at 6 Rutland Square in 1877, selling it in 1885 for £2,100. The rectory has been at *1 Anslie Place* since 1953.

Randolph Cliff

This row of houses, along the north-east side of the Queensferry Road, joins *Randolph Crescent* to the Dean Bridge, which was built in 1833. Only the south end is in the Moray Feu, but the whole street has been included here. *Numbers 2 to 6* were whole houses and *no. 7* comprised three spacious flats, with *no. 8* below them as a maindoor house; while *no. 9* was reached by a path at pavement level, and faced the Water of Leith. *No. 1* was built later than the rest. It extended underneath *17 Randolph Crescent*, which is reached by an elaborate external stone stairway.

In the little private garden to the north of the houses is a statue of a seated, barefoot sailor, visible from the pavement. It is shown on the Ordnance Survey map of 1852, but the origin, sculptor and history are all unknown. There is a possibility that the sculptor was Robert Forrest, who had an exhibition of statuary on Calton Hill from 1832 until the exhibits were sold at auction in 1876. One story about the sailor is that, for a wager, he jumped over the Dean Bridge using an open umbrella as a parachute. On repeating the exercise, a bystander slit his umbrella and he plunged to his death. Another version of this story is that 'Jack the Sailor' was a boy from the Lawnmarket and that he died because the umbrella was too weak.

Number 1

James Gowans built no. 1 in 1852 and lived in it for four years, having previously had his home on the opposite side of the main road, at Lynedoch Place. He was a builder and contractor, but had started his working life as a stone mason with his father Walter. James Gowans was to become one of the foremost architects in Scotland.

The Dean Sailor

Gowans became very interested in railway engineering in 1846, with the coming of new railways, but he soon returned to building and architecture. He was concerned to improve housing for the working man and he designed a scheme of two storey cottages at Rosebank, Fountainbridge. He lived there for four years after leaving Randolph Cliff.

He then moved to Rockville, a house he had designed and built at 3 Napier Road. This was a three-storey house with a five-storey tower, an elaborate and fantastic structure, known locally as 'The

133

Rockville, designed by Sir James Gowans
(Reproduced with permission from the George Washington Wilson Collection,
Aberdeen University Library: Ref. F3886X)

Pagoda'. Always interested in different colours of stone, he created a panchromatic effect on his house, within the two-foot square frames of wood covering the outside walls of the house. He installed hot water and gaslight throughout the house. Rockville was demolished in 1966. His first wife, Elizabeth Mitchell, died in her bath in 1858, aged 28. His second wife, Mary, daughter of William Brodie RSA, was an artist and she painted some of the windows of Rockville.

Gowans designed the striking tenement development at the south end of Castle Terrace, where he established his office. Further along Castle Terrace, he designed the New Edinburgh Theatre in 1875, which soon became the United Presbyterian Synod Hall.

In 1885, Gowans was appointed Lord Dean of Guild in Edinburgh. In that capacity, he advocated the provision of baths at work for coal miners, and he urged the appointment of a Minister of Health, which was not achieved until 1919. He was chairman of the committee which planned the International Exhibition of Industry, Science and Art in the Meadows in 1886. He installed electric lighting throughout the Exhibition, and he designed the two Memorial Masons' Pillars which can still be seen at the north–west entrance to the Meadows. Queen Victoria knighted him at the Exhibition.

George Gibson (1854–1913) was destined, by his father, for a career at the Bar, which did not attract him. Instead, he was a physician by the time he moved to 1 Randolph Cliff in 1880, and he remained there for four years. By the age of 23 he had become President of the Royal Medical Society.

Dr Gibson had boundless energy and was interested in everything. He was large-hearted and genial, bubbling over with vitality. His entrance into a sick room was described as a ray of sunshine. He was much loved by doctors and patients alike. He had knowledge of a wide range of medical subjects and possessed the gift of explaining the most abstract problems in simple language. He wrote a great many medical articles: his great work was *Diseases of the Heart*, published in 1898. For ten years from 1884, he was Secretary of the Royal College of Physicians of Edinburgh.

Number 2

for Pringle family, see *no. 5*

Norman Macpherson (1825–1914) was Professor of Scots Law from 1865 to 1887. After their marriage in 1873, he and his wife Georgina (whose father was William Manson, Professor of Medicine in Glasgow), lived at 2 Randolph Cliff until 1893. His father, Hugh Macpherson, was Professor of Greek and sub-Principal of King's College Aberdeen (and married to the daughter of the Principal).

Hugh Macpherson bought the island of Eigg for £15,000 in 1827, and his children inherited the island after his death in 1854. Four of his sons served in India: Samuel was a political agent there, William

Professor Norman Macpherson

was Secretary of the Indian Law Commission. John was a surgeon in the EICS and published reports on insanity among Europeans and on native lunatic asylums, and Arthur was a judge of the High Court at Calcutta and then Judicial Secretary, India Office. Only Norman remained in Scotland and, as Laird of Eigg, visited the island at every opportunity. The island was prosperous in the 1870s when the population was over 300. Eigg was sold in the 1890s to Robert Thompson.

Norman Macpherson edited reports of Court of Session cases from 1856 to 1865 and he also edited the *Journal of Jurisprudence* for some years. In 1868 he was Secretary of the Law Courts Commission leading to the Act dealing with procedure in the Court of Session. From 1880 he was Sheriff of Dumfries and Galloway for ten years, succeeding 'the venerable and beautiful Mark Napier' (W. Hole).

Number 3

for Bell, 1840 to 1843, see *3 Forres Street*

General Sir John Sinclair, 6th baronet of Dunbeath, and his wife Margaret (daughter of John Learmonth of Edinburgh) were lodgers at 3 Randolph Cliff at the 1871 census. They brought with them two small grandchildren, Mary and John Sinclair, aged nine and six, whose father Alexander had died in February of the same year while serving with the Bombay army. The children had already lost two sisters who had died from whooping cough in 1869. The young John succeeded his grandfather as seventh baronet in 1873.

Probably Sir John had come to Edinburgh for the burial in the Dean cemetery of his son George, a Captain in the Bengal army, who died in March 1871, ten days before the date of the census. George's wife was Agnes, daughter of John Learmonth of *6 Moray Place.*

John Maitland and two of his sisters, all unmarried, moved from *3 Ainslie Place* to 3 Randolph Cliff in 1871, a year after the death of their father, Edward Francis Maitland. He had been Solicitor-General and then, as Lord Barcaple, a judge. The next generation had a more modest lifestyle than their father, with three resident servants instead of six: one who had been nursery maid in 1861 became a lady's maid by 1881. John, an advocate, was MP for Kirkcudbright from 1874 to 1880.

Number 4

The second occupier of no. 4 was the Rev. George Smith (1793–1866) who lived there with his wife and two sons from 1844 until his death. He was appointed minister to the Tolbooth Free Church Parish in 1844, a year after Queen Victoria had laid the foundation stone of the building on Castle Hill. This church was designed by William Playfair and was to have a dual purpose, serving also as College and Assembly Hall for the new Free Church of Scotland.

Number 5

for Wauchope, 1851, see *8 Moray Place*

Alexander Pringle, of Whytbank and Yair in Selkirkshire, and his wife Agnes Joanna Dick had four homes in succession on the Moray feu. They lived at *2 Forres Street* from 1846 for three years, then at *4 Randolph Crescent* until 1854 before joining his two unmarried sisters Mary Agnes and Charlotte who were already at *2 Randolph Cliff*. In 1856 they all moved down the road to 5 Randolph Cliff.

Alexander Pringle had been a neighbour of Walter Scott in Selkirkshire, and they had travelled together to the field of Waterloo in 1815. He later entered politics, being MP for Selkirkshire from 1830 to 1832 and again from 1837 to 1845. From 1841 he was a Lord of the Treasury in Sir Robert Peel's ministry for four years, and was also a Commissioner of Revenue Inquiry. He then came to Edinburgh and from 1846 was Principal Keeper of the Register of Sasines. He died in 1857.

The Pringle sisters remained at 5 Randolph Cliff until 1879, being joined by another sister Margaret, widow of William Elmsley QC. Meanwhile, their sister-in-law Ann Elizabeth Pringle, widow of their brother William (an officer in the Bengal Civil Service) spent six years at *6 Randolph Cliff* from 1859 with her three adult daughters. Later, a nephew Robert K. Pringle WS was a lodger at *3 Randolph Place* from 1884 for eight years.

for Simpson, 1881 to 1886, see *2 St Colme Street*

Number 6

John A. Ballantyne, at no. 6 from 1839 to 1843 with his wife Frances, was a son of James Ballantyne, a school friend and close companion of Walter Scott in Kelso. James printed Scott's early works from 1799, and was persuaded by Scott to move to Edinburgh in 1802, setting up the printing firm of Ballantyne and Company at Paul's Work, North Back of Canongate, very near to Holyroodhouse. John came of age after his father's death in 1833 and then became a partner in the firm, along with John Hughes, a compositor, whose father also came from Kelso. Ballantyne and Hughes opened a branch in Thistle Street, with John A. Ballantyne in charge.

for Pringle, 1859 to 1865, see *no. 5*

Number 7

The Rev. Dr Thomas Brown FRSEd (1811–1893) was appointed minister of Dean Church in 1849 and lived at 7 Randolph Cliff until 1853. At the Disruption in 1843, the minister and practically the whole of the congregation adhered to the new Free Church. The minister, James Manson, was interdicted from occupying or preaching in the church, which the congregation themselves had built and supported. They next met for worship in a granary. A church was then built at the west end of Lynedoch Place (on the north side of what is now Belford Road) and opened for services in December 1844. However, this was too close to Free St Andrew's Church, and the Dean congregation had to move again. A new church was built at Belford Bridge and opened in October 1889, in which year Dr Brown retired, after four years as senior minister.

[I must make an incursion into the twentieth century, for my parents-in-law, John and Sheila Mitchell, lived for over 30 years from 1948 in the top flat of no. 7, with magnificent views over the Water of Leith and out to sea. In their seventies, they began to provide an important service to family historians all over the world by systematically recording and publishing the information on pre-1855 gravestones throughout the central belt of Scotland.

At the age of 86, my mother-in-law learned that Jacques Cousteau had discovered the wreck of the hospital ship *Britannic* (sister ship of the *Titanic*), sunk in 1916 while she was on board serving as a nurse. Cousteau arranged for her to be flown out to join him on the island of Kea and on his ship *Calypso*, to share her vivid memories with him. At the end of a week, she went down in the soucoupe (a two-man mini-submarine) to inspect the wreck, at a depth of 300 feet. A year later, Sheila Macbeth Mitchell spent six weeks touring the United States to promote Cousteau's film *The Search for the Britannic*.]

Number 8

Early in the morning of 16 January 1850, a fire was discovered at no. 8, the home of James Mitchell WS. Fire engines were soon in attendance but the fire, found to be in a press in the parlour, was less serious than at first thought. It was quickly extinguished by the firemen without the operation of the engines, the only damage having been the ignition of a portion of the floor and a partition.

Robert Cathcart WS, living upstairs at *no. 7* with his uncle John Dunlop, wrote that 'the safety of other houses above was much endangered.'

William Lyon, who had earlier lived in George Square, spent nearly twenty years at 8 Randolph Ciff from 1877. He established the auctioneering firm of Lyon and Turnbull in 1864 at 51 George Street, where it is still. The business had been started in 1825 by William's father, Jonathan Lyon, in Market Street. William continued the business in Melbourne Place. In the early 1840s he joined Messrs Dowell at 18 George Street, forming the firm of Dowell and Lyon, which was successful but was dissolved in 1864. By 1891, he was widowed and one of his daughters, also widowed, lived with him as housekeeper, along with her own eleven year old daughter.

Margaret, mother of Robert Louis Stevenson spent the last few months of her life at no. 8, where she died in 1897. She had joined her sister Miss Balfour, who had gone there in the previous year.

Soon after RLS's father's death in 1887, Mrs Stevenson accompanied RLS, his wife and stepson on their extensive travels. They spent some time in crossing America from New York to San Francisco. Then for over two years they sailed through the Pacific. Mrs Stevenson senior remained in Honolulu in June 1889 while the others continued their journey, eventually settling in Samoa in September 1890. RLS's mother rejoined them there in the spring of 1891; she was with him when he died there in 1894. A photograph shows her walking on a beach in Samoa, dressed as for Edinburgh streets, and being quite unperturbed when she came face to face with a native woman dressed in next-to-nothing.

Number 9

Thomas Constable, son of Archibald, one of Walter Scott's printers, came from Bellevue Terrace to live at no. 9 for two years from 1839. This was two years after his marriage to Lucy, one of the twenty children (by two wives!) of Alexander Cowan, papermaker in Penicuik. Thomas and Lucy eventually had nine children and lived next door to her father in Royal Terrace. Thomas, who had 'a sweet and genial nature and a fund of genuine Scottish humour' was appointed Her Majesty's printer and publisher in Edinburgh in 1839. His son Archibald was similarly appointed thirty years later. Thomas ceased publishing in 1860 and concentrated on writing, notably a biography of his father.

Philadelphia Hughes, who was the widow of William, a surgeon in the HEICS, was briefly at no. 9 at the time of the 1851 census. Her son William Lewis Hughes was then described as a civil engineer student, aged 26. He married Grace, daughter of Leitch Ritchie (editor of *Chambers' Journal*) in her family home at *8 Great Stuart Street* in 1858. By then he was a Doctor of Medicine, living in Manchester.

Number 10

This late seventeenth century house, which stands on the north–west end of the Dean Bridge, is not really part of Randolph Cliff. Basil Skinner, in *The House on the Bridge* (1982), gives a fascinating history of the house.

The Scotsman reported that, at 6 p.m. on 8 March 1881, there was a serious landslip at the south-east end of the Dean Bridge. This was caused by heavy rain during the day, following a thaw. A mass of earth, some 20 or 30 yards in length, fell from the 80 foot high cliff which overlooks the Water of Leith. The landslip carried with it a large portion of a garden wall and iron railing behind Randolph Cliff. The mill lade, which was conveyed in big wooden ducts raised upon posts, was completely choked. The lade supplied water to the Greenland, Stockbridge and Canonmills flour mills as well as to other businesses whose work was stopped.

At the 1891 census, there were ten households in *numbers 1 to 9* Randolph Cliff (only two flats at *no. 7* were occupied). Of these, eight were headed by women, three widowed, and five unmarried. The remaining two were headed by one widower and one unmarried man. There were only three children in the street, one aged six and two aged eleven.

Randolph Place

The first two houses of Randolph Place face onto the Queensferry Road at the south end of Randolph Crescent, the others being round the corner, forming the north side of a cul-de-sac. Unusually, the other side of the cul-de-sac has another name, Charlotte Place, which lies outside the boundary of the Moray Feu and of this book.

Numbers 1, 3, 5 and 8 were built as flats. *No. 1* was first occupied in 1834, and the remaining houses between 1850 and 1855.

Number 1

The first resident of this stair with three flats were John Corsar, a coal merchant and John Horsburgh, a baker. They, and other early residents, solicitors and shop keepers such as a grocer, a chemist and druggist, were birds of passage and did not stay for long.

After three years at *11 Darnaway Street*, John Steell (1804–1891), sculptor, moved to no. 1 Randolph Place with his wife and five small children and two female servants in 1841. Somewhat restlessly, they next had one year in 1847 at *12 Darnaway Street* before removing to *19 Great Stuart Street*, where the family remained for seven years. Steell

Duke of Wellington's statue, by Sir James Steell

clearly found Randolph Place a congenial place in which to work, for he had his studio at *no. 3* for two years from 1850 and then at *no. 9* for the next 35 years, sharing the studio accommodation from 1870 with his son William, an architect.

John Steell had been apprenticed to his father (also John Steell) as a wood carver before going to Rome for several years, to study as a sculptor. He was elected RSA at the age of 25. When not yet 30 years old, he made the colossal model of Alexander taming Bucephalus, which was later cast in bronze and can today be seen in the City Chambers courtyard. He was appointed sculptor to the Queen in Scotland in 1838 and was responsible for many other statues: notably that of Queen Victoria atop the Royal Institution (now the Royal Scottish Academy), the Duke of Wellington on his horse outside General Register House ('Iron on bronze by Steell'), and the 1876 memorial to the Prince Consort in Charlotte Square gardens, for which he was knighted. The Duke of Wellington was so pleased with Steell's work that he ordered two busts of himself.

As well as producing a great many busts of subjects who included Queen Victoria, Thomas de Quincey, Lord Cockburn and Florence Nightingale, Steell was responsible for the original figures illustrating the parable of the five wise and five foolish virgins, adorning the Standard Life Assurance building at the east end of George Street (see also *no. 4*).

for Hibbs, 1852 to 1855, see *1 Great Stuart Street*

The Halkett family occupied a flat at no. 1 from 1859 into the twentieth century. Two unmarried sisters, Isabella and Amelia (then aged 62 and 58), were the first to arrive followed some twenty years later by their widowed sister-in-law Catherine Halkett with her three unmarried daughters Helen, Catherine and Mary, all of whom were still living with their mother, at the ages of 55, 46 and 44 at the 1891 census. Throughout their years here, they had one resident domestic servant.

Number 2

George Mackay, MD, FRCSEd, MRCSEng, who lived here from 1887 until his marriage in 1896, was a consultant ophthalmic surgeon. He was born in Madras, where his father (of the same name) was Deputy Surgeon-General in the Madras Army. He became President of the Royal College of Surgeons, Edinburgh, from 1919 for two years. He was also Vice-President of the Ophthalmological Society of the UK, and President of the Caledonian Medical Society. He was a member of the Royal Company of Archers and a founder member (later, President) of the Clan Mackay Society. He was a dapper figure who used to walk to and from the Royal Infirmary in a well–cut morning coat and a shining tall hat. When operating, he wore neither gown nor mask.

Number 3

John Watherston lived for some years from 1852 with his wife and five children in the third floor flat at no. 3. He was a builder who, at the 1861 census, employed 57 men (47 masons). His only son James was a partner in the firm, which built houses in a number of nearby streets, including 4-6 Melville Street, 1-2 Lynedoch Place and Drumsheugh Place.

for Pringle, 1884 to 1892, see *5 Randolph Cliff*

Number 4

The first resident at no. 4 was Gourlay Steell (1819–1894), the younger brother of Sir John Steell (see *no. 1*). He and his second wife and his children spent sixteen years in this house from 1853. He, too, was a sculptor but also a painter, in both cases specialising in animals. He first exhibited at the Royal Scottish Academy in 1832, aged 13, showing a model of a greyhound. He went on to model many groups of horses, dogs and cattle which were afterwards cast in silver. He taught modelling at the Watt Institute in Adam Square. He painted equestrian portraits and many large pictures in oil, tempera and charcoal of animals, for display in highland mansions. In 1865 he exhibited *A Cottage Bedside at Osborne*, a painting of Queen Victoria reading the Bible to a sick fisherman. In 1872 he was appointed animal painter to Her Majesty in Scotland, succeeding Landseer in that post. Ten years later he succeeded Sir William Fettes Douglas as curator of the National Gallery of Scotland.

For two years before going to St Andrews in 1875 as Professor of Medicine and Anatomy, James Bell Pettigrew, a bachelor, lived at no. 4. He came to Edinburgh from Airdrie in 1855, as a medical student. In 1858 he was awarded the senior gold medal in anatomy. In that year he was engaged in dissecting the heart. One day after dinner, he happened to roll his newspaper obliquely into a cone and was surprised to find that the print of the paper assumed spiral forms, the spirals on the outside of the cone being the opposite of those on the inside, an arrangement identical with that revealed by his dissections. He exclaimed 'Eureka!' and informed his favourite sister, who was sitting beside him, that 'The structure of the heart is now an open secret.'

He was awarded a gold medal in medical jurisprudence in 1860 for an essay on *The Presumption of Survivorship*, and he gained yet another gold medal in 1861 for his MD dissertation on the ganglia and nerves of the heart.

After graduating in 1861, he was Professor Syme's house surgeon in the Royal Infirmary. As such, he had to attend all cases of accident on four days a week, and was in charge of 84 beds. He personally dressed all primary amputations, set fractures and performed minor operations.

He was appointed assistant in the Hunterian Museum at the Royal College of Surgeons in England in 1862 and spent five years there. As the result of re-organising the work rooms of the museum, his health suffered. Thousands of specimens, preserved in spirit, gave off semi-putrid vapours and he had to work at an open window throughout the year.

To recuperate, he spent some time in the south of Ireland, extending his knowledge of the flight of insects, birds and bats. According to him, fishes swim, birds fly and bipeds and quadrupeds walk, all by spiral and double-curve figure-of-eight movements. He experimented with artificial flight with steam models, and was convinced that aerial navigation would soon be possible. He published a paper on aeronautics in 1873.

On returning to Edinburgh in 1869, Bell Pettigrew was appointed curator of the museum of the Royal College of Surgeons of Edinburgh.

Number 5

Henry Kay, in a third floor flat at no. 5 from 1860 for three years, was a plumber and gasfitter, whose business was at 18 Charlotte Place, immediately opposite his home. In 1861 he employed six men and six boys. With a small family (wife and eight year old son), he had two resident domestic servants,

The occupier of the other third floor flat at no. 5 from 1860 to 1877 was William Kenward, a widowed music teacher. His mother and sister (a daily governess) lived with him. His father William, who died in 1860, had been an alto vocalist, composer and music teacher as well as being precentor of the High Church and conductor of the Edinburgh Harmonists' Society.

Number 6

Dr G. Lovell Gulland (1862–1941), physician, came to no. 6 in 1888 on his marriage to Helen, one of the daughters of Professor David Masson. He had graduated only two years previously but had already been President of the Royal Medical Society for one year.

While in general practice, he bicycled, dressed in morning coat and bowler hat. Later, when he had charge of hospital wards, he used taxis, eventually obtaining his own car. He executed sketches and water–colours, always aiming at a good picture rather than a reproduction of the landscape. If he preferred the effect, he would move a castle from east to west and, on occasion, he would move mountains.

Dr Gulland later became physician to the Victoria Hospital for consumption and diseases of the chest, but by the time that he became consulting physician to the Royal Infirmary in 1911, he was a specialist in diseases of the blood. At the same time, he became Principal Medical Officer of the Scottish Widows' Fund. From 1915 to 1928 he was Professor of Medicine at Edinburgh University. He was President of the Royal College of Physicians of Edinburgh from 1923 for two years. He was Manager of the Royal Infirmary from 1932 to 1938.

Number 7

No. 7 was built as a hall and for twelve years from 1852 it was known as St Cecilia Hall, not to be confused with St Cecilia's Hall in Niddry Street, Cowgate, which was built a century earlier. No records can now be found of the use of the hall in Randolph Place, apart from that of Thomas Hunter, who lived next door at *no. 8.* Mary Cooper, a widow, was the resident hall keeper, with her daughter and son-in-law (a messenger) and three grandchildren.

The name of the hall was changed in 1864 to St George's Hall and it became the home of the Edinburgh Choral Society, whose conductor until 1872 was T. K. Longbottom, a celebrated sol-fa teacher. For several years he was choirmaster at St George's parish church in Charlotte Square.

Women were hungry for the education which was available to their brothers. In 1867, the Edinburgh Ladies' Educational Association was formed, with Mrs Mary Crudelius as its dynamic honorary secretary. Advanced instruction was offered to women in physical and natural sciences, mental philosophy, literature, history and languages. The first lecture, given by Professor David Masson in the Hopetoun Rooms in Queen Street, was free and was attended by over 400 women, of whom 265 enrolled for the course. This included thirty one-hour lectures, given twice a week, with essays to be written and exams to sit. The women were aged 16 to 60.

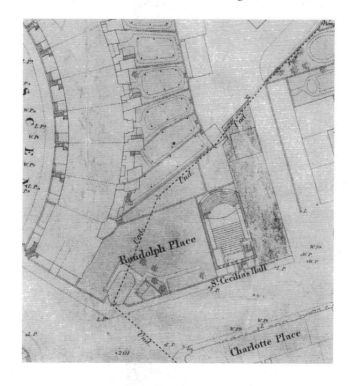

Ordnance map, 1852, showing St Cecilia's Hall

From the mid 1870s, classes were held at St George's Hall, Randolph Place. After the death of Mrs Crudelius in 1877, Louisa Stevenson of *13 Randolph Crescent* became honorary secretary. Women were offered the opportunity to study for Edinburgh University Local Examinations, and a correspondence course was available for those who lived further away. Most had already attended classes of the Edinburgh Ladies' Educational Association which, in 1879, changed its name to the Edinburgh Association for the University Education of Women. All of the students were found to be weak in arithmetic and geography and many had never been taught any English grammar.

Number 8

Thomas Hunter (1820–1886), another music teacher, had his home at no. 8 from 1855 for seven years. He and his wife had four daughters and two sons but no resident servants. A tenor vocalist, he was precentor of Rose Street United Presbyterian Church from 1845 until shortly before he died. His death was the result of being thrown out of a gig when out riding with a friend. He had charge of the St Cecilia Hall music classes as well as others.

Number 9

for Steell, from 1852, see *no. 1*

Randolph Place Lane and Mews

Randolph Place Lane is a square of stables behind Randolph Place and it had residents before most of Randolph Place. At the 1851 census, there were two households: one was that of a cabinet maker, William Hunter. The other was of a butler, Andrew Gillam, with his wife and daughter and his two brothers, one also being a butler and one a bookseller's shopman. By 1871, there were ten households, all headed by a coachman, all except one with a wife. Between them they had 14 young children, so the stable courtyard must have been a lively place.

This pattern continued, with eight coachmen and two grooms in 1881. One coachman then had a son who was a groom and two others had a boarder, one groom and one joiner.

Randolph Crescent Householders

1.
1835 Mrs McCallum
1837 Misses Gray
1840 A. Fletcher, advocate
1845 Archibald Ewart and John Ewart
1847 Kirby Dalrymple
1856 Mrs Rennie
1860 Ellerington Reed, sheep farmer
1862 Alexander Craig Sellar, advocate
1872 Tyndall B. Johnstone
1880 & Henry B. Johnstone
1898 J. Lamond Lackie MD FRCPE; George
    R. Wilson MD

2
1836 Murdoch Maclaine of Lochbuy
1840 J. B. Atkinson esq.
1841 John Brodie WS
1847 Edward Strathearn Gordon, advocate
1897 H. D. Gordon, advocate; Miss
    Somerville, ladies' school

3.
1838 Miss McKerrell
1841 George Cleghorn esq. of Weens
1847 Mrs Blackwood
1854 & James Blackwood WS
1876 & John Blackwood

4.
1834 William Scott esq.
1840 Patrick Orr esq. WS
1849 Alexander Pringle
1857 Mrs Sprot
1861 Mrs Ogilvie
1862 Arthur F. Campbell junior WS
1886 & George Campbell WS

5.
1833 Patrick Boyle, advocate
1835 Prof. Robert Christison FRCP
1847 John Marshall, advocate
1856 W. McHutchen
1898 John McHutchen Dobbie

6.
1833 George Dickson esq.
1838 Robert Haldane esq.
1840 Miss Milne, boarding school
1848 David McFarlane HEICS
1874 John Marshall, advocate
1875 Hon. Lord Curriehill

1882 William Mackintosh, advocate
1889 Hon. Lord Kyllachy
1895 & W. E. Mackintosh, advocate

7.
1831 Miss Hill & Mr P. Hill
1837 William Stothart esq. of Cargen
1843 Charles Forbes esq.
1848 Robert Horn, advocate
1876 & William Horn, advocate
1888 George Bayley WS

8.
1835 Mrs Williams
1843 Henry Williams esq.
1844 Miss A. Brown
1845 Robert Bruce, advocate
1852 –
1857 Mrs Renny
1858 Francis George Souter
1861 William Grant Henry
1864 John Bruce WS
1870 Angus Fletcher, advocate
1875 Prof. James Muirhead
1880 A. F. M. Lockhart, advocate
1887 Charles W. Cathcart MB FRCS, lecturer
    in surgery

9.
1832 Hon. Misses Mackenzie of Seaforth
1840 Rev. R. Candlish
1841 Mrs Cox; Mrs Henderson
1844 J. B. Gracie WS
1845 Mrs Kellie
1848 Mrs William Loch
1853 Donald Mackenzie, advocate
1856 David Jeffrey
1864 Arthur Dingwall advocate
1875 Middleton Rettie, advocate
1878 James Mylne, junior, advocate
1893 Miss Robertson

10.
1853 James F. Scott
1859 Arthur Fraser of Colrossie
1870 John Macandrew
1875 G. F. Melville, advocate
1880 Mrs Trotter

11.
1835 E. D. Sandford, advocate
1861 David Baxter, merchant

1862 Thomas Graham Murray, WS

12.
1840 J. Shaw Stewart, advocate
1841 John Stuart Hay, independent
1842 A. Morrison esq. of Bognie
1884 Lt. Col. Duff
1889 Colin R. Dunlop, coal & iron master
1896 William Campbell, advocate

13.
1839 Sir John Robison, KH
1844 Lt. Col. George Cadell
1859 James Stevenson

14.
1844 Charles Baillie, advocate
1866 David Jeffrey

15.
1853 Hugh Blair, WS
1864 & Alexander Blair, advocate
1867 & Patrick Blair WS

16.
1852 J. W. Crowe
1854 Robert Paul
1859 Mrs Thomson
1871 James Gowans
1876 Mrs Johnston
1881 George D. Mackay, manufacturing
      chemist
1882 Miss Borrie
1888 & William Francis Wood, advocate to
      1895
1895 & Hugh J. E. Fraser, advocate
1897 Thomas F. S. Caverhill, MB FRCP

17.
1852–61 Francis Russell, advocate
1853–55 Miss Augusta Stodart
1855–61 Misses Murray
1861–62 Rev. D. F. Sandford, St John's
         church
1861–66 J. Thorne Harris
1862–72 Mrs Clark
1862–72 Mrs Rutherford
1866–67 Mrs Swanson
1868–80 Mrs Coley Bromfield
1872–82 Mrs Aitchison
1881–82 Duncan McGregor, builder
1882–   Colin Sinclair, fancy stationer
1885–88 John Taylor CA
1888–90 Miss Dunlop

1891–94 W. Percival Lindsay WS
1894–97 Mrs John Binny & Graham Binny
1897–   Miss Lowson; Charles H. Brown,
         advocate

Randolph Cliff Householders

1.
1852 James Gowans, builder & contractor
1856 Mrs Edward Forbes
1861 Misses Davidson
1867 Alexander M. Stewart
1871 Mrs Susan Henderson, lodgings
1876 George S. Dundas, advocate
1880 George A. Gibson MB DSc
1884 J Gordon Stuart WS
1886 Miss Wotherspoon

2.
1841 J. H. McKenzie WS
1847 John Wilson Pillans
1849 Misses Pringle
1854 & Alexander Pringle
1856 Miss Weir
1859 Mrs James Maitland Robertson
1860 William Henry
1862 Mrs Le Blane
1871 John Spence, lodgings
1872 Prof. Norman Macpherson LLD
1895 Mrs Russell

3.
1840 Charles Bell MD FRCP
1846 Mrs Warden
1870 Miss Robertson
1871 John Maitland, advocate, MP
1885 Miss Maitland

4.
1839 John Grieve, accountant
1844 Rev. George Smith DD
1867 Alexander Robertson WS
1868 Hugh James Rollo WS
1892 Eneas Macdonell, advocate
1895 Misses Dalmahoy

5.
1840 Misses Erskine
1843 Thomas Innes, advocate
1846 Miss Anne Forbes
1851 Mrs Eliza Wauchope
1852 Mrs A. F. Crawford
1856 Alexander Pringle (1 yr only); Misses

Pringle
1873 & Mrs Elmsley
1881 Sir Walter Simpson, bart, advocate
1886 Miss Sanders; Miss Maughan, school for
     boys & girls

6.
1839 J. A. Ballantyne, printer
1843 John Miller esq.
1851 William Cadell
1857 John Miller esq.
1859 Mrs W. A. Pringle
1865 Edward Chancellor WS
1873 Mrs Daun
1893 Robert B. Armstrong

7.
1838–39 William Turnbull, Inspector, Royal
     Bank
1839–52 John Dunlop Esq.
1839–41 Major Veitch
1841–43 Mathew Wingrave
1842–45 James S. Robertson WS
1844–54 Miss Catharine Burnside
1845–49 Mrs Christie
1850–51 R. A. Cathcart WS
1850–53 Rev. Thomas Brown
1852–58 Alexander Macarthur, builder
1854–56 James Robertson, civil engineer
1856–58 Mrs Beilby
1857–73 John Macdonald, accountant
1859–64 J. Moxon, painters
1868–73 Alexander Mackenzie
1869–73 William Drummond WS
1872–77 Thomas Dewar
1873–77 A. & H. Cruickshank
1877–78 George A. Wilson
1877–79 William Raeburn
1877–78 R. T. Hamilton Bruce
1878–   Mrs Login
1879–91 Miss Corlett
1881–   Alexander Bowman
1891–96 Alfred Sutherland WS
1897–   Arthur H. Dickson WS

8.
1838 James L. Mitchell WS
1853 Misses Eyre
1863 Mrs Anstey
1867 Miss Tennent
1877 William Lyon, auctioneer
1896 Miss Balfour
1898 & Mrs Thomas Stevenson
1898 Mrs H. L. Hunt

9.
1839 Thomas Constable, printer
1841 V. H. Nelson, stationer & book-seller
1843 William Curle
1851 Mrs Philadelphia Hughes
1856 Miss Campbell
1864 Miss Stewart & Alexander Stewart
1868 James M. P. McHardy
1870 Miss Maclaurin
1873 Miss Spens
1899 Patrick J. Blair, advocate

Randolph Place Householders

1.
1834   John Corsar, coal merchant
1834–40 John Horsburgh, baker
1837–49 Mrs Oliphant
1837–40 R. Dall of Cedar Valley
1840–49 George Barron WS
1840–41 William Menelaws, grocer
1841–47 John Steell, sculptor
1847–48 James Campbell
1849–51 Mrs Capt. Hunter
1849–50 Robert Legget, skinner, tanner
1850–53 John Mackay, chemist & druggist
1851 & 1853–59 Robert Haig
1853–59 James Hogg
1853–56 Rev. Richard Hibbs
1856–59 Mrs Crichton
1859–99 John Cuthbertson
1859–69 Robert Wilson
1859–99 Misses Halkett
1862–72 Alexander Nevay, advocate
1871–81 John Wilson, merchant
1874–81 William Ramsay
1881–82 George McArthur
1882–84 Miss Walker
1884–87 Robert H. Shaw
1888–96 Miss Wilson
1895–   Heinrich Weisse

2.
1854–56 Mrs Bruce
1856–79 Mrs John Babington
1879–93 Misses Williamson
1880–83 John Home WS
1881–85 Alexander Tod
1887–96 George Mackay MB, CM, MRCS,
     FRCSE
1888–98 J. Edward Graham, advocate
1893–   Miss Janet Laidlaw, apartments
1893–95 Mrs Leech

1896–98	J. Lamond Lackie MD, MRCPE
1897–99	George R. Wilson MD

3.

1850–52	John Steell RSA
1852–53	William Jamieson
1852–61	John Watherston, wright
1852–56	J. F. Alexander, surgeon
1853–64	John Kirkhope, grocer
1856–61	Mrs Macara
1861–69	Mrs Adam
1864–69	John Reid, plumber & gas-fitter
1867–83	Mervyn Pillman
1869–76	Mrs Robertson
1870–71	Mrs Brown
1871–76	P Lawrence
1876–81	Thomas Page
1876–78	P. Stewart
1876–	Miss Adam
1879–84	Mrs George Park
1883–87	John Lamont
1884–92	Robert R. K. Pringle WS
1884–	Miss C. M. Fraser
1887–89	Mrs Taylor
1890–95	Miss Mowbray
1890–92	Robert Holland, greengrocer
1893–99	William Adam White CA
1893–95	Fraulein Klingenberg, teacher
1894–95	Miss Agnes Johnston
1896–97	J. Hussey Robertson CA
1896–	Miss Ferguson Smith
1897–	Fraulein Klingenberg

4.

1853–65	Gourlay Steell ARSA
1869	Miss Anderson
1874	J. Bell Pettigrew MD FRS
1876	George Dunlop WS
1883	Miss MacAllan

5.

1853–80	David Laing, writer (later, Miss)
1853–82	Mrs Cochrane (later, Misses)
1853–62	H. Morrison, draper
1853–62	Mrs P. Orr
1855–59	Edward Jackson
1856–60	M. Wallace
1860–77	W. Kennard, music teacher
1860–63	Henry R. Kay, plumber
1862–84	Robert Scott Sorlie
1863–	Thomas Strachan, land surveyor
1864–81	Miss Ross

1877–81	James Dow
1880–	William Rogers
1880–84	Miss Muir
1882–85	John Spence
1882–84	Mrs Lamb
1884–85	Mrs Pringle
1884–	William Barclay
1884–88	Henry Ramsden
1885–86	John S. Gillies
1886–89	Mrs M Robertson
1888–89	Miss Brodie
1895–	Miss Graham
1896–	Miss Ferrall

6.

1854–57	Miss Tower
1861–68	Mrs Dryborough
1873–86	Mrs J. E. Traquair
1889–94	G. Lovell Gulland MD, FRCPE
1894–	Fred J. Turnbull LRCP & SE, LDS

7.

1852–64	St Cecilia Hall
1864–	St George's Hall
1866–72	Edinburgh Choral Society

8.

1855–62	T. M. Hunter, teacher of music
1863–65	John Mushet & Son, house agent & undertaker
1866–71	James Wood, cabinet maker
1869–75	James Hepburn
1870–74	Mme Clemandot, teacher of French
1874–87	Miss Reid
1875–78	Mrs Wilton
1878–86	David S. Kennedy, bookkeeper
1880–86	Miss Kennedy, dressmaker
1886–	David Watson, wine & spirit merchant
1887–88	Miss M. R. Walker
1888–89	John Lorrain Wright
1889–96	Miss Ferrall
1895–	Miss Wilson
1895–96	Miss Stirling
1895–96	Miss M. Ritchie
1896–	John Drysdale

9.

1853–88	John Steell, studio
1870–	William Steell, architect
1888–	Macfarlane & Wallace, painters & dealers in paper hangings

Glenfinlas Street

This is the shortest street on the Earl of Moray's estate, consisting of only five houses on the west side of the spur leading south from Ainslie Place. It was named after part of the Earl's estates at Glen Finglas in the Trossachs. *Numbers 2, 3 and 4* were occupied by 1837. The gap site between these houses and Charlotte Square was not built on until very recently, in the 1990s. The original numbers 1 to 4 were then renumbered 6, 8, 10 and 11.

Number 6 (number 1 until 1990)

One of the most distinguished physicians of the nineteenth century, John Hughes Bennett (1812–1875), lived for the last twenty-two years of his life at no. 1, where he was the first occupier. His children were taught by a governess at home. The household also had a butler, a cook and two other female servants.

Bennett graduated MD in Edinburgh in 1837, with a gold medal for the best surgical report. He would have had a second medal for his dissertation on the physiology and pathology of the brain, but no candidate was allowed two medals. A fluent French speaker, he worked in Paris for a few years. As the founder, and first President, of the Parisian Medical Society, he wrote widely on diseases of the nervous system.

Bennett returned to Edinburgh in 1841 and published a treatise on the use of cod liver oil in the treatment of gout, rheumatism and tuberculosis. This proved to be so popular that, by 1847, one Edinburgh druggist dispensed 600 gallons of cod liver oil in one year, compared with one gallon in 1841. For many years, and even after Bennett's death, a fish merchant – G. Dickson Moffat in Dundas Street – advertised cod liver oil to be bought in any quantity, from an ounce to hundreds of gallons. In a bottle, it cost three halfpence per ounce. Bennett also considered that bloodletting weakened patients, especially those with pneumonia, and that, instead, they should be strengthened with good food, rest and fresh air. Nevertheless, the availability of leeches continued to be widely advertised.

At the same time, he was the first doctor in Britain to teach his students the use of a microscope in the clinical investigation of disease. He formed a private museum of morbid anatomy, with 800 wet and 300 dry preparations.

Partly thanks to his upbringing, he was an excellent lecturer. His father had been a comedy actor and his mother's family owned the Sadler's Wells Theatre in London. His mother taught him elocution, setting him to read Shakespeare aloud from an early age. Every lecture of his was said to be a work of art, with elegant language and appropriate gestures.

Bennett reported the first recorded case of leukaemia in 1845. This was, for many more years, expected to be fatal in all cases. In 1848, he was appointed Professor of the Institutes of Medicine at Edinburgh University. He was deeply disappointed in 1855 not to be appointed Professor of the Practice of Physic, a post which had long been his highest ambition.

In 1872, the 19 members of the medical staff of the Royal Infirmary were asked whether they were in favour of the admission of women medical students to clinical instruction. In spite of his advice to the girls of the Scottish Institution in Moray Place in 1867 not to become doctors of medicine, Professor Bennett was one of the only three who were in favour, with the caveat that, if expedient, the women could be taught separately from the men. He subsequently offered extra-mural classes to women students. The University of Edinburgh did not allow women to graduate in medicine until 1894.

Number 8 (number 2 until 1990)

The first resident was Thomas Bruce of Langlee, WS, who came to no. 2 in 1828 from Frederick Street, with his wife and five small children and four female servants. His office was nearby, at 5 South Charlotte Street. After his death, his widow and some of their children remained in the house until the 1890s.

Number 10 (number 3 until 1990)

In 1830, Charles Fergusson, advocate, (1800–1849) came to no. 3 with his wife Helen, daughter of David Boyle, Lord Justice General of Scotland. They left Edinburgh when he succeeded his father, as fifth baronet, in 1838, and took up residence at the family home at Kilkerran, Ayrshire. Of their four sons and seven daughters, two sons should be mentioned. The eldest, James, born in 1832, succeeded his father as sixth baronet in 1849. He had a distinguished career, being Governor of South Australia, of New Zealand and of Bombay. He was Under Secretary of State for Foreign Affairs from 1886 to 1891 and then Postmaster-General for one year. Sir Charles's third son, another Charles, took the surname of Dalrymple on succeeding to the estates of Hailes and Newhailes in Midlothian on the death of his father. He was created a baronet in 1887. The National Trust for Scotland acquired the 18th century mansion of Newhailes in 1996.

The family of James Simson (1796–1876) began a long occupancy of no. 3 in 1845. He was surgeon to the Calton Jail and medical officer to the New Town Dispensary. He had the unusual distinction of being twice elected President of the Royal College of Surgeons of Edinburgh, in 1844 and again for the last two years of his life. He had been Honorary Secretary of the College for many years. He was also known for his unostentatious generosity to the poor. After his death, his son David, an advocate and a graduate of Oxford, took over the house.

Number 11 (number 4 until 1990)

Duncan Dempster, a master sugar refiner, moved into no. 4 in 1875 with his wife and five daughters and a son. One daughter was Margaret (1863–1935), a painter in oil of portraits, portrait miniatures and flowers. She exhibited 37 times at the Royal Scottish Academy. She moved to Comrie in 1898 on her marriage to another artist, Robert Nisbet RSA.

Number 14

This house straddles the corner between Ainslie Place and Glenfinlas Street. From its first occupation in 1859, it was briefly numbered *20A Ainslie Place.* From 1862, it became *21A*, although it was next to *20 Ainslie Place*, while *21 Ainslie Place* was across the road, beyond Ainslie House. The confusion continued until the 1950s, when it was renumbered 14 Glenfinlas Street.

James Spence (1812–1882), who lived here from 1859, was a leading surgeon. He was Professor of Surgery in Edinburgh from 1864 until his death, and was President of the Royal College of Surgeons of Edinburgh 1867–1869. Earlier he had been a candidate for the post of conservator of the museum of the College, but he withdrew because of a feeling in the college that the conservator should not also be engaged in practice. His widow and two unmarried children remained in the house into the next century. As a surgeon James Spence was noted for the extreme care he gave to the preparation of the patient and of his surgical instruments. He was nervous until the moment that he made his first incision.

Glenfinlas Street Householders

6.
1853 Prof. John Hughes Bennett, FRCP
1877 R. Jamieson Torrie, accountant

8.
1828 Thomas Bruce of Langlee, WS
1853 George Bruce
1858 & Charles Bruce, Bank of Scotland

10.
1830 Sir Charles D. Fergusson, bart.
1839 Col. H. D. Robertson
1840 Col. Macpherson
1842 George McKillop WS
1843 Mark Napier, advocate

1845 J. Simson, PRCS
1887 David J. Simson, advocate

11.
1837 W. Hastie, lodgings
1841 Miss Lang
1843 Miss Mansfield
1847 T. G. Murray WS
1863 Mrs James Noble
1864 William Moir, lodgings
1875 Duncan F. Dempster, sugar refiner

14.
1859 James Spence FRCS
1895 Lewis Spence, stockbroker

St Colme Street

St Colme Street and Albyn Place together form the south east boundary of the Earl of Moray's former estate.

One of the titles held by the Earl of Moray is that of Baron St Colme. This title was given in 1611 to his ancestor Henry Stuart, whose father and grandfather had both been Commendator of Inchcolm Abbey (dedicated to St Columba) in the Firth of Forth.

The first houses were built at the same time as the earliest houses in Moray Place and began to be occupied in 1825. All were lived in by 1828 except for numbers 5 (1830), *10* and *11* (1858). What is now *no. 11* was originally *20B Ainslie Place*, straddling the junction of the two streets. It has always been called Ainslie House.

The man who recorded details of St Colme Street at the 1841 census described himself as 'the enumerator of this fashionable district'. He must have been impressed by the opulence of the houses he had to visit.

Number 1

There were at first two households here. George Angus, architect, (1792–1845) made his home at no. 1 from 1827 until his death. He designed the Subscription Baths and the Drawing Academy at 17 to 19 Hill Street in 1825 to 1828. In 1833 he won a competition for new gaols, police offices and a court-house in Dundee, where he did a great deal of work. He designed the High School there, which was the terminal feature of Reform Street, for which he was also responsible. He rebuilt Alloa House for the Earl of Mar and Kellie from 1834 to 1838.

Graham Speirs, advocate, lived at no. 1 from 1828 for four years. Later, from 1837 to 1842, he lived at *23 Ainslie Place*. He had been a Lieutenant in the Royal Navy, but switched to the law. He was appointed Sheriff of Edinburghshire in 1841. Lord Cockburn wrote an obituary of Speirs, giving muted commendation: 'sensible without what could be called talent', 'intelligent without learning', and 'I don't think I ever knew a layman to whom such religious authority attached in virtue of mere solemnity of character and gravity of manner'. By his death-bed directions, Speirs was buried beside Dr Thomas Chalmers (see *3 Forres Street*) in the Grange Cemetery.

Numbers 1 St Colme Street and *2 Forres Street* were combined into Gunn's Hotel from 1874 to 1881. The Forres Street half then returned to private ownership and the hotel occupied 1 and 2 St Colme Street until 1891, when it was reduced in size and renamed as Queen Hotel at no. 1 only.

The proprietor throughout was John Gunn who, with his wife (at the 1881 census) had a governess for their three small children. They also had seven resident servants, including a waiter, as well as three men as lodgers (two solicitors and a retired Lt. Colonel). Two families were also hotel guests, including Coutts Trotter who later lived at *13 Randolph Crescent*. Ten years later Gunn and his second wife had two more children and seven servants, including a 'boots'. There were then six hotel guests, including Harry Younger, brewer, and his wife.

Number 2

Hugh Williams (1773–1829) spent the last year of his life at no. 2, coming from Castle Street. His father was a sea captain and his mother the daughter of the Deputy Governor of Gibraltar: both died when he was young and he was brought up by his maternal grandparents.

Williams, who painted many water colours of Scottish scenery, was a pupil of David Allan and Alexander Nasmyth. In 1820, after a Grand Tour of Italy and Greece, he published an illustrated account of his journey: *Travels in Italy, Greece and the Ionian Islands*. Many of his paintings were small and informal but some of his Greek paintings were on a large scale, which earned him the name of 'Grecian' Williams. He continued working on similar subjects until the end of his life. After returning from the Mediterranean, he married Miss Miller of Earnock in Lanarkshire: she came from a wealthy family. Lord Cockburn, in his 'Memorials', described his friend Grecian Williams as 'warm-hearted and honourable, of singular modesty and almost feminine gentleness'.

for Wood, 1854 to 1858, see *no. 10*

The connections with medicine continued with the arrival at no. 2 in 1871 of Sir Walter Grindlay Simpson 2nd baronet (1843–1898), son of

Sir James Y. Simpson, who first used chloroform in 1847. Walter, an advocate, was called Wattie by his father, and had inherited the baronetcy in 1870, his elder brother David, a doctor, having died from appendicitis at the age of 24.

A year after moving to St Colme Street, Sir Walter joined his friend R. L. Stevenson in Frankfurt and wrote, 'It is an awful joke to be living – two would-be advocates and one a baronet – in this supremely mean abode.' Two years later both men enjoyed a yachting trip in the Western Isles. In that year, Walter married Anne Fitzgerald Mackay and they had two sons and two daughters. In 1881 the family moved to *5 Randolph Cliff* for five years.

Number 3

for Bell, 1849 to 1852, see *3 Forres Street*

An advocate, Andrew Jameson (1845–1911), came to 3 St Colme Street on his marriage in 1875. He was later Chairman of the Board of Conciliation between the coal owners and the Scottish Miners' Federation; and was also Commissioner to inquire into the telephone system in Glasgow. He and his wife and four children moved to *14 Moray Place* in 1892. He was one of the first Scottish advocates to be nominated as QC in 1897.

After being Sheriff of several areas from 1886 (the last being Perthshire), Jameson was raised to the bench in 1905 as Lord Ardwall, taking his title from the estate in Galloway inherited by his wife Christian Brown from her uncle Walter McCulloch of Ardwall. Lord Ardwall had a robust constitution, and was a good trencherman. He walked to and from the court until the year of his death.

for MacFarlane, from 1891, see *14 Moray Place*

Number 4

R. J. Blair Cunynghame spent three years at no. 4 from 1867. After retiring from the Army Medical Service, he returned to Edinburgh where he had graduated. He devoted special attention to diseases of the throat, and was described as an expert physiologist and an excellent teacher. He was conservator of the museum of the Royal College of Surgeons of Edinburgh for many years.

He gave up his private practice when he was appointed Superintendent of Statistics to the Registrar-General for Scotland. In that post, he delighted in analysis of the census returns and issued an invaluable report on the census of 1901. He became, successively, President of the Royal Medical Society of Edinburgh (1862), Secretary and Treasurer of the Royal College of Surgeons of Edinburgh (1887) and President of the College in 1891.

for Readman, 1881 to 1889, see *9 Moray Place*

Number 5

This was the home of only one family from 1830 until past the end of the century. Adam Urquhart, advocate and later Sheriff of Wigtonshire, lived here until his death in about 1860, after which his

Snowball Riots, 1838

wife Mary Lydia remained until her death and then two of their daughters maintained the family home. After the Sheriff's death, Mrs Urquhart increased the complement of resident servants from three to four, which number her daughters continued to employ.

As Sheriff-Substitute in 1838, Adam Urquhart presided at a three-day trial of five Edinburgh University students who were charged with mobbing, rioting and assault. The incident had been started by parties of working men who waylaid students on their way to classes, attacking them in Old College with snowballs and insults. The police were called and attacked the students, ignoring the outsiders, and arrested 35 students. Urquhart found the five not guilty.

Number 6

William Watson (1827–1890) lived at 6 St Colme Street from his marriage in 1868 to Margaret Bannatyne (18 years his junior) until 1879, and then at *34 Moray Place* for the next four years. After being called to the Bar in 1851, he had very little work. It was said that he spent many solitary hours in the curious employment of arranging the loose sheets of music in the Advocates' Library. But in 1862 he began to make his name at the Bar, having by chance taken the place of a friend who was ill.

Watson acted as junior counsel in 1864 to Andrew Rutherford Clark for the defence of Dr Edward Pritchard, who was found guilty of using antimony and aconite to poison his mother-in-law and his wife in the expectation of inheriting large sums to pay off his debts. Dr Pritchard had earlier aroused the suspicions of medical colleagues with his suspected fraudulent credentials. He was the last person to be publicly executed in Glasgow, in 1865 with, it was estimated, a crowd of 100,000 onlookers.

Watson's career continued well. He was, successively, Solicitor-General (1874), Dean of Faculty (1875) and, in 1876, Lord Advocate and Conservative MP for the Universities of Glasgow and Aberdeen. The Lord Advocate's office was then moved to the Home Office, where three rooms were provided. In 1880, Watson was appointed Lord of Appeal, as Baron Watson of Thankerton. He was then said to be the greatest lawyer on the British bench. But he was also a shy man who loved to talk for hours in the company of colleagues or friends.

At the 1871 census, he and his wife had two children under two, with six resident servants.

Number 7

Archibald Alison, advocate, (1792–1867) and his wife Elizabeth Tytler began their married life in Heriot Row at the home of his father, the Rev. Archibald Alison, essayist and minister of St Paul's episcopal chapel. A few months later, in November 1825, as he wrote in his autobiography, he 'took possession of a new house which I had built in St Colme Street, Edinburgh [no. 7] in one of the best situations in town. (Hitherto I had constantly lived under my father's roof.) The furnishing of the house was a source of interest to us both. Seated in the smaller of the two drawing rooms, with our books and pictures around us in the winter evenings, we heard the roll of the carriages outside conveying people to the evening parties, in which we no longer cared to participate.'

Their first son, another Archibald, was born in the house in January 1826. That summer, the family joined the grandfather in a house he had taken at Pilton, Lasswade. In spite of temperatures ranging from 78°F to 84°F for two months, the young advocate walked eight miles to his office in Edinburgh every day and back in the evenings at 7 or 8 o'clock. The following two summers, the family spent together at Whitehouse in Bruntsfield, and at Canaan Lodge, 'a villa two miles from Edinburgh'.

Alison had done so well at the Bar before his marriage that he could afford four extensive continental tours, and also to accumulate an excellent library. He was also a historian and in December 1828 he finished writing his book *Population* at 11 o'clock one night, sitting in the drawing room in St Colme Street beside his wife. Next month, he started writing his *History of Europe*: he wrote in the evenings, after finishing work on his legal papers.

In 1830, when the Duke of Wellington's government was defeated, Alison lost his post as Advocate Depute. At the same time, two firms of writers (i.e. solicitors) to which he had been standing counsel, both failed. His hopes of becoming Solicitor-General and then Lord Advocate were dashed. Instead, he increased his income by writing *Principles and Practice of Criminal Law*. He was paid 250 guineas by Blackwood in 1833 for the first two volumes of his *History of Europe*, with a first edition of 1000. The work eventually ran to 19 octavo volumes, being finished in 1842. After that he gave up writing after dinner – he had completed the last volume in one long stretch of 17 hours, after which his amanuensis broke down, and he wrote the rest himself in a further three hours.

By then, the family had left Edinburgh. In October 1834, Alison heard at 4 o'clock in the morning of the death of the Sheriff of Lanarkshire and, 'after consulting with Mrs Alison for an hour', he decided to apply for the post to which he was subsequently appointed. Literary, rather than legal, ambition led him to a post which gave him time for writing. In 1852 he was awarded a baronetcy. After his death in 1867, his widow returned to their house in St Colme Street for another seven years.

During the absence of the Alison family in Lanarkshire, a widow, Mrs Anne Strangeman, used the house at no. 7 as a boarding house from 1855 to 1867. She had ten girl boarders, aged 13 to 19 at the 1861 census.

On his marriage in 1874, Graham Murray (1849–1942) came to live at no. 7 where he and his wife stayed until 1886. His wife was Mary Clementina, 7th daughter of Admiral Sir William Edmonstone of *11 Ainslie Place*. Murray was at the Scottish Bar and in 1888 he was appointed Sheriff of Perthshire (said to be a stepping-stone to further promotion, because of a tradition that the Sheriff of Perthshire never dies).

In 1889, Murray became Solicitor-General and also took silk. At that time, the honour of being a QC was conferred in Scotland only on law officers of the Crown and the Dean of Faculty. This practice continued until 1897. From 1891 to 1905, Murray was Conservative MP for Buteshire, having been appointed Lord Advocate in 1896 and Secretary for Scotland with a seat in the Cabinet in 1903. Two years later he became Lord Justice-General and Lord President of the Court of Session and was raised to the peerage as Lord Dunedin. He left Scotland in 1913 to become Lord of Appeal in Ordinary until 1932. He later liked to boast that he had pleaded before four Lord Chancellors and sat as a colleague with nine.

Lord Dunedin also had time for many outside interests. He was Captain of the Royal and Ancient Golf Club in St Andrews, was one of the earliest cyclists and enjoyed photography and dancing.

Number 8

A Captain in the Royal Navy, Basil Hall (1788–1844), spent three years in Edinburgh from 1828 – at 8 St Colme Street – with his wife Margaret, daughter of Sir John Hunter, consul-general in Spain, and their three infant children. His mother was Lady Helen Douglas, daughter of the fourth Earl of Selkirk. She was present at St Mary's Isle when the noted Paul Jones landed on the coast of Galloway with the intention of seizing her father but, finding him absent, instead carried off the family silver, returning it all some years later. Paul Jones was the son of a Scottish gardener: he went to sea and, after many courageous exploits, became known as the 'father of the US Navy'.

Basil Hall published a number of books about his travels. In a later edition of *A Voyage of Discovery to the Western Coast of Corea and the Great Loo-Choo Island in the Japan Sea* (first published in 1817) he gave an account of his meeting with Napoleon in St Helena in 1817. The great man was astonished to hear that the people of Loo-Choo never had any wars and also had no money, being uninterested in gold and silver coins. Contrary to general belief in England, the former emperor appeared to be in excellent health and spirits.

Hall also published a lively account of his journey – lasting fifteen months, in 1827 to 1828 – accompanied by his wife and small daughter: they travelled 8,800 miles within North America. He gave fascinating descriptions of the fire service, of prisons and of slavery. As guests in a house at West Point, they found that, at 3 p.m., they had missed dinner and 'the black cook had gone out to take a walk – whoever heard before of a cook taking a walk! – and carried the key of the larder in his pocket!' Staying near Niagara Falls, it was he who got up in the night to attend to his daughter. The little girl later fell ill with cholera but recovered on removal to mountain air in the Allegheny mountains.

Whitelaw Ainslie (1767–1837) spent the last six years of his life at no. 8. He went to India as an assistant surgeon in the East India Company Service at the age of 21. There, he became keen to improve the health of the British troops and was credited with the proposal although his own plan was rejected. He rose to become medical superintendent of the southern division of the army in India but a year later he resigned, apparently after 27 years without home leave. He then devoted himself to writing, especially on the *Materia Medica* of India. He was knighted in 1835.

Ainslie's brother Robert was a friend and correspondent of Robert Burns. The two brothers married two daughters of Col. James Cuninghame of Fife.

Number 9

Another advocate, Andrew Rutherford (1791–1854), moved to no. 9 from 141 George Street in 1826, living there until his death. His wife was Sophia, daughter of Sir James Stewart Bt MP. They had no children and spent their summers at Lauriston Castle, Kincardineshire. In Edinburgh, he kept an excellent cellar and liked to entertain interesting people, such as the author William Thackeray. In 1851 he and his wife had six resident servants, including a butler and footman (Census).

Andrew Rutherford was Lord Advocate from 1839 to 1841 and again from 1846 to 1851, while sitting as Whig MP for Leith. Lord Cockburn wrote of him: 'I have known all our Lord Advocates since 1793 and there has not been one of them so well qualified for that situation.' In 1851, Rutherford became a judge, taking the title of Lord Rutherford. He was a member of the Royal Commission on the British Museum.

After Rutherford's death, the auction of his library of rare books (including nine editions of the *Decameron*) lasted for eleven days. He also collected marble busts of Greek gods and goddesses and silver, china and curios as well as many paintings.

Number 10

Alexander Wood (1817–1884) and his wife lived at *no. 2* for four years from 1854 and then no. 10 for a further 13 years before removing to *36 Moray Place* until 1874. His father was Dr James Wood of Cupar. After graduating MD at Edinburgh in 1839 he became medical officer at the Stockbridge Dispensary and later at the Royal Public Dispensary in the New Town. According to the DNB, 'his chief claim to remembrance as a physician is the fact that he introduced into practice the use of the hypodermic syringe for the administration of drugs... not necessarily limited to the administration of opiates.' He was strongly opposed to homeopathy and mesmerism and he wrote a paper entitled 'Homeopathy unmasked: being an exposure of its principal absurdities and contradictions'.

for Trayner, 1871 to 1878, see *27 Moray Place*

Number 11 (AINSLIE HOUSE)

When houses were built on the two gap sites on either side of the south-east of Ainslie Place, there were no numbers available for the houses built on the two corners, facing each other. Ainslie House, on the angled corner of Ainslie Place and St Colme Street was originally numbered 20B Ainslie Place, changing to 20 in 1861. From 1871 or earlier, Ainslie House had no number, but remained in Ainslie Place until 1913. In 1916, it became 11 St Colme Street.

Ainslie House was first used, from 1858, as a boarding house for Dr William Graham's Scottish Institution at *9 Moray Place*. The superintendent was Miss Helen Haswell, with Miss Prynne to help her. In 1861 they had two resident teachers (one for English and one for German) and 24 girls aged 11 to 21, with four domestic servants

Jessie Carrick with her family

(a cook, a waitress and two housemaids). Miss Haswell closed her boarding house in 1863, when she was aged 42.

We have a delightful vignette of life as a school boarder here from Jessie Carrick, sister of the photographer William Carrick. Jessie's correspondence with Frank Forbes, with whom she had fallen in love when on a visit to England, was discovered by Miss Haswell, who made her destroy his letters. However, her letters to him, tied up in pink ribbon, were found at the back of a drawer in the early 1930s by Felicity Ashbee and her mother, Jessie's niece and great-niece.

Jessie wrote to Frank in 1858, when she was 16 and he was 14:

> We have just removed to a new house, it is very large and handsomely fitted up; I have chosen a nice little bedroom, which one of the girls, my FRIEND, and I are to occupy.... To my great disappointment, this former arrangement is changed and ... my friend Lilly Dawson and I ...sleep in a double bed in a large room, two other girls are in it as well ... it is large, light and square, with two windows in and a closet off it. Its furniture consists of two double beds, a large press, a chest of drawers, four chairs, a small night table and a dressing table. The latter is covered with a white muslin cover and decorated with all sorts of little ornaments. Our mantelpiece is also covered with pretty books, fancy boxes etc.... WE have never tried BLINDMAN'S BUFF in our bedroom. However, I am going to follow your example.
>
> Sometimes at night, when we are hungry, Lilly (who has brought loads of provisions with her in a LARGE box) produces some eatables and we have a SORT of supper. ...Lilly and I have great fun up in our room; we undress as quickly as possible after we get up to our room at half past nine, and lie in bed talking (nonsense of course), laughing etc, until one and two in the morning. The only unpleasant thing at school is getting out of one's warm bed at half past six on a cold winter's morning and going downstairs to practise or to learn lessons.

After leaving school, Jessie rejoined her parents in St Petersburg. She and Frank did not marry until 1868, because of his father's insistence that they should wait until Frank could support a wife.

Mrs Grace Brown lived in Ainslie House from 1867 to her death in 1882, after which her son Captain William Brown, RN and her daughter Mrs Louisa Anderson took over the house. Grace Brown was the widow of Robert Brown, a landed proprietor and daughter of Samuel Anderson of Moredun. Her brother David and their three sisters lived at *24 Moray Place* from 1858. Louisa, the widow of another Samuel Anderson, lived there until 1913.

St Colme Street is now mainly occupied as offices.

St Colme Street Householders

1
1827–45 George Angus, architect
1828–32 Graham Speirs, advocate
1833 Mrs Dr Hunter
1835 Dr J. D. Hunter FRCP, surgeon, MD
1841 Miss Cadell of Tranent
1844 Alexander Donald, WS
1847–48 Gordon & Barron, WS
1847–51 John Purdie
1849–51 Mrs Glen
1851 Mrs W. Douglas
1853 Miss Ferguson
1863 Richard Denson, lodgings
1865 & James Keir, advocate
1867 & Rev. Decimus Brigstocke
1869 Rev. William Douglas
1873 A. E. Henderson, advocate
1874 Gunn's private hotel
1891 Queen Hotel (prop. John Gunn)

2.
1828 Hugh William Williams, painter
1832 Miss Millar
1836 Ralph Bruce Esq. & Miss Bruce
1849 Charles G. Reid WS
1851 Mrs McKenzie
1854 Dr Alexander Wood
1858 John Gowans
1861 Miss H. Carruthers
1862 Charles R. Couper, advocate
1871 Sir Walter G. Simpson, bart
1881 Gunn's private hotel (with no. 1)
1891 Leslie M. Balfour
1894 A. Makgill

3.
1828 Miss Keay
1849 Dr Charles Bell
1852 Charles G. Reid, WS
1858 Mrs William Stewart
1865 & William Stewart WS
1875 Andrew Jamieson, advocate
1892 George L. Macfarlane, advocate

4.
1826 Miss Campbell
1854 Mrs Purves (later, Robert R. Purves)
1867 R. J. Blair Cunynghame, MD, FRCSE
1870 Thomas Brodie, WS
1877 George Vertue
1881 George Readman, advocate
1887 Miss Violet C. Brown
1893 W. B. Dunlop

5.
1830 Adam Urquhart, advocate
1865 Mrs Urquhart (later, Miss & Miss M. J.)

6.
1826 Thomas Guthrie Wright, auditor, Court
  of Session; Swedish & Norwegian consul
1850 Miss Brodie; & William Turner
1853 C. F. Shand, advocate
1862 Mrs Symons
1865 William Webb
1867 William Watson, advocate
1879 Miss Forbes
1888 J. Sharp Callendar
1890 George Kerr MB

7.
1826 Archibald Alison, advocate
1837 John Hay, EICS
1843 W. S. Walker, advocate
1856 Mrs Strangeman
1868 Lady Alison
1875 A. Graham Murray, advocate
1886 David Dundas, advocate
1899 Robert Barclay Pearson, advocate

8.
1828 Capt. Basil Hall, RN
1831 Dr (from 1836, Sir) Whitelaw Ainslie
1840 Mrs Gilchrist
1862 Mrs Anderson
1881 Henry Johnston, advocate
1893 James L. Greig, advocate

1899 Harold Jalland Stiles, MB, FRCSE

9.
1826 Andrew Rutherford, advocate
1855 John Fraser, actuary
1870 Francis Deas, advocate
1875 S. F. R. Deas, WS
1899 J. & J. Gelletley, SSC

10.
1858 Dr Alexander Wood, FRCP

1871 John Trayner, advocate
1878 D. J. Brakenridge, MD, FRCPE, LRCSE
1896 Robert Abernethy, MD, FRCPE

11. (AINSLIE HOUSE)
1858 Miss Haswell
1863 W. Grant Henry
1867 Mrs Grace Brown
1882 Capt. Wm. Brown RN & Mrs S.
      Anderson

Forres Street

This street is named after Forres, a small town in Morayshire, the site of the Earl of Moray's Darnaway Castle.

Forres Street enters Moray Place from the south. It is short, with odd numbers 1 to 11 on the east side and even numbers 2 to 10 on the west. The first resident – Mrs Janet Lyon at no. 1 – arrived in 1825 and all the houses were occupied by 1830. Apart from no. 1 (at the south end) every house was used as lodgings or furnished apartments at some period during the nineteenth century, usually, but not always, with a landlady rather than a landlord. The four corner houses were each built as four flats.

Number 1

The basement of no. 1 housed a chair office from 1827, where sedan chairs could be hired from Alexander Stewart. Two years later he

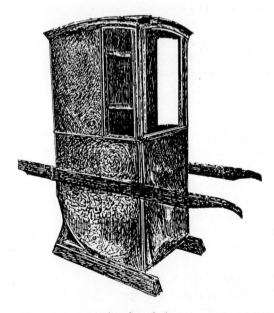

A sedan chair

was followed at no. 1 by Peter Stewart, a post-horse and coach hirer, who lived there until 1847 with his wife and seven children as well as one male and two female servants. He kept his horses and carriages at Wemyss Place.

Meanwhile, Alexander Stewart moved to *no. 10*

A sedan chair, which carried one passenger, was an unusual form of transport in that it could be taken into the home and destination of the passenger, who was therefore never exposed to the weather. John James Cowan, in his memoirs, wrote that, in 1852 when he was seven years old, 'on account of the delicacy of my sister of 18 or thereby,' we had a sedan chair to carry her from one house [Abercromby Place] to the other [Royal Terrace] and I was put in along with her in the hall of our house, and the chair was carried into the hall of the other so as to protect her from the night air'.

Sedan chairs could also serve another purpose. Towards the end of the eighteenth century, Lord Monboddo used to walk from the Court of Session to his home in St John Street but employed a sedan if it rained, to carry his wig!

In the early 1850s, regulations and a table of fares were published for access by sedan chairs to the Assembly Rooms in George Street. Chairs had to approach along the north side of George Street and enter by the 'right-hand division' and 'retire by the east division of the New Front Door'. The fare from Moray Place to the Assembly Rooms was eighteen pence.

In 1847, William Fraser took over the office and home of Peter Stewart at no. 1. He was a jobbing postmaster and coach hirer. By 1861, he employed two men but he also farmed fifty acres, employing another man. He and his wife and six children lived at no. 1 with a cook and a housemaid. One son, Robert, was initially a quarrier but he took over his father's business as a coach proprietor in 1870. At that time, the firm advertised first class carriages and job horses for hire (by the month or the year). Cabs were available at Lothian Road station, at the west end of Queen Street and at Lynedoch Place. Also for hire from Young Street North Lane were 'carriages, dog carts, other machines and spring vans for luggage, at the shortest notice'.

Thomas De Quincey (1785–1859) came to Edinburgh in 1828, his wife and eight children following him within two years. He and his family spent some months at 1 Forres Street in 1832. He then moved from one lodging to another, finding that the noise made by his children was too disturbing. He collected so many books that, when his lodgings became overcrowded, he abandoned his books and sought fresh lodgings. His landladies were trusted not to disturb his papers and, after his death, six store-houses of his books were found.

De Quincey was aged seven when his father died after some years of ill-health. The young Thomas gained a reputation as a classical scholar while in his teens, but ran away from Manchester Grammar School, where he was miserable and unwell. Later, at Worcester College, Oxford he turned to money-lenders and, to reduce the pain from toothache and rheumatism, he began to eat opium. His *Confessions of an Opium Eater*, published as a serial in 1821 in the *London Magazine*, made him famous. He lost all his teeth at an early age and thereafter could eat nothing except bread with soup or coffee.

He married Margaret Simpson in 1816 and for her sake he greatly reduced his consumption of opium. Embarked on a literary career, his contributions to *Blackwood's Magazine* (edited by his friend Professor Wilson) led to him moving to Edinburgh. Two of his children died in 1833 and 1835 and his wife in 1837, after which he settled his remaining children in a cottage at Lasswade, where he often visited them. There, he set his hair on fire on many an evening, but would never allow water to be used for extinguishing a fire near his precious papers.

Although he was in debt for much of his adult life, De Quincey was recklessly indifferent to money and gave away what he earned. He would also drop in on friends unexpectedly and then stay for several weeks.

for Dowling, 1875 to 1880, see *11 Darnaway Street*

Number 3

The Rev. Dr Thomas Chalmers (1780–1847) came from Argyle Square in 1830 to live at 3 Forres Street for seven years. He had been Professor of Moral Philosophy at St Andrews University from 1823 and of Theology in Edinburgh from 1828. In Edinburgh, his lectures were well attended: by distinguished members of various professions as well as by students (his predecessor, because of old age and infirmity, had given lectures which were inaudible, and classes had therefore dwindled).

As assistant to the minister of Cavers, near Hawick, from 1799 to 1802, Thomas Chalmers, 'for lack of a black surplice, addressed his audience from the pulpit in a dressing-gown of grey duffel which unfortunately on one occasion gave way under the armpits during the fervour of his declamation' (Crombie).

In Glasgow, as a parish minister, he established schools for the children of his parishioners. He was strongly opposed to the growing custom of a compulsory tax for the support of the poor, and demonstrated that, by helping the poor to help themselves and by rejecting applications for relief from the idle and the drunken, the expenditure could be met by voluntary church door contributions.

A prolific writer, his *Astronomical Discourses* – his sermons on the connection between astronomy and Christianity – sold 20,000 copies within a year of publication in 1817.

In 1832, as Moderator of the General Assembly of the Church of Scotland, he objected to the expense of public dinners given on the Sundays during the General Assembly, and also to the daily public breakfasts traditionally given by the Moderator. He succeeded in having these abolished.

Thomas Chalmers was the leader of the Free Church movement and in 1843 played a major part in the Disruption against interference by the law in affairs of the church, particularly the appointment of ministers to parishes against the wishes of their congregations. He demitted his chair after the Disruption and became Principal of the Free Church Theological Institution which later became New College.

Chalmers was an imposing figure with a fine shock of hair. He was once delighted when a London barber clipped out all his white hairs, leaving only the black, making his customer look forty years younger!

An unnamed chairman, whose office was at no. 3, showed in his account book for 1844 under 'Sabbath chair hires', a regular entry for taking a French governess to chapel.

Charles Bell (1805–1891), surgeon and physician to the Royal Dispensary and accoucheur to the maternity hospital, moved from one house to another with his wife and children. First he was at *3 Randolph Cliff* from 1840 for three years, next at 3 Forres Street for six years and then at *3 St Colme Street* for three years to 1852. His particular interests were midwifery and diphtheria. His 'suavity of manner with his massive and truly physician-like appearance' endeared him to his maternity patients, in spite of his occasional manifestations of temper. The son of an advocate, he was a nephew of Sir Charles Bell of *6 Ainslie Place*.

Number 5

for Borthwick, 1829 to 1832, see *10 Darnaway Street*

Forres Street had connections with many baronets. Sir Alexander Kinloch, 10th baronet, of Gilmerton (1830–1912) married Lucy Charlotte, daughter of Sir Ralph Anstruther, baronet, and they had a large household at no. 5 from 1890 until his death, with two adult children, two grandsons and seven resident domestic servants at the 1891 census. Sir Alexander had served as a Captain in the Crimea with the Grenadier Guards, earning a medal with four clasps and a Turkish medal.

Number 7

Catherine Sinclair, author of more than twenty books, including *Modern Accomplishments* and *Holiday House*, was instrumental in obtaining seats for crowded thoroughfares in Edinburgh, instituted public drinking fountains and set up soup kitchens. Her brother was Sir George Sinclair, 2nd baronet of Ulbster (1790–1868). Sir George (MP for Caithness for many years) was the eldest of fifteen children of Sir John Sinclair, the celebrated originator of the *Statistical Account of Scotland*, published in twenty volumes in 1798.

One of Sir George's daughters, Emilia, was divorced at the Court of Session in July 1841. Her mother and two sisters, as well as her three year old son (Wilbraham Tollemache), were listed at 7 Forres Street at the June 1841 census, probably having come to Edinburgh for Emilia's divorce case.

Emilia had married Henry Bertie Tollemache, her mother's first cousin, at Gretna Green in August 1837 and, a few days later, at St George's Church, Hanover Square in London. The couple lived in Edinburgh until March 1841, the last few months in Mrs Peacock's lodgings at *4 Darnaway Street*. They did not get on with each other and their friends advised them to divorce. Emilia agreed that she and their son should live at Leamington in England and they left Edinburgh with a nursemaid but travelled no further than Glasgow. There, the nursemaid was instructed to take the child back to

Edinburgh. Emilia, together with a man who went by the name of Williams, also travelled back to Edinburgh, where they took up residence as a married couple at the Black Bull Inn in Catherine Street. Emilia was divorced in Edinburgh on 3 July 1841 and married Major John Power of Waterford two days later.

Emilia's father, Sir George, had been arrested as a spy at the age of 16 after going to Germany to study in Göttingen. He and a companion, travelling from Gotha to Leipzig in October 1806, soon found that all horses had been commandeered by the Prussian army and they had to travel on foot, hiring a man to take their luggage in a wheelbarrow. They were arrested by the invading French army and were questioned by Marshal Murat and then by Napoleon himself, about their knowledge of the strength of the Prussian army. Napoleon declared himself satisfied with the naivety of George Sinclair's replies and declared both men innocent.

Number 9

James Dalmahoy, a retired surgeon of the HEICS, spent many years at no. 9. He arrived in 1855 with his wife Helen: they had a cook, housemaid and tablemaid. At the 1881 census, when he was aged 81, he was described as retired merchant, which possibly shows that the enumerator misheard 'surgeon' for 'merchant'.

Number 11

John Maclaren Barclay (1811–1886) and his family occupied one of the four flats at no. 11 from 1866 to his death. He was a portrait painter, but he also painted genre and figure subjects; he was treasurer of the Royal Scottish Academy for the last two years of his life.

Number 10

Alexander Stewart moved here from *no. 1* in 1829, remaining for eight years. He was one of the eleven chairmasters listed in the 1832 Edinburgh street directory. He was succeeded there by James Gow, another chairmaster, until 1847.

Music teachers were much in demand, and Charles Hargitt (c.1785–1865) taught piano at the Scottish Institution, with ten

Professor James Syme, assisted by his staff and students, employed in reducing a dislocation of the shoulder

Rev. Dr Thomas Chalmers

assistants. He was also an organist. He and his wife Mary and, eventually, their six children lived at no. 10 from 1829 to 1842. Their eldest son Charles was later organist at St Mary's Roman Catholic Cathedral and was a well-known composer and conductor: he was the first conductor of the Edinburgh Choral Union from 1858 until he went to London four years later.

Number 8

The new Edinburgh Academy opened in 1824 and one of the first teachers of classics there was Robert Mitchell, living at no. 8 from 1830 to 1836. He had previously been Rector of Kirkcudbright Grammar School. Lord Cockburn noted, of Mitchell's application to Edinburgh Academy: 'A very good-natured sensible person. His certificates are not so good as he deserves, for they don't adequately explain the substantial fact that he prodigiously improved the Kirkcudbright Academy. Keep this man in view' (Magnusson). The first specially endowed prize at Edinburgh Academy was the Mitchell Medal.

Number 6

David Rhind (1808–1883) joined his father John (cashier, Edinburgh Friendly Insurance Company) and brothers Macduff (advocate) and Williamson (WS) at no. 6 in 1834 for two years. Later in his life he was the architect of a number of large buildings, notably Daniel Stewart's College in 1848 and the Life Association Assurance office in Princes Street in 1855. Sadly, the latter was demolished in the 1960s.

Daniel Stewart, of the Scottish Exchequer, left money for the education of poor boys, with a preference for those named Stewart or Macfarlane. The resulting school, on the Queensferry Road, is one of Edinburgh's landmarks for travellers from the north.

David Rhind had an unusual commission in designing the Miller mausoleum in Craigentinny Crescent, built between 1848 and 1856. William Henry Miller, who died in 1848, left £300,000, of which £20,000 was for his burial in a grave not less than 40 feet deep, with walls to be lined with dressed stone, and his body to be encased in a series of lead coffins. The whole was to be surmounted by a monument which *The Scotsman* reported was to be 'in commemoration of the private virtues of the deceased for, as a public character, he was unknown'. The vast mausoleum has marble panels depicting the Overthrow of Pharoah and the Song of Moses and Miriam. Miller was an eccentric book collector, known as Measure Miller, for his habit of measuring shelf space required for his purchases. He had once been Conservative MP for Newcastle-under-Lyme.

for Trotter, 1841, see *10 Randolph Crescent*

Sir James Colquhoun, 4th baronet of Luss, was briefly in lodgings at no. 6 at the time of the 1851 census, with two male servants and his own coachman. His wife, Jane, daughter of Sir Robert Abercromby, baronet, had died in 1844. Sir James was MP for Dunbartonshire from 1837 to 1841. His niece, Lucy Bethia Walford (née Colquhoun), in her *Recollections of a Scottish Novelist*, wrote about the death of her uncle, whom she described as 'the shyest man in Scotland'. He used to make a deer-stalking expedition to the island of Inch Lonaig on Loch Lomond, to provide Christmas venison for the poor people on his lands of Luss. In December 1873, the weather became very stormy and, on the return trip, the boat carrying four oarsmen with Sir James at the helm, disappeared. Two days later Sir James's high white felt hat was washed ashore, followed by the upturned boat. Some days later, his body was recovered.

Number 4

Lord Robert Kerr (1780–1843), the fourth son of the fifth Marquess of Lothian, lived at no. 4 with his wife Mary from 1826 to 1831 and then at *38 Moray Place* until his death. Probably at least some of their four sons and five daughters lived with them. He was assistant adjutant-general to the army in Scotland and, from 1837, aide-de-camp and military secretary to Lord Greenock (later, Earl of Cathcart), who was Commander-in-Chief of the Forces in Scotland. Lord Robert's office was at 2 Young Street.

Lord Robert was secretary to the Order of the Thistle and was also one of the first Directors of the Scottish Naval and Military Academy, founded in 1825. He finished his military career as a Major-General.

John Montgomerie Bell and his family went to no. 4 in 1841 and, after his death in 1862, his wife and then two daughters continued to live in the house into the early twentieth century. He was Sheriff of

Kincardineshire from 1851 and he published a *Treatise on the Law of Arbitration in Scotland* in 1861, which became the standard work on the subject. When staying at Linnhouse, Midlothian, where he had been living during the summer, a quiet horse, which he had ridden regularly, bolted with him whilst they were still in the yard. It rushed back to the stable, knocking him out of the saddle as he was trying to throw himself off. He died from his injuries. He had been tipped to be appointed Professor of Scots Law, his brother Robert having previously held that post.

Number 2

At the age of 17, James Syme (1799–1870) discovered the method of applying rubber in solution in the preparation of waterproof cloth, later patented by (and named after) Charles Macintosh. He lived at 2 Forres Street from 1831 to 1837.

Although he never attended any lectures on surgery, in 1818 he was appointed a dissecting room demonstrator. Two years later he became Superintendent of the Edinburgh Fever Hospital and in 1823 he began to give lectures on anatomy. He soon abandoned anatomy for surgery. Annoyed that the managers of the Royal Infirmary had failed to appoint him to a post, he made Minto House into the Edinburgh Surgical Hospital in 1829. This had once been the town residence of the Elliots of Minto, on the east side of Argyle Square, overlooking the Cowgate. It was demolished when Chambers Street was taken through Argyle Square.

Syme was appointed Professor of Clinical Surgery in 1833 and he gradually became recognised as the greatest living authority in surgery. In 1833, without anaesthesia, operations demanded coolness, dexterity and rapidity of action. Major operations were mainly amputation of limbs, removal of stones from the bladder and ligation of arteries in the treatment of aneurysm. Patients often died from haemorrhage or septicaemia. Professor Syme revolutionised the teaching of clinical surgery by bringing patients to his lectures for demonstration purposes. He introduced into Britain the excision of diseased elbows, and he amputated at an ankle joint instead of removing the whole leg. He also introduced improvements in plastic surgery especially of the lower lip.

for Pringle, 1846 to 1849, see *2 Randolph Cliff.*

Forres Street Householders

1.
1825–47   Mrs Lyon
1826–27   Robert Mueller, prof. of music
1827–29   George Nicholson, house painter
1827–29   Alexander Stewart, chair master
1829–30   Mrs Napier
1830–39   Mrs Dr Hunter
1831–39   Capt. Thomas Leighton, E. India Co.
1831–39   Donald Mackenzie, teacher
1832–39   Misses Laing, dressmakers
1832–33   Thomas De Quincey
1832–47   P. Stewart, post horse & coach hirer
1833–37   Mrs Wylie of Annatfield
1837–39   Mrs & Miss Rae
1841–42   Charles Doig, writer
1841–47   Dr P. S. Samuells
1842–45   William G. Spindler, teacher of guitar
1842–44   E. Spindler, teacher of piano & violin
1845–49   George Calder, SSC
1847–   William Fraser, coach hirer
1849–53   Adolph Maussion, French consul, Scotland
1849–66   John Milne
1858–62   Mrs Learmonth of Parkhall
1862–64   Mrs John Buist
1865–71   Mrs Gibson
1866–68   Mrs Houston
1871–76   Miss Maxton
1872–73   Servants' Friend Society
1875–80   Charles Dowling
1877–   William Rae Macdonald
1877–78   Miss Burdon Sanderson
1878–82   Thomas Ker, sharebroker
1883–89   Miss Helen C. Sanderson
1888–98   William N. Granger
1890–94   James Stuart
1894–   Mrs Learmonth
1897–98   Miss Johnston
1898–   Duncan MacGillivray
1898–   Thomas Mackintosh WS

3.
1830 Rev. Prof. T. Chalmers
1838 Mrs J. Woolard, lodgings; & Thomas S. Brown, surgeon & dentist
1844 Dr Charles Bell, FRS
1850 Rev. Dr Bannerman
1851 Miss McKay
1853 William P. Wilkie, advocate
1862–74 Mrs Dickson

1867–70   Henry James Moncreiff, advocate
1874–91   George Watson, advocate
1874–78   Mrs P. C. Macdougall
1892   Miss McCosh Smith

5.
1829 Dr George Borthwick
1832 Miss Porteous
1838 Mrs Brown, lodgings
1840 James Denniston, Esq.
1849 John Babington
1851 Thomas Lee
1852 Miss Brown
1853 John Myles, tavern keeper
1855 Mrs Reid
1857 George Dingwall Fordyce, advocate
1876 John Aiton
1878 John Henry Davidson
1890 Sir Alexander Kinloch, bart; & Francis Kinloch, advocate

7.
1828–35   William Moncrieff Scott, accountant
1832–33   Archibald Gibson, accountant
1835–36   Miss Parker, lodgings & Mr M. Parker
1845–49   Rev. Robert Ferguson
1850–55   Miss Fairbairn
1853–55   Alexander Howe, WS
1855   George Lockhart Ross, jun., advocate

9.
1830 Mrs Rollo
1840 Rev. John Hunter
1841 Miss Marshall, boarding-house
1855–96 Dr Dalmahoy and James Dalmahoy. HEICS
1893–94 J. A. Fleming, advocate
1896 John Macpherson
1897 Rev. Archibald Fleming, MA; & Maxwell Fleming

11.
1826–28   Mrs Rutherford
1827–31   Wm. Lindores, grocer, spirit dealer
1827–30   John McLaren, lodgings
1829–30   Arthur Dingwall, advocate
1830–32   William Swan, writer
1831–32   Miss Potts
1831–39   Miss White
1832–39   Thomas Thorburn WS

1832–34 R. Wharton Jones, surgeon
1833–34 D. S. Threshie
1833–36 Charles Muirhead, poulterer
1833–42 Mrs Dr Hodgson
1835–39 Miss Margaret Davidson
1836–37 E. Ricateau, teacher of French
1838–44 Donald McDonald, lodgings
1840–46 James Watson, writer
1841–46 Robert Stewart, writer
1844–45 James Meikle, solicitor
1844–45 Robert McCredie, lodgings
1845–52 Mrs Dr Sanders
1846–60 William Fraser, writer
1847–48 Walter Black, agent
1852–59 H. Callender, accountant
1853–66 Fred. Stevens Sansome, silk mercer, draper
1859–66 Thomas S. Paton, advocate
1860–63 Miss Davidson
1861–95 William Morrison (later, only Miss)
1863–65 Adam Currer
1863–70 Charles Stewart, advocate
1866–68 Lawrence Sinclair
1866–87 J. M. Barclay, portrait painter
1867–68 J. Campbell Lorimer, advocate
1868–72 Hon. Mrs Hugh Arbuthnott
1869–72 John Rhind, advocate
1872–74 Alexander Nevay, advocate
1872–73 Miss Forrester
1873–74 P. Devine
1874–89 A. Le Harivel, Prof. of French
1877–78 Holmes Ivory, WS
1878–82 George A. Wilson
1883–86 Henry Smith
1886–90 William Simpson
1887–   T. Mitchell
1889–93 Mrs Rennie
1890–94 James H Brown
1892–95 Miss Morrison
1893–95 E. M. Montague
1894–   Mrs John Hill
1895–   Alexander Leitch
1896–   Mme Agnes D. Hamilton (Mrs Kedslie) teacher of violin
1896–   Andrew Kedslie

10.
1828–32 Walter McCulloch Esq.
1828–31 George Monro Binning, advocate
1829–42 Charles Hargitt & son, teachers of music
1829–37 Alexander Stewart, chairmaster
1833–39 James Maidment, advocate
1833–37 James Stevenson, fishmonger

1838–47 James Gow, chairman (area)
1838–41 W. S. Ogilvy, house painter & paper-hanger
1841–43 Mrs Sarle
1843–46 Miss Anderson
1843–46 Miss Lewis & Miss Jane Lewis
1846–69 Thomas Ponton, architect
1869–82 Miss Ponton
1846–53 Alexander McGregor, architect
1852–54 Miss Kissock
1853–54 Francis Jardin
1853–54 Alexander Martin
1855–65 D. Douglas, foreign booksellers
1856–57 Richard H. W. Brown
1856–60 Robert Chisholm, clothier
1857–65 William & F. & Miss Hanson, music teachers
1859–63 Michael Sanderson
1865–69 Heinrich Weisse, teacher of German
1865–69 Mrs Weisse, teacher of music
1865–73 Miss Kerr
1865–66 James A. McIntosh & Mrs Lachlan McIntosh
1866–82 Miss Mary Sinclair
1867–68 Mrs Ferguson & Mrs Grant, ladies' nurses
1874–83 Miss Kay
1878–80 Miss Morrison
1879–88 James Alex Gardner; Matthew Gardner
1882–83 James Connell
1883–85 Mrs McArthur
1885–86 Mrs Graham
1885–   Miss Jane A. Couston
1886–93 John Wilson, advocate
1888–   George P. McNeill, advocate
1888–92 Grant T. McNeill
1893–   Robert J. Hamilton (10A)
1894–   Miss Isbister
1896–   Hugh J. E. Fraser, advocate

8.
1830–36 Robert Mitchell, Edinburgh Academy
1830–39 J. W. Semple, advocate
1831–32 John Alison, WS
1831–48 Mrs Helen Black, lodgings
1843–51 Mrs Taylor
1851–65 John Dewar, lodgings
1865–80 James Archibald, lodgings
1870–74 William Fredk. Hunter, advocate
1880–85 Mrs William Scott, apartments
1886–   Mrs Archibald, apartments
1889–95 F. L. Callender

1891–95 Misses Muirden
1899–   Maxwell Fleming, advocate

6.
1830 Mrs Anderson, lodgings
1831 John Rhind, Edin. Friendly Ins. Soc.;
Macduff Rhind, architect; Williamson Rhind,
WS; David Rhind, architect
1836–39 & 1842–48 Cosmo Innes, advocate
1841–42 Archibald Trotter, younger, of
Dreghorn
1848   William Stewart
1852–76 John Macdonald (1867, only Mrs)
1856–59 William Leslie WS
1863–66 S. M. D. Currie, MD
1865-66 Major Ramsay,
1874-77 William Fredk. Hunter, advocate
1876-80 Mrs Weatherley, lodgings
1877-81 T. C. Frost
1880-81 J. G. Lorrain
1881   Miss Cuthbert, apartments
1885   Mrs H. P. Macpherson, apartments

1888–91 J. Nolan, apartments
1890–91 J. A. Fleming, advocate
1892   David Paulin, manager, Sco. Life
Ass. Co.

4.
1826 Lord Robet Kerr, asst. Adj. Gen.
1831 Dr Robert Omond, FRCS
1841 J. M. Bell, advocate
1865 A. Montgomerie Bell, MD, surgeon; M.
Montgomerie Bell, WS
1886 Miss Montgomerie Bell

2.
1828 Alexander Errol Monteith, advocate
1831 James Syme, surgeon
1837 Alexander Errol Monteith
1843 James Glassford Esq.
1846 Alex. Pringle of Whytbank
1849 Henry Oliver
1854 R. B. Moore, private hotel
1873 John Gunn, private hotel

Albyn Place

The origin of the name Albyn is thought to be *Albainn*, the Gaelic for 'Scotland' or for 'men of Scotland' (referring to the Highland Society at *no. 24*). A newspaper of October 1823 reported that 'several noble houses' in Albyn Place 'are newly finished as to masonry'. The first two to be lived in were nos. *2* and *10*, both in 1825. All of the eleven houses were occupied by 1831.

Number 1

Andrew Scott, the collector of the poor rates for the West Church (St Cuthbert's) parish, spent the last three years of his life at no. 1 from 1826.

This was one of several houses used as lodgings. Miss Margaret Falkner, a milliner at no. 1 for a few years from 1849, had nine lodgers in 1851, including another milliner and two dressmakers. Two other flats in the house were also lodging-houses then, making a total of 17 people living at no. 1.

James Muirhead (1831–1889) spent one year here in 1879. He was Professor of Civil Law from 1862 to his death. He introduced the idea of history of law, and of changes in it (as in a living organism); he also stressed the importance of the history of legal institutions. During lectures he held the attention of the students by giving human interest to a topic. Muirhead gained a European reputation in Roman Law. In 1885 he became Sheriff in Chancery and, a year later, Sheriff of Stirling, Dumbarton and Clackmannanshire. His father Claud was the proprietor of the *Edinburgh Advertizer*.

Sir George Washington Browne, the architect of Edinburgh Central Library and of the Hospital for Sick Children, had his office at no. 1 from 1892 and then at *no. 8* from 1896.

Number 2

Some of the first families to live in Albyn Place remained in their homes until the turn of the century.

John Archibald Campbell (1788–1866) and his family were at no. 2 from 1825 for over 80 years. He was Clerk to the Signet and

Commissioner for taking affidavits in the Court of the Exchequer, King's Bench and Common Pleas. From 1843 he was Sheriff-Clerk of Midlothian. He had married Emma Legh, daughter of the High Sheriff of Cheshire, in 1822. Of their three daughters, Caroline inherited the house on her father's death and described herself as 'a lady of independent fortune' in 1871 (census). By 1891, her unmarried brother, the Rev. John A. Legh Campbell, had displaced her as head of household (or perhaps the census enumerator preferred a male head of household). The family was never short of servants, having four until 1871 (census) and five at the two succeeding censuses.

Number 3

Mrs Margaret Steuart and her adult children James, Charles (both WS), and Agnes moved into no. 3 in 1826. A year later James went to *8 Doune Terrace*, but the others remained in Albyn Place for the rest of their lives. They always had two or three resident servants. Charles never married and by 1891 he additionally had a resident 'invalid gentleman's attendant' (census) when he was aged 87. By then, his faithful cook Martha Knight, who had been with the family since at least 1841, was 74.

Number 4

No doubt Charles Steuart (from *no. 3*) was latterly sometimes mistaken for his next door neighbour Charles Stewart. This second Charles and his widowed father John Stewart of Eskgrove, came to no. 4 in 1875: both were WS and John died in 1890.

Colin Campbell of Jura (1772–1848) had his town house at no. 4 from 1828 to 1839. He was the Heritable Keeper of Craignish Castle in Argyllshire, parts of which were said to date from the twelfth century. One of his seven daughters, Isabella, married Lachlan Macquarie of Jarvisfield in 1836, the only son of General Macquarie, Governor of New South Wales. The Macquarie family mausoleum in Mull is a place of pilgrimage for many Australians.

John Swain and his wife Elizabeth let furnished apartments at no. 4 from 1849. In 1851, as well as their baby and John's sister (a dressmaker) and his mother-in-law with three servants, they had three other households at no. 4, two of them headed by a landed proprietor, evidently high-class tenants. This made a total of 23 people living here.

In 1853 the Swains expanded into *no. 5*, making Swain's Private Hotel out of the two houses until 1874. Thereafter, the hotel was at *no. 5* only until 1888.

Number 5

John Bowie of Camiscan and William Bowie Stewart Campbell of Glenfalloch, both WS, lived at no. 5 from 1826. Bowie, who was solicitor to the GPO and to the Inland Revenue, came from Albany Street. He and his wife Margaret had two sons (one of them a clerk in the GPO) and three daughters at the 1851 census. He died in 1862. William Campbell (whose mother was a Bowie) had been apprentice to John Bowie, and together they had their office of Bowie and Campbell WS in their home from 1826 until 1837. At that time, Campbell left to remarry, having been widowed after a short marriage of four years. He then took the territorial title of his second wife, Janet Maxwell Stewart, only child of Robert Stewart of Cloichfoldich.

for Swain, 1853 to 1888, see *no. 4*

William Forbes Skene DCL, LLD (1809–1892), son of James Skene of Rubislaw (see *46 Moray Place*) had an office at no. 5 from 1888 to his death. He was Historiographer-Royal for Scotland from 1881 to 1892.

Number 6

Number 6 Albyn Place was built in 1827 for the Highland (later, Highland and Agricultural) Society of Scotland at a cost of about £4000, to be their offices and hall and also the home of their Secretary. The Society's Museum of the Vegetable Productions of the UK, begun in the late eighteenth century, was also housed there. The collection became large and valuable and a new museum was built on George IV Bridge in 1841, but this was burned down in 1851. The insurance covered a gradual replacement of the collections, which were transferred in 1855 to the Museum of Science and Art in Chambers Street (now the Royal Museum of Scotland).

Charles Gordon and his wife Helen Fletcher of Dunans lived in the house from 1828 to 1846. They had two daughters and four sons, one of whom became Bishop of Jamaica. In 1841 they had one male and five female resident servants (Census). Charles Gordon was Depute Secretary of the Society, jointly with his uncle Mr Lewis Gordon. His title was changed to Secretary in 1834, and he then bought the estate of Drimmin in Argyllshire. He was very highly thought of by the Directors of the Society and was knighted in 1837.

As a solicitor, Gordon also had his office of Gordon and Burnett WS at no. 6 from 1829 to 1843 (Burnett being replaced by Mackay in 1834).

John Hall Maxwell, an advocate, succeeded Gordon as Secretary of the Highland and Agricultural Society (as it had become) in 1845. During his management over the next twenty years, the membership nearly doubled to 4,200. For his services to agricultural statistics (relating to stock and crops) he was appointed a Companion of the Bath in 1856. He also greatly improved his own estate of Dargavel in Renfrewshire, especially by reclaiming waste land.

He and his wife and their two sons and four daughters lived in their town house in style. They had six resident servants in 1851 and 1861, as well as a governess. By 1861 they had a butler and a coachman, so must have had their own carriage; their servants wore the family livery.

A booklet entitled *What's to become of the Highland Society?* was published in 1859. The author was 'Investigator' but was thought to be John Wilson, Professor of Agriculture. It alleged that discontent with Hall Maxwell's management had led to resignations from the Board of Directors. He had been imperious and insolent and had changed the dates of the Society's exhibitions to the inconvenience of exhibitors. 'He names the Directors, appoints the Committees, cooks the report and treats with the most severe disdain, not to say insolence, everyone who ventures to object to his arrangements.' He had absorbed the Society's hall into his own domestic use and had replaced the brass plate at the door by one with his own name.

Hall Maxwell immediately published a letter to the members, refuting all the allegations. He denied, for instance, that he had opposed the appointment of John Wilson to the chair of agriculture and produced letters to show that he had supported the nomination. He averred that the Directors themselves had changed the dates of exhibitions at the request of farmers.

There was no mention of this dispute in the history of the Society, published in 1879, but Hall Maxwell remained in post until shortly before his death in 1866. On retirement, he was presented with 1000 guineas and a service of plate.

Number 7

Mrs Amelia Kirkaldy of Baldovie came to no. 7 as a widow in 1830 but died soon afterwards. Her children, George and Mary, lived there until Mary's marriage in 1838 to Thomas Mackay, WS, whom she had met because his office was next-door at *no. 6*. George then left Edinburgh. Thomas Mackay, who died in 1864, and Mary, who died in 1884, always had five or six resident female servants. Their son Aeneas, who was an advocate, lived with his parents (and then with his mother) before becoming the householder himself. He did not marry until 1891 and had no children. He inherited the estate of Hearnesbrook in Co. Galway from his mother's brother George, who died in 1871.

Aeneas Mackay was Professor of Constitutional Law and History from 1874 to 1881. The chair had been renamed 'History' in 1862, but the holder of the chair still had to deliver a series of lectures in each winter session on Constitutional Law and Constitutional History, which were necessary for a degree in law. His predecessor, Professor Cosmo Innes, had been delighted to have a large attendance at his lectures when he gave them without charge. As soon as he asked students for a fee, the attendance dropped until the lectures became mandatory.

Aeneas maintained his home in Albyn Place when he was Sheriff of Fife and Kinross from 1886 to 1901.

Number 8

The Postmaster-General for Scotland, Sir David Wedderburn, baronet, made his home at no. 8 from 1829 for three years. He had been MP for Perth from 1805 to 1818 before taking up this government appointment, a post which was later abolished. As well as succeeding to the Scottish baronetcy of Blackness, he was created first baronet of Balindean, a UK baronetcy, in 1803, 'with remainder, failing heirs of his own body, to the heirs male of Sir Alexander Wedderburn, his great-grandfather.'

Number 9

George Handyside Pattison and his family lived at no. 8 from 1870 to 1887. He was Sheriff of Roxburgh and Kelso, while continuing to practise as an advocate. One son, William, was a WS.

Alfred Gallrein was a lodger at no. 9 from 1888 for four years. He was born in Magdeburg but went to England and was appointed musical professor at Uppingham College. Two years later, he joined the orchestra of Glasgow Choral Union. In 1885 he moved to Edinburgh, and established himself as a teacher of cello and piano; he organised annual chamber concerts and composed an operetta *The Squire* as well as songs.

Number 10

The Professor of Medical Jurisprudence, Thomas Traill (1781–1862) lived at no. 10 from 1835 to 1842,before moving to Rutland Square. He had graduated in medicine in Edinburgh before practising in Liverpool, where he was a founder of the Literary and Philosophical Society.

For many years, Traill was curator of the library of the Society of Antiquaries of Scotland. He was occupied for ten years as editor of (and contributor to) the eighth edition of the *Encyclopaedia Britannica.*

The professor was described by William Gibson MD as 'a short, thick, squat-looking man, with bushy black head and queer expression, who skellies [looks sideways] slightly out of one eye, and is very busy, bustling and important.' He continued lecturing to within twelve days of his death.

Number 11

During Hall Maxwell's tenure of office as Secretary of the Highland and Agricultural Society (see *no. 6*), John Wilson's predecessor as Professor of Agriculture, David Low, had lived at no. 11 from 1835 for five years. He was also editor of the quarterly *Journal of Agriculture*. Students were stimulated by his museum of agriculture to attend lectures on the subject. Among David Low's published books was *Breeds of Domesticated Animals of the British Islands*, with coloured plates, which was translated into French.

Towards the end of the century the face of Albyn Place was

changing. A number of businesses had their offices in nos. 1, 5, 6, 8, 9 and 11. These were mainly lawyers, surveyors and financial offices.

Albyn Place Householders

1.
1826–38 Andrew Scott collector of West
  Church's poor rates
1827–34 James Dennistoun of Colgrain,
  advocate
1830–31 J. Gray Farquahar WS
1833–35 A. G. Sutherland WS
1835–39 James Crawford, advocate
1837–38 Alex Stewart, coach hirer
1838–40 John Davidson, grocer
1840–42 Elizabeth Davidson, lodgings
1840–45 Graham Weir MD
1842–43 W. H. Forrist, accountant
1845–47 James Griffith, accountant
1847–48 Capt. Patrick MaLeod Petley
1848–60 Mrs Stevenson
1849–52 Misses Falkner & Macausland
1849–54 Mrs Greig
1852–58 Mlle Angelica, teacher of dancing
1854–60 Robert Lee, advocate
1859–79 Miss Cockburn
1860–62 Abercromby Dick, advocate
1860–65 William Lamond, advocate
1862–63 William Clow
1863–66 J. C. Thomson, advocate
1865–66 William Adlington, ARA, prof. of
  music
1866–69 Mrs Taylor
1867–82 Miss C. Dunlop
1869–73 Henry Tod, jun. WS
1873–76 Robert M. Boyd
1876–96 R. S. Patterson, upholsterer
1879–80 Prof. James Muirhead
1880–93 Mylne & Cook, CA
1882–87 Miss Maclaren
1885–87 Town & Country Bank of S.
  Australia Ltd
1887–96 J. S. Anderson, Mus. Bac. Oxon.
thereafter, offices

2.
1825 John Archibald Campbell WS
1888 Rev. J. A. Campbell

3.
1826–29 James Steuart, jun. WS
1827 Charles Steuart WS

4.
1828 Colin Campbell of Jura
1840 W. Scott Moncrieff, accountant
1848 Angus Hossack, lodgings
1849 Mrs Swains, lodgings
1862 Thomas Mackie, advocate
1875 John Stewart WS
1877 Charles Stewart WS
1894 William Whyte SSC

5.
1826–53 John Bowie WS
1826–33 William Bowie Campbell WS
1836–38 Hamilton Russel WS
1852–53 W. R. Skinner SSC
1853–88 Swain's Private Hotel (with no. 4)
1875–76 James Pringle CA;
thereafter, offices

6.
1827 Highland Society of Scotland
1828 Charles Gordon of Drumnin
1851 John Hall Maxwell
1867 William W. Gibson, corn merchant
1875–89 Mrs John W. Walker
thereafter, offices

7.
1830 Mrs Kirkaldy of Baldovie
1840 Thomas G. McKay WS & Mrs Mckay
  (nee Kirkaldy)
1866 Aeneas J. G. McKay, advocate

8.
1829 Sir David Wedderburn bart,
1832 D. Mure, advocate
1856 Thomas Brown, advocate
from 1896, offices

9.
1831 Miss Wardlaw
1853 Mrs William Herris Ker
1855–70 Misses J. and I. Fairbairn
1855–61 Alexander Howe WS
1870–87 G. Handyside Pattison, advocate &
William R. Pattison WS
1883 David J. Mckenzie, advocate
1887 E. M. Cuthbert, apartments
1887 Robert W. Will SSC
1888 Alfred Gallrein, prof. of music
from 1892, offices

10.
1825 Adam Paterson, advocate; & Alex
Paterson, wine merchant; & David Paterson,
accountant
1835 Prof. Thomas S. Traill
1842 Misses Harriman
1852–56 William Stewart, lodgings (& no.11)
1855–56 Benjamin R. Bell, advocate
1856–70 Robert Williams, lodgings (& no.11)
1857–58 James Walker of Dalry, advocate

1870–95 Miss Moffat, lodgings
1870–81 James Keir, advocate
1881 G. Vertue, wine merchant
1887 J. Horne Stevenson, advocate
1891 J. A. Fleming, advocate
1892 William J. Kippen, advocate
1896 Robert D. Barclay

11.
1827 Misses Whyte, milliners & dressmakers
1830 Mrs Dr Deans
1835 Prof. David Low; & Alex Low,
accountant
1841 Robert Omond MD
1843 Alexander Crawford esq.
1847 John M. Lindsay CS
1851 Miss Robertson
1858 see no. 10
1870 Mrs McKey
1878 Mrs R. Moffat
1881 Alexander James FRCP
from 1888, offices

Wemyss Place

Wemyss Place, the eastern boundary of the Moray Estate, was built on the site of Wood's Farm which had been for many years in the family of Mr Wood of Warriston. Chambers, in 1824, wrote of the area: 'Many still alive remember the fields bearing as fair and rich a crop of wheat as they can now be said to bear houses.' Game used to be plentiful on the farm, especially partridges and hares.

An anonymous Australian emigrant who had been brought up in Queen Street in the 1820s remembered that, 'at the foot of Wemyss Place, there was the ancient domain of Moray Park which was entered through an iron-railed gate, between dark-grey stone pillars, each surmounted by a stone lion couchant.' At that time a bull was kept in a shed in the field between Queen Street and Heriot Row.

A stone wall ten feet high, with a gardener's hut behind it, which had been the western boundary of Queen Street Gardens, was removed and replaced by an iron railing. The western section of Queen Street Gardens was the property of the Earl of Wemyss who had his town house in Queen Street, opposite to Wemyss Place, which was named after him.

The houses became occupied between 1825 and 1836.

The character of Wemyss Place was different from that of any of the other streets in the Moray Estate, since it was the only one allowed by the Earl of Moray to include shops. The first residents made good use of this concession.

Number 1

First came John Hill who was a tailor and clothier at no. 1 from 1825 to 1831. Number 1 became a bakery for the rest of the century, with only three proprietors. George Aitchison was the first baker, from 1833 until 1866. He remained unmarried but had six employees living with him in 1841. At the next two censuses he lived alone but by 1851 he employed twenty men. The next baker, from 1866 to 1887, was John Neill, who occupied both *nos. 1 and 2*, and employed eight men and four boys in 1871. He was followed by R. McDowell who lived at 60 George Street and had shops there and at 19 Frederick

Street as well as at 1 Wemyss Place.

Number 2

Mrs Johanna Grant had a silk and worsted furnishing shop, as well as her home, at no. 2 from 1829 to 1846.

Number 3

Joseph Stewart, a spirit dealer and grocer, lived and had his shop at no. 3 from 1827 to 1835. He was followed by William Swan (in a similar business) until 1841 and then by Adam Scott, a fruiterer, until 1848. Scott and his wife were able to employ two resident female domestic servants.

John Kennedy had his business at no. 3 from 1848 for ten years, advertised as a 'cheap ironmongery, gas-fitting and bath establishment'. He sold American rocking-chairs ('no invalid should be without one'), portable shower baths ('very convenient for the country and sea-bathing quarters at £1.12s') and Victorian shower baths from £3.3s upwards. He also supplied plunge, Roman, spunging, vapour, children's and foot baths.

Lodging with Mr and Mrs Kennedy and their two children in 1851 were a journeyman tinsmith and a 14 year old gunmaker apprentice.

After Mr Kennedy left in 1858, no. 3 was occupied by G. K. Kent and Weston, painters, until 1871. Then Miss Jane Dunn, milliner and dressmaker, and her school teacher sister Rebecca were in the house for ten years. They were followed by Charles Dussell, tailor and clothier, who had his business there.

Number 4

The ladies in the area were able to have their tailoring done by the Misses Jane and Mary Johnston, milliners and dressmakers at no. 4 from 1835 to 1849. In 1841, they had living with them two assistants and four apprentices as well as two domestic servants (Census).

William Fettes Douglas (1822–1891) was a largely self-taught artist who rose to become President of the RSA from 1882 until his death. He and his wife spent three years in this house from 1854 and returned to it in 1871 for a further two years, after three years at *1 Great Stuart Street*. After leaving the Royal High School, he worked for about ten years in the Commercial Bank but spent his leisure hours in drawing and painting. He exhibited at the RSA for the first time in 1845, eventually contributing nearly 200 pictures to exhibitions there, mostly of portraits, historical subjects or still-life. In the late 1840s, he was so fascinated by the subject of anatomy (and, especially, of dissecting) that he nearly gave up his artistic career for a medical one.

After his first visit to Italy in 1857, William Fettes Douglas began to collect 'dainty and precious things' but especially Renaissance medals. He was also interested in archaeology, book-binding, coins and ivories. He was curator of the National Gallery of Scotland 1877–1882, but fell seriously ill in 1879. Thereafter, he painted mostly water colours, on small canvases. As President of the RSA, he was knighted. He was the great-great-nephew of Sir William Fettes whose legacy of £166,000 was used to found Fettes College in 1870.

The Edinburgh Institution for Music occupied no. 4 from 1873 for three years. The Honorary Visitor was Sir Herbert Oakley (1830–1903), Reid Professor of Music and director of music at St Paul's Episcopal Church. In 1866 he founded the Edinburgh University Musical Society, whose annual concerts were popular and included piano solos by himself, as well as glees and madrigals, overtures and symphonies. He also gave many organ recitals. From an early age he had shown evidence of a good ear: at the age of four, after being shown the notes on a piano and told their names, he could, without seeing the keys again, name any note or combination of notes which was played.

Number 5

James Arnott WS and his wife made their home at no. 5 from 1835, where they were the first occupiers. They brought up four daughters and one son there with, usually, four resident servants. By 1871, Mrs Arnott was a widow and remained in the house for a further five years.

Number 6

From 1838, no. 6 was Henry Maitland's home as well as his wine shop. The house was next used as an infant school for two years from 1840 by Miss Margaret Syme and Miss Mary Allan.

Rowand Anderson, architect (1834–1921), lived at no. 6 from 1878 to 1882. He designed the McEwan Hall and the Scottish National Portrait Gallery, among other buildings, and was knighted in 1902.

Number 7

The Caledonian Museum of Practical Science was at no. 7 (Straiton House) from 1834 for five years. Among models exhibited was one of the Liverpool and Manchester locomotive engines by George Stephenson, a Barker's water mill, a complete kitchen range, a portable warm-air stove heated by gas, specimens of stained glass, a stomach pump, a portable printing press and patent copying press and many other inventions. A special attraction was a 'mermaid'! There was also a canal 60 feet by 4 feet for experiments with vessels: on this canal was a steam-ship with engine, boiler and fire.

On the same premises was the Caledonian Bazaar, in a room 85 feet by 42, with nearly 400 feet of counters. Fancy, ornamental and useful articles as well as paintings were for sale. A 'powerful organ' was played in the bazaar and a 'valuable musical clock' was shown. There was also the Johnston Gallery, a public exhibition of over 600 paintings, mostly Old Masters.

As a result of the Disruption of the Church of Scotland in 1843, Straiton House, at no. 7, was rented as a temporary place of worship in early 1845 for the adherents of the Free Church among the congregation of St Stephen's Church. Above the arch leading to the mews beyond were two storeys, entrance to which was from the back of the arch. The second storey, or upper chamber, immediately under the roof, was rented as the temporary church. There was also a small inner gallery at the sides.

The first minister was the Rev. Dr James Buchanan (1804–1870) who left a few months later to become Professor of Apologetics at New College (Free Church of Scotland) and who succeeded Dr Thomas Chalmers there in 1847 as Professor of Systematic Theology. He was succeeded at St Stephen's Free Church by the Rev. Francis Gillies. The congregation purchased the property at Straiton House in 1846. However, in that year, during public worship, ominous sounds were heard, indicating that the church fabric was in much need of repair. The two upper storeys were then made into one. The whole interior of the church was renovated in 1893.

The building remained in use as a church until 1901, when a new

Straiton House, 1834

church was built in Comely Bank. Straiton House was later used as an army drill hall, before becoming office accommodation.

Number 8

An artist, John R. Ballantyne RSA (1815–1897), lived briefly at no. 8 from 1847 for two years. He was best known for a series of portraits of artists in their studios.

When the Misses Johnston left *no. 4* in 1849, another milliner and dressmaker – Miss Jane Mackie – came to live and work at no. 8 until 1864. She had two dressmakers and two milliners living with her as boarders as well as four servants.

Number 9

This was a lodging-house from 1844 until 1895, with a series of lodging-house keepers. One lodger in 1861 was Thomas Shephard, a landed proprietor, possibly in Edinburgh for a short visit. He had with him his wife and six daughters and one son, with an age range of 33 down to 11, as well as their three female servants.

Number 10

Dr James Keith MD, FRCS lived at no. 10 from 1835 to 1870, with two daughters and one son and three servants. They were followed by Donald McKay, the City Officer, who lived here for the next five years.

Number 11

for Marshall, 1856 to 1861, see *5 Randolph Crescent*

Dr John Smith MD, LLD, FRCS (1825–1910) made his home at no. 11 from 1861 until his death. As well as being consulting dental surgeon to the Royal Infirmary, he was surgeon-dentist to Queen Victoria and Vice-President of the British Dental Association. In 1859 he was a founder of the Edinburgh Hospital for Sick Children and in 1860 he opened the Edinburgh Dental Dispensary in Drummond Street and established the teaching of dental surgery as a special branch of surgery. John Smith was President of the Royal College of Surgeons of Edinburgh in 1884, at the time of the University's tercentenary, and he wrote a brief history of the College in 1905, to mark its quatercentenary.

Smith enjoyed painting, music and occasionally wrote songs and verses; his son-in-law said he had music in his soul. For Walter Scott's centenary, he wrote a dramatised version of *Waverley* which was produced by Robert Wyndham, the theatrical manager.

William Guy FRCS, FRSE, LLD (Penn) (1859–1950) whose mother was a first cousin of Mrs John Smith (above), came to Edinburgh as a dental student in 1890, having been a general practitioner in Cumberland. He had a bedroom at *no. 10* but had his meals with the Smiths at no. 11. Five years later, he married Helen, one of the six children of John and Elizabeth Smith. They had no children and, after living at Brunstane Cottage for some years, they moved to 11 Wemyss Place in 1912, after the deaths of her parents, and lived there until his death.

William Guy was greatly concerned with dental education, dental legislation and the techniques of anaesthetics. When he joined his father-in-law's practice at 11 Wemyss Place, gas was administered for the extraction of teeth until the patient was black in the face. For many years Guy fought for the prohibition of the practice of dentistry by unqualified people and the establishment of a Dental Board to regulate the profession. He gained an international reputation for his reforms.

Like his father-in-law, he became President of the British Dental Association. They both also wrote comic verse.

Throughout the First World War, Guy was in charge of a special centre for wounds of the face and jaws at the 2nd Scottish General Hospital at Craigleith in Edinburgh. After retiring, he wrote *The Story of the Edinburgh Dental Hospital and School* and also his autobiography, *Mostly Memories, Some Digressions*.

Wemyss Place Lane

Behind Wemyss Place, and entered via the archway under *no. 7*, are mews houses and former stables, originally called 'pavement yard'. These housed coaches, carriages, horses and coachmen and grooms. The first census to list residents in the lane was that of 1871. No family in the Mews houses was listed at more than one census. Some of them were crowded together: in 1871, there were three families, including a van driver called Craven and his wife with two daughters and four sons, of whom two were gardeners and one was a flesher. Another, John Cameron, coachman, and his wife had two children. His 70 year old mother-in-law, a former housemaid, also lived with them.

In 1881, there were three households, each headed by a coachman – one was Humphrey Autridge. He and his wife Sarah had a son aged 20 who was a writer in the civil service mercantile marine department, as well as an 18 year old groom as a lodger. By 1891 there were five households, four headed by coachmen and one by a vanman. James Inglis, coachman, had three sons and two daughters aged from 4 to 14, while Peter Rud, who was an unemployed coachman, had three children aged 2 to 8.

In the late 1880s, Edwin Knowles, riding master, had property in the mews at Wemyss Place Court, probably for his horses as he lived at 32 Castle Terrace.

Church Lane

On the north-eastern outer edge of the Moray Estate is Church Lane (called Gloucester Lane since 1966). This is a continuation of Wemyss Place and contained coach-houses as well as people with a variety of occupations. Alexander Bulloch, stabler, lived here from 1829. By 1833, there were six householders: a meal dealer, a shoe maker, a cabinet maker and three spirit dealers, as well as livery stables. Nine householders were listed in the 1841 census, including mason, book-binder, letter-carrier, brass founder, livery stabler and coach hirer. Most had wives and children but none had resident servants. Ten years later, there were eleven householders, including master carpenter, shoemaker, cabinet maker, four gentlemen's coachmen and a mangle-keeper (offering a useful service to those who did not have their own mangle for use on wash days). In addition, Church Lane Court housed another two gentlemen's coachmen and one coach proprietor.

Sixteen householders were listed in 1861, six of them being coachmen as well as a grocer, a mason and a spirit merchant, with a further four coachmen in Church Lane Court. By 1871, there were nineteen householders, with a greengrocer, vulcanite mill worker, mason, plumber and laundress as well as seven coachmen, two grooms, a cabman and a livery stable keeper. The centre court had been renamed Church Lane Square.

The 1881 census listed 18 householders in the Lane and six more in the Square, most of them coachmen or grooms.

Wemyss Place Householders

1.
1825 John Hill, tailor and clothier
1833 George Aitchison, baker
1866 John Neill, baker
1887 R. McDowell & Sons, bakers

2.
1829–46 Mrs Grant, silk & worsted shop
1899 James Kitchin

3.
1827 Joseph Stewart, spirit dealer
1835 William Swan, grocer
1841 Adam Scott, fruiterer

1848 J. Kennedy, ironmonger
1862 G. K. Kent & Weston, painters
1871 Miss J. H. A. Dunn, milliner
1882 Charles O. Dussell, tailor and clothier

4.
1835 Mrs Johnston, milliner & dressmaker
1849 Pelican Life Insurance; Manchester Fire
   Assurance
1854 William Fettes Douglas RSA
1857 Mrs Malcolm, lodgings
1864 William Sharp, lodgings
1871 William Fettes Douglas RSA
1873 Edin. Institution for Music; P. F. L.

Stalker, teacher; W. Adlington, ARA, prof. of music
1878 Miss Smitton
1885 Dr D. Berry Hart, med. practitioner
1888 J. Eaton Dykes, advocate & William Shedden Dykes WS
1896 William Babington

5.
1835 James Arnott WS
1877 Alexander Crombie, jun. WS
1879 Henry Cook WS
1885 F. F. Roget, teacher of mod. languages
1894 Gen. E. Ghuznee Morrogh, Madras Army
1895 John Ferguson

6.
1834 Dr Spittal
1837 Henry Maitland, wine merchant
1840 Misses Syme & Allan, infant school
1842 Capt. Thompson
1844 Mrs Alex. Stewart
1847 Peter Stewart, coach-hirer
1851 Dr Duncan & James Matthews
1853 Wm. H. Thomson, advocate
1856 Robert Maclachian
1867 Major J. P. Carruthers Wade
1873 Miss Rose Watson
1878 Rowand Anderson RSA
1882 David J. Hamilton MB, FRCS
1893 D. S. Meikleham, grain merchant
1896 Alexander Nish; also J. D. Boswell

7.
1834 Caledonian Bazaar; Museum; Johnston gallery
1845 St Stephen's Free Church

8.
1834 George Smith, architect

1847 John Ballantyne ARSA
1849 Miss Mackie, dressmaker
1864 J. D. Morrison, dentist
1868 Miss Gunn
1871 John Neill, baker
1888 Miss McKie
1891 Miss M. C. Lees

9.
1834 David Davidson
1838 William Marshall WS; James Marshall esq.
1840 George Farquharson WS
1844 George Craigie, lodgings
1858 James Robertson, lodgings
1870 Thomas M. Mure, advocate
1883 James A. Gardiner, advocate
1885 Mrs Keith
1890 Mrs Bydewell; Mrs Addison; Arthur Dewar
1895 John Craigie, advocate

10.
1835 James Keith FRCS
1870 Donald McKay, City Officer
1873 Thomas M. Mure, advocate
1879–92 Mrs Stewart; & J. M. Thomson, advocate; & J. C. White, advocate; & Wm. Walker Johnstone DCS
1890 John Maitland Thomson, advocate & Miss Low
1892 James Ferguson, advocate

11.
1836 Dr Peebles FRCP
1841 Mrs James Dunlop
1856 Lord Curriehill; & John Marshall, advocate
1861 John Smith, surgeon & dentist
1895 William Guy, surgeon & dentist

Darnaway Street

One of the seats of the Earl of Moray was – and still is – Darnaway Castle, near Forres. The name of the castle was chosen for the short street entering Moray Place from the east, a continuation of Heriot Row.

There are six houses on each side, those on the north having odd numbers and those on the south even numbers. The houses at both ends (1, 2, 11 and 12) were each built as three flats, while the rest were whole houses.

Number 1

Alexander and George Fowler, builders of some of the houses in Darnaway Street, lived at no. 1 from 1826. George moved out three years later, but Alexander remained there until 1848 with his wife, three sons and a daughter.

for Fletcher, 1828 to 1830, see *1 Randolph Crescent*.

Thomas Duncan (1807–1845) lived at 1 Darnaway Street from 1831 to 1837. As a schoolboy, he drew likenesses of his friends and also painted the scenery for a performance of Walter Scott's *Rob Roy*, to be presented in a stable loft. His father considered these activities to be a waste of time, and apprenticed him to a WS. As soon as Thomas had served his time, he entered the Trustees' Academy and embarked upon his career as a portrait painter, being elected RSA in 1830.

Duncan painted a great many scenes from Scottish history (especially the 1745 Rebellion) and from Scottish literature. He became professor of colour and then of drawing at the Trustees' Academy and was headmaster for the last year of his life. A tumour which led to near-blindness was treated, but it spread to his brain, resulting in his early death.

Robert Familton, resident at no. 1 from 1847 for four years, was a teacher of mathematics and also writing master at Edinburgh Academy from its foundation in 1824 until his death in 1852. The boys called him Hamilton (shortening it to Hammy), and he soon used that name himself. He was Clerk to the Directors of the Academy from 1825 to 1850. In his writing-classes, he allowed boys to chat to each other as they 'executed copperplate scripts decorated with highly ornamental capitals, for which they mixed their own colours from poppy petals and other plants gathered on the way to school' (Magnusson: *The Clacken and the Slate*).

Early on, this street provided lodgings for families or individuals. In 1851, no. 1 showed seven heads of household ranging from a surveyor of buildings (William Laurence), a master tailor (Samuel Gilles) and a mason journeyman (Charles Paton) to a coachsmith journeyman (James Petrie). In all, 28 people were listed at no. 1 in 1851.

A variety of shopkeepers and tradesmen lived in Darnaway Street, all in the flatted houses. In 1851, John Dick, a dealer in spirits at *4 Church Lane*, was at no. 1.

From 1860 to 1864, John Jamieson (at no. 1) was a fishmonger at 60 Queen Street, where he employed nine men and two boys: he and his family had two female servants.

Number 3

A solicitor's office was at no. 3 from 1826 for two years. The partners, Henry J. Burn WS and Patrick Orr WS, both lived on the premises: Burn and his mother moved next door to *no. 5* in 1830. Patrick Orr then lived successively at *3 Moray Place* for five years, *15 Moray Place* for five years and *4 Randolph Crescent* from 1840 to his death in 1848. By then he was Sheriff Clerk of Forfarshire.

Mrs Eliza Makgill of Kemback, in Cupar, Fife, spent two years at no. 3 from 1832. Her husband, John Makgill, de jure 8th baronet, had died in 1817. Possibly she was in Edinburgh to enable her only son George to prepare the family home for the arrival of his English bride Harriet Utterson in 1833. Their son Arthur, an advocate, lived at *no. 7* for three years from 1876.

Number 5

From 1843 to 1854, Mrs Elizabeth Borthwick, a widow, was a boarding house keeper here. In 1851, as well as three lodgers, she had two visitors: Thomas and Mary Stewart, being a 'gentleman, retired merchant' and 'lady'. Possibly they brought with them some of the eight resident servants, who included three ladies' maids and two footmen.

Number 7

for Ramsay, 1825 intermittently to 1844, see *23 Ainslie Place*

The Dowager Lady Ramsay, who had fourteen children and who died in 1844, spent the last four years of her life here, with her granddaughters Elizabeth and Jane Ramsay. She had six resident servants, including one man.

Number 9

A private hotel was opened here in 1830 by David Sutherland, who moved to Abercromby Place two years later.

William Wood FRCS (1782–1855), whose father Alexander had also been a FRCS, spent twenty years at no. 9 from 1835 until his death. As President of the Royal College of Surgeons of Edinburgh, he had, in 1830, laid the foundation stone of Playfair's impressive new building for the College.

William's son Andrew (1810–1881) came with him from George Street in 1835, following in his father's footsteps as a surgeon in general practice and as President of the College in 1855–56. He, too, lived at no. 9 until his death, after which his widow and children remained there. He was medical officer at the New Town dispensary and surgeon to three schools – Heriot's Hospital, the Merchant Maiden Hospital and the Trades Maiden Hospital. As a manager of the Edinburgh Royal Infirmary, he was active in superintending the progress of the new Infirmary, opened in 1879. In 1840 he married Grace Collyer and they had six sons and three daughters, all of whom were listed in the 1861 census return for no. 9, together with five female domestic servants.

As recreation, Andrew Wood wrote many songs for social gatherings. When he suffered from what was thought to be gout in the soles of his feet, he went to Aix-la-Chapelle (Aachen) to take the waters. Ordered to relax, he spent several hours a day reading with a German governess to improve his knowledge of her language.

In the mid-1870s, soon after the loss of three of his adult children (including one from pulmonary consumption and one – Adelaide, aged 15 – from 'atrophy'), he learned that he had a fatal condition himself. Anxious to spare his wife further distress, he kept the information from her and from the rest of his family, finally dying of a ruptured heart.

Royal Infirmary of Edinburgh, 1878

At least one of his surviving sons, Russell, was a registered medical practitioner who, with his sister Jane, lived with their widowed mother.

Number 11

for Stark, 1830 to 1833, see *no. 6*
for Steell, 1838 to 1841, see *1 Randolph Place*

William Tait, at no. 11 in 1866, was a chemist and druggist and a partner in the firm of Duncan, Flockhart and Co. At the same time another partner, Wardlaw MacFarlane, lived at *no. 1*. At Tait's death in 1876 he had worked for more than thirty years at the branch at 139 Princes Street. The firm was one of the first producers of chloroform and supplied it for Sir James Young Simpson's historic experiment in 1847 at his home at 52 Queen Street. Between January 1847 and October 1848, Simpson delivered 150 obstetric cases under ether or chloroform. In 1853 Queen Victoria had chloroform for the birth of her eighth child, Prince Leopold: she called it 'this blessed chloroform'.

A. The Urn with its stopper, into which the ether is poured.
B. Valve which admits the air.
C. Contains sponge saturated with ether.
D. Valve which opens at each inspiration, and closes at each expiration.
E. Ferule for regulating the quantity of atmospheric air admitted.
F. Valve for the escape of expired air.
G. Mouth-piece.
H. Lower vase.
I. Spring for closing the nose.

**Squire's ether inhaler, used by J. Y. Simpson in 1847
in the Royal Infirmary, Edinburgh**

James Ferrier lived at no. 11 for four years from 1882. He was an Edinburgh landscape artist, specialising in water-colours which were full of detail and incident. Two brothers and two sisters of his were at the same address. William was the Secretary of a public company, Gilbert and Rosina were teachers of music, while Euphemia was in charge of the household.

Lucy Bethia Walford (née Colquhoun), in her *Recollections of a Scottish Novelist*, wrote of lessons in the early 1860s: 'Our dear little drawing-master, Mr James Ferrier, whose landscapes were the delight of lovers of Scottish scenery, ...having a large family to provide for, he supplemented his income by teaching, and his lessons were eagerly sought for. He never spoke; he sat at an impromptu easel and we clustered round and watched. When he had finished for the day, he produced his watch, murmured, "Good morning, ladies" and was off.' Each pupil was expected to produce a copy of his painting and he presented his original to the painter of the best copy. Later in life, he had a stroke and for some years was unable to paint, until he learned to paint with his left hand.

James K. Munro, at no. 11 from 1867, was a draper and hosier with his business at 9 Baker's Place, but by 1881 he had become a house agent in West Nicolson Street (Census).

Charles Dowling, after five years at *1 Forres Street*, was at no. 11 from 1880 until his death in 1896. He was a commercial traveller while his wife was superintendent of female staff at the General Post Office.

(returning along the other side of the street)

Number 12

D. F. Surenne, a portrait painter and a teacher of drawing, came from George Street in 1832 to live at no. 12 for nine years. His brother John was a composer and organist at St Mark's Church, Portobello, and afterwards at St George's Episcopal Church, York Place. He was 'a man of refined taste and scholarly attainments, a sound musician and most courteous gentleman' (Baptie).

Mary (Mrs James) Lacon had a 'ladies' school' at no. 12 from 1840 for two years. At the 1841 census she had another resident teacher and nine girls aged from 14 to 19.

for Steell, 1847, see *1 Randolph Place*

The 1851 census showed David Taylor living here. He was a master upholsterer, employing 110 men in his business at 109 Princes Street, including decorators, cabinet and picture-framers, carvers, gilders, auctioneers and appraisers.

Robert Jameson, who was here from 1869 to 1885, was a fruiterer, greengrocer and confectioner, with his shop at 79 Queen Street. He and his wife had ten children and two servants, making quite a crowd for one flat.

Number 10

The first occupier was Dr George Borthwick, from 1832 to 1844. He was a consulting physician and had lived at *5 Forres Street* for the three previous years. His four children had company in the house in the form of three students who were boarders.

An advocate, George Readman, lived here from 1889 to 1897. with his wife and at least four children, looked after by a nurse and an under nurse. For his father, see *9 Moray Place*.

Number 8

From 1847 to 1852, this was a boarding house for girls from the Edinburgh Institution. The Edinburgh Institution was then in Hill Street but later moved to Queen Street, and eventually it became Melville College. The widowed Lady Superintendent, Charlotte Bentley, had two children of her own as well as her mother living with her. In 1851, it was an entirely female household – apart from 11-year-old William Bentley – with a resident governess and six girl pupils aged 12 to 16, two further boarders in their early twenties and three domestic servants.

Number 6

Mrs William Stark (coming from 3 North Charlotte Street) was one of three occupiers sharing no. 6 in 1828, moving to *no. 11* two years later. She was the widow of the architect William Stark of Drumsheugh, who had made his reputation in Glasgow. In January 1813 he had been one of eight leading architects invited to comment upon plans entered for a competition for designs for an extension of the New Town to the east of Princes Street and Leith Walk. He did not accept the invitation, probably because he was ill, but wrote his 'observations'. He stressed that the contours of the ground on the slopes of Calton Hill were more important than any symmetry of layout, and that trees should be integrated into the architectural plan.

William Stark died in October 1813 before his ideas could be acted upon, but his observations were later published and used. Walter Scott commented that 'more genius has died than is left behind among the collected universality of Scottish architects'. In February 1818, William Stark's former pupil William Playfair was appointed architect for 'the proposed New Town between Edinburgh and Leith' (see Mitchell: *The People of Calton Hill*).

George Bell (1770–1843), brother of Sir Charles Bell of *6 Ainslie Place*, came to no. 6 in 1837 for four years. He was Professor of Scots Law from 1822 and, ten years later, was appointed Principal Clerk of

Session by Francis Jeffrey, then Lord Advocate. According to Cockburn, Jeffrey would have made Bell a judge if there had been a vacancy. His classic great work was his *Commentaries on the Laws of Scotland and on the Principles of Medical Jurisprudence considered in Relation to Bankruptcy.*

In spite of having several children of his own, Bell helped to support the widow and children of his brother Robert who died in about 1816, having been Professor of Conveyancing to the Society of Writers to the Signet. There was no such post in the university until 1825.

for Hill, 1854 to 1856, see *32 Moray Place* (Anderson)

Number 4

for Ramsay, 1826 to 1830, see *23 Ainslie Place*
for Tollemache, 1841, see *7 Forres Street* (Sinclair)

Robert Campbell of Skerrington in Ayrshire (1814–1868) and his family occupied no. 4 from 1848 to 1892, with two brief gaps when the house was rented to others. He could trace his family back to 1266. An advocate, he married Anne Carr from Durham in 1843: they had one son and six daughters and always had five or six resident servants, making for a full household. The only son, William, was also an advocate who, in 1880, married Alice Mary, daughter of Lord Fraser of *8 Moray Place*. From 1896 they lived at *12 Randolph Crescent.*

After Robert Campbell's death, his widow let their house at no. 4 for a brief period in 1871 to Sir William Forbes, 8th baronet of Craigievar. He brought with him his second wife Frances, daughter of Sir Robert Abercromby, baronet, and four of their children (they later had three more).

Sir William Forbes divorced his first wife, Caroline, daughter of Sir Charles Forbes, baronet of Newe, in 1851 after only three years of marriage. He charged her with adultery. 'From the month of August 1850 the defender, casting off the fear of God, and disregarding her matrimonial vows, has alienated her affections from the pursuer, and has had carnal conversation and intercourse with a man or men other than the pursuer, at different times and in different places.' She was said to have committed adultery in Scotland with Captain Thomas Bayly Gibbard, a guest in her husband's home at Fintry, in October 1850, and with Captain Bayly, 'probably the same man', on a number of occasions in Brighton in January 1851. This must have scandalised Scottish society, at a time when divorces were rare.

Number 2

The first resident in Darnaway Street was Miss Fitzmaurice at no. 2 from 1824 to 1833.

Mrs Catherine Crowe (1800–c.1870), at no. 2 from 1840 to 1851, was a popular author. In 1841 she published anonymously her first novel, *Susan Hopley*, which was immediately successful, and other books followed. She became interested in the supernatural and paranormal, showing an ability to investigate painstakingly all evidence of precognitions of the future, telepathy and poltergeists. Her best-known book, *The Night-side of Nature or Ghosts and Ghost Seers*, a collection of supernatural stories, was published in 1848. She hoped to stimulate inquiry. The book remained in print for over a hundred years.

Catherine Crowe held select literary gatherings in her house and Thomas De Quincey was a frequent guest. His daughter told the story of De Quincey and a friend accompanying Mrs Crowe to a lecture by Ralph Waldo Emerson, the American poet and essayist. Both men needed much nudging by Mrs Crowe to prevent them from being overtaken by drowsiness caused by Emerson's American nasal sing-song. Mrs Crowe was the only lady outside his family whom De Quincey addressed by her first name.

In 1860 Catherine Crowe suffered a brief but violent attack of 'insanity', after which she published no more books. Charles Boog-Watson, the Edinburgh historian, later wrote; 'It is related of Mrs Crowe that one day she was found walking along Queen Street, stark naked, with an apple in one hand and a handkerchief in the other. She was hurriedly taken into shelter where she explained that our Lord had bidden her to go out thus unclad and carrying the two articles mentioned, assuring her that she would be invisible. Unfortunately, instead of carrying the apple and the handkerchief in the proper hands as directed she had reversed them – and therefore the promise of invisibility failed! She was quite mad!'

It is not known what happened to her husband, Lt. Col. Crowe, whom she married in Kent in 1822, but he did not live with her in Darnaway Street, although she described herself in the census as married. Her married son John, living on private means, was the head of her household at the 1851 census. They then moved to *16 Randolph Crescent* until 1854, when they probably left Edinburgh.

John Ritchie Findlay (1824–1898) lived at no. 2 for two years before his marriage to Susan Leslie in 1863. With their ten children they subsequently lived at *3 Rothesay Terrace*.

Findlay spent all his working life at *The Scotsman*, starting as a clerk addressing labels and rising to become editor and proprietor. Under his direction, *The Scotsman* developed from being a local newspaper to one with a national circulation, incidentally making a fortune for Findlay. He became a public benefactor, committed to social reform. He was President of the Association for the Medical Education of Women: *The Scotsman* vigorously supported Sophia Jex-Blake in her fight for women to be admitted to the University's medical faculty.

As Secretary of the Society of Antiquaries, Findlay developed a plan for a Scottish National Portrait Gallery and, in 1882, he anonymously offered to finance such a project. His identity was not revealed until 1889 at the opening of the building in Queen Street, which was then named the Findlay Building; one of the stained glass windows shows his head. In 1900 a Findlay memorial, designed by Rowand Anderson (see *6 Wemyss Place*), was unveiled, enshrining a posthumous portrait of Findlay by Sir George Reid.

From his home in *Rothesay Terrace*, Findlay overlooked the Dean Village and he planned and financed the reconstruction of part of it, at Well Court, including accommodation for working men.

Two artists lived at no. 2, not necessarily in the same flat. Thomas Brown was there for one year from 1866: he painted mostly rural and coastal scenes and also taught drawing. Peter Cleland, another teacher of drawing, followed him, from 1868 for six years; he painted still life and dead game. He later taught at Aberdeen School of Art.

After training at the Royal Academy of Music in London, Alexander Campbell Mackenzie (1847–1935) came to Edinburgh as choirmaster of St George's Church, Charlotte Square, from 1865 to 1879, living at 2 Darnaway Street for his last five years in that post. He came from a musical tradition, his father having been leader of the orchestra at the Theatre Royal, Edinburgh and his grandfather in the same position at the Theatre Royal, Aberdeen. He was latterly also conductor of the Scottish Vocal Music Association, and composed orchestral and chamber music.

He left Scotland for reasons of ill-health caused by overwork, and settled in Italy where his compositions included an oratorio *The Rose of Sharon*, a violin concerto and many other works.

In 1887 Mackenzie was appointed Principal of the Royal Academy of Music in London, where he initiated many administrative reforms. With the composer Sir Hubert Parry he formed an examining body later known as the Associated Board of the Royal Schools of Music. Mackenzie was knighted in 1895 and received honorary degrees from seven universities as well as many other distinctions.

Darnaway Street Householders

1.
1826–30 Mrs Fleming
1826–48 Alexander Fowler, builder
1828–30 J. Gray Farquhar WS
1828–30 Angus Fletcher, advocate
1829–30 John F. Stodart, advocate
1831–37 Thomas Duncan, portrait painter
1831–34 John Taylor Gordon WS
1834–39 James McArthur, dancing teacher
1837–38 G. W. Strathy, music teacher
1840–41 Miss Buckham
1843–47 John B. Bell, writing master
1847–51 Robert Hamilton, teacher
1848–59 Charles H. Schneider, teacher of French
1850–55 William Lawrance
1851–53 Miss Rainforth, teacher of singing
1851–64 Wardlaw H. McFarlane
1853–60 Miss Blackwood
1860–64 John Jameson
1862–67 Miss Jane Cleghorn
1864–66 Alexander Strahan
1866–87 Mrs Veitch
1866–67 William Tait
1868–77 John Tait
1869–70 Heinrich Weisse
1872–73 James Peddie
1876–77 James Gardner
1876–79 W. Gardner Hill
1877– Mrs James McArthur
1878–83 Charles S. Dickson, advocate
1882–88 H. G. Stewart
1884–85 John F. McLennan, advocate
1887–90 John Smith
1887–88 Herbert Strachan
1889–91 C. E. W. Macpherson CA

1893–96 Alex F. Hunter CA
1894–96 Misses Gordon
1896– Jane C. Ogilvie
1899– Signor Vittorio Ricci

3.
1826–30 Mrs Burn
1826–28 Orr & Burn WS
1827–30 Henry J. Burn WS
1827–28 Patrick Burn WS
1832–34 Mrs Makgill of Kemback
1836–38 Miss Young, boarding school
1841–48 Alex S. Cook, advocate
1848–51 John Graham, advocate
1853–59 George E. Balfour, advocate
1861–68 M. & Mme Brouneau, dancing teachers
1868–73 Mrs Duncan
1873–75 James Peddie
1875–77 Robert C. Cumming
1879–94 Arch. C. Gloag
1894–97 William J. Cullen, advocate
1897– W. K. Dickson, advocate

5.
1826 Thomas Hamilton esq.
1830 Henry J. Burn WS
1834 Mrs Dunn, lodgings
1843 Mrs Borthwick, lodgings
1854 George Monro, advocate
1876 George M. Thomson WS
1883 G. R. Gillespie, advocate
1892 G. Munro Thomson WS

7.
1825–44 *passim* Dowager Lady Ramsay of

Balmain
1838–40 James H. Burnett WS
1844 Dandeson C. Bell
1858 Archd. Campbell Swinton
1861 James Seton Wightman of Courance,
advocate

9.
1830 David Sutherland, private hotel
1835 Dr Andrew Wood FRCS

11.
1830–32 Miss Maxwell
1830–33 J. M. & Robert Mueller, music
teachers
1830–33 Mrs William Stark
1833–39 James Newton WS
1834–36 William Rae, accountant
1835–41 Henry C. Graham WS
1837–40 John Steell, sculptor
1842–50 John Penman esq.
1842–43 Mrs Nembhard
1844–51 J. C. Kieser, music teacher
1851–59 James Lamond SSC
1851–56 A. D. Hughson
1851–62 Thomas Macfarlane, Writer
1857–60 Mrs Matilda Hamilton
1859–64 William Tait
1861–65 Arch. C. Lawrie, advocate
1865–67 Mrs Murray, lodgings
1866–73 Miss Rollo
1867–73 J. K. Munro
1868–80 Charles Wilson
1873–78 John Sherar
1874–78 David Crichton, advocate
1878–80 Daniel Macbeth, advocate
1880– Charles Dowling
1880–87 William S. Harris
1882–93 Gilbert J. Ferrier, music teacher
1882–86 James Ferrier, artist
1882– William Ferrier
1888–90 Mrs Macleod
1890– John Moir DCS

12.
1831–32 Mrs William Russell
1832–33 William Swan, Writer
1832–36 A. Roxburgh, lodgings
1832–35 Alex. Graham, advocate
1832–41 D. F. Surenne, portrait painter
1835–41 Mrs Craigie
1835–37 Robert Horn, advocate
1840–42 Mrs James Lacon
1843–50 William H. Forrest, accountant

1844–45 Mrs Nembhard
1844–47 T. S. Fairley SSC
1844–47 Mrs Wilkie
1847–48 John Steell RSA
1847–49 Mrs Ross
1849–66 Miss Pearson
1850–56 David Taylor
1852–62 Matthew Tunnock, Writer
1859–60 Mrs Valance
1860–63 J. S. Oliver
1860–69 John McLaren, advocate
1863–68 John McEwan, Writer
1866–72 Mrs Cockburn
1869–72 George Andrew SSC
1869–85 Robert Jameson, greengrocer
1872–75 Walter Hately
1875–78 Lt. Col. James D. N. St George
1875–83 David Lang, advocate
1879– D. Howard Smith
1886– Miss Reid
1887–97 E. B. Thomson
1897– W. A. Ramsay, advocate
1899– Colin M. Black

10.
1832 George Borthwick, consulting physician
1844 Mrs W. McKenzie, lodgings
1845 John Gray WS
1854 John Sprot
1856 Misses Mure
1889 George Readman, advocate
1897 William J. Cullen, advocate

8.
1832 James Buchanan esq.
1847 Mrs William Bentley
1852 D. J. McBrair SSC
1857 Aeneas McBean WS

6.
1827 Robert Mueller, music teacher
1828 Miss Maxwell; & Mrs William Stark
1832 James Balfour, manager, wine co.
1837 Prof. George Joseph Bell
1841 Capt. Cameron
1844 Archd. Boyd, merchant
1848 John S. Wood
1854 J. M. Hill
1857 Mrs J. Y. Black
1885 Finlay Dun, land agent
1891 Susanne Jane Hooper, boarding
establishment

4.
1826–30 Dowager Lady Ramsay of Balmain;
 Rev. E. B. Ramsay
1833 David Scott WS
1837 Mrs Peacock
1843 Mrs Eckford
1848 R. Campbell, advocate
1853 James Hunter of Hafton
1856 Henry Johnston
1857 Robert Campbell of Skerrington,
 advocate
1892 J. McKie Lees, advocate

2.
1824–33 Miss Fitzmaurice
1834–39 Mons. W. F. Chaumont, teacher of
 French
1834–36 Mrs Stewart
1836–37 Graham Binny WS
1838–39 Mrs Boyce
1840–50 John Cairns, Writer
1840–51 Mrs Crowe, author
1850–51 James Richardson
1850–53 J. L. Smith
1851–55 Misses Welsh
1852–54 Misses Dunlop
1853–56 Mrs Christie

1855–60 Donald Duff
1856–60 Alex. Ramsay
1861–64 J. R. Finlay
1862–64 William Mitchell SSC
1864–66 S. H. Salom & Co., opticians
1866–67 Thomas Brown, artist
1868–74 P. Cleland, drawing teacher
1868–70 T. Chalmers Hanna CA
1870–74 George Cockburn, tea, wine & spirit
 mercht.
1873–80 Kenmure Maitland; & J. Gordon
 Maitland, advocate
1874–79 A. C. Mackenzie, music teacher
1877–82 George Ellis
1880–92 Miss Helen Jamieson
1880–82 J. W. Hope
1882–87 Heinrich Weisse, German master
1883– Mrs Kynoch
1887–88 Mrs Veitch
1887–89 J. R. N. Macphail, advocate
1890–92 Lt. Col. D. N. Potter
1892– Alexander Dow
1892–98 Mrs Rainy
1893– Andrew White WS
1894– W. B. Rankin WS
1898– Mrs D. Ralph

In Conclusion

If the 10th Earl of Moray were to return today, he would find that there are still judges, professors, architects and other professionals who consider his estate to be a desirable and convenient place in which to live. However there are no longer lodging-house keepers, who often provided rooms for young lawyers, plumbers, tailors, shop keepers and other such service-providers. Mews no longer provide stables and coachmen – instead they contain garages and much sought-after small homes.

The traffic, of course, is heavier and faster, but there were problems even in the early days. In June 1825, the *Edinburgh Courant* reported that 'a new married couple and their friends, proceeding home in a hackney coach, were precipitated into the foundation of a new house, in one of the unfinished houses of the New Town. The carriage was destroyed and the horses were damaged. The happy pair said they were not hurt but very much astonished.'

Throughout the nineteenth century, many householders were tenants and not owners of their homes. Quite a number moved from one home to another within the Moray feu, often after a very few years at any one address. Not surprisingly, there were neighbouring families who inter-married, with the next generation also making their homes in the Moray feu.

Overall, there are now fewer residents: for instance, there are 205 names on the voters' roll for Moray Place compared with 363 adults at the 1841 census and 428 in 1871. Households are smaller and many houses have been divided into flats or offices. Children and resident servants have almost completely disappeared. When every family had resident servants, wages were higher for men than for women. In 1836, a footman was paid £28 a year, a lady's maid £20, a cook £16 and a housemaid from £11 to £15. They had no electrical equipment; coal and water had to be carried up endless flights of stairs. Domestic servants worked long hours, but had companionship from each other.

Today, Lord Moray's feuars include residents as well as proprietors of offices. They all pay an annual assessment, in proportion to the value of their property, for the maintenance of the extensive gardens.

The Moray feu is still a prestigious place in which to live and work. The residents are a close-knit community, conscious of their heritage. This book is intended to discover something about their predecessors. Inevitably, there were too many to include mention of them all, and apologies are offered for the omission of other interesting families and individuals.

Principal Sources

Baptie, D., *Musical Scotland* (1894)

Books of the Old Edinburgh Club

Burke's *Landed Gentry*, various dates

Burke's *Peerage and Baronetage*, various dates

Census returns for 1841, 1851, 1861, 1871, 1881 & 1891

Cockburn, Henry, *Memorials of His Time* (1856; 1910 edition)

Crombie, B. W., *Modern Athenians* (1857)

Dictionary of National Biography

Edinburgh Medical Journal

Gifford, John, McWilliam, Colin and Walker, David, *The Buildings of Scotland: Edinburgh* (1984)

Grant, Alexander, *The Story of the University of Edinburgh* (1884)

Grant, James, *Old and New Edinburgh* (1882)

Harrison, Wilmot, *Memorable Edinburgh Houses* (1898)

Knight, W. A., *Some Nineteenth-Century Scotsmen* (1903)

Magnusson, Magnus, *The Clacken and the Slate* (1974)

Mitchell, Ann, *The People of Calton Hill* (1993)

Omond, G. W. T., *The Lord Advocates of Scotland: Second series, 1834–1880* (1914)

Post Office Street Directories

Youngson, A. J., *The Making of Classical Edinburgh* (1986)

Various published memoirs

Personal communications

Index

Abbott, Francis, 28
Abercromby, James (Baron Dunfermline), 80
Adam, Lord, 37
Addison, Berkeley, 85
Agnew, Lady, 28
Agnew, Miss Mary, 37
Agnew, Sir Stair, 28
Ainslie, David, 47
Ainslie, Sir Philip, 1, 72
Ainslie, Sir Whitelaw, 164
Aitchison, George, 191
Alison, Archibald, 162
Alison, John, 16
Allan, Jessy & John, 64
Allan, Miss Mary, 193
Anderson, David, 12, 28, 167
Anderson, Findlay, John, 35
Anderson, John (fishmonger), 59
Anderson, Mrs Louisa, 167
Anderson, Sir Rowand, 194, 209
Andrews, Anna, D. A., Miss M., 101
Angus, George, 157
Anstruther, Wyndham C., 63
Ardwall, Lord, 159
Armstrong, John, 115
Arnott, James, 193
auction, disaster at, 7
Aytoun, William F., 66, 111

Baillie, Charles (Lord Jerviswoode), 130
Balfour, John (Baron Kinross), 108,113
Balfour, Miss, 140
Balfour, Thomas, 65
Balfour, William, 7, 65
Balfour of Burleigh, Lord, 40
Balfour-Kinnear, George, 8, 60, 66, 112
Balfour-Kinnear, James, 66
Ballantyne, John A., 138
Ballantyne, John R., 195
bank: City of Glasgow, 8; Clydesdale, 15; Commercial, 193; Union, 28;
Western, 7
Banks, Miss Eliza, 45
Barcaple, Lord, 137
Barclay, John Maclaren, 175
Barker, Frederick, 64
Bartholomew, Misses, 44
Baxter, Sir David, 10, 98
Begbie, James Warburton, 112
Bell, Benjamin, Isabella, Robert, 106, 131
Bell, Sir Charles, 75, 174
Bell, Charles, 173
Bell, George, 206
Bell, John Montgomerie, 178
Bennett, John Hughes, 15, 153
Bentley, Mrs Charlotte, 206
Bewicke, Mrs Margaret, 12
bishop of: Argyll, 114; Brechin, 85; Durham, 131; Jamaica, 185; Sydney NSW, 64; Tasmania, 131
Bissett, Alexander, 20
Blackburn, Jemima, 91
Blackburn, Robert, 104
Blackburn, Robert (Lord), 104
Blackwood, John, 74, 122
Blackwood, Miss Mary, 123
Blackwood, William, 73
Blackwood, William jnr., 73
Blackwood's Magazine, 74, 112, 122, 172
Blair, Alexander, Hugh, Patrick, 131
Blair, Patrick, 108
Board of Commissioners in Lunacy, 82, 85
Board of Education for Scotland, 82
Borrie, Miss, 131
Borthwick, Mrs Elizabeth, 201
Borthwick, George, 205
Bowes-Lyon, Lady Constance, 104
Bowie, John, 185
Boyd, Sir Thomas, 42
British Association for the Advancement of Science, 83

Index

De Quincey, Thomas, 58, 74, 123, 171, 208
Dick, John, 201
divorce, 174, 207
domestic servants, 49, 92, 109, 213
Don-Wauchope, Sir John, 81
Douglas, Sir Hugh, 90
Douglas of Cavers, James, 37
Douglas, Sir William Fettes, 144, 192
Doune, Lord, 56
Dowling, Charles, 205
Drummond, Mrs, 37
Drumsheugh House, 1, 120
Duchess of Kent, 89
Dun, Barclay, 102
Duncan, John, 78
Duncan, Thomas, 200
Duncan, Flockhart & Co., 203
Dunedin, Baron, 163
Dunfermline, Lord, 63, 80
Dunlop, John, 140
Dunn, Miss Jane, 192
Dussell, Charles, 192

East India Company, 33, 35, 47, 48, 63, 73, 77, 85, 87, 136, 141, 164, 175
Edinburgh Academy, 59, 113, 177, 200
Edinburgh Choral Society, 147
Edinburgh Collegiate School, 44, 48, 59, 103
Edinburgh Fever Hospital, 179
Edinburgh Hospital for Sick Children, 196
Edinburgh Institution, 17, 18, 48, 206
Edinburgh Ladies' Educational Association, 147
Edinburgh Review, 27, 75
Edinburgh Royal Infirmary *see* Royal Infirmary
Edinburgh School of Medicine for Women, 68
Edinburgh University Musical Society, 193
Edmonstone, Sir William, 79, 81, 163
Educational Institute of Scotland, 15, 130
Eigg, island of, 135
Eldin, Lord, 7

Elgin, Lady Matilda, 105
Elmsley, Mrs Margaret, 138
Erskine, Miss Magdalene, 68
Ewart, Cossar, 100

Fabiani, H. B., 115
Falkner, Miss Margaret, 183
Familton, Robert, 200
Ferguson, Robert, 17
Fergusson, Charles, James, 154
Ferrier, Gilbert, James, Rosina, William, 204
Fettes College, 26, 28, 84, 138
Findlay, John Ritchie, 209
Fishery Board for Scotland, 42
Fitzmaurice, Miss, 208
Fletcher of Dunans, Angus, 121, Helen, 185
Fletcher, Miles Angus, 30, 97, 121
Forbes, Alexander, William, 85
Forbes, James David, 83
Forbes, John Hay (Lord Medwyn), 84
Forbes, Sir William, 207
Forbes, Miss Louisa, 81
Forrest, Mrs Catherine, 33
Fothringham, Thomas & Charlotte, 22
Fothringham, Frederick, James, Thomas 22, 26
Fowler, Alexander, George, 200
Fox Talbot, William, 106
Fraser, Alexander, 20
Fraser, Miss Alice Mary, 207
Fraser, Hugh J. F., 131
Fraser, Patrick (Lord), 12
Fraser, William, Robert, 171
French royal family, 45
Froebel, Karl & Joanna, 23, 25, 126
Fullerton, Lord, 36
Fulton, Sir Robert, 102
furnishings, estimate for, 8

Gallrein, Alfred, 188
General Post Office, 28, 34, 109, 205
Gibson, George, 135
Gillam, Andrew, 148
Gilles, Samuel, 201
Gillespie Graham, James, 2, 5, 73
Gillies, James, 104

Index

Randolph, Earl of Moray, 120
Rankine, John, 90
Readman, George, James, 15
Readman, George jnr., 15, 206
Reid, Mrs William, 84
Reith, Lord, 38
residents, number of, 48, 92, 213
Rhind, David, John, Macduff, Williamson, 177
Ritchie, Leitch, 115, 141
Robertson, James, 91
Robertson, William, 19
Robison, Sir John, 128
Romanes, Robert, 60
Royal Academy of Music, 210
Royal College of Physicians, 41, 70, 74, 86, 135, 146
Royal College of Surgeons, 39, 76, 87, 143, 144, 145, 155, 159, 160, 196, 202
Royal High School, 44
Royal Infirmary, 42, 78, 80, 84, 85, 129, 145, 154, 179, 196, 202
Royal Medical Society, 135, 146, 160
Royal Scottish Academy, 21, 103, 114, 115, 175, 192
Royal Society of Edinburgh, 41, 83, 128
Russell, Claud, 82
Rutherford, Andrew (Lord), 165

St Cecilia Hall, 146, 148
St Colme, Baron, 157
St George's Church, 107, 125, 151, 209
St George's Episcopal Chapel, 89, 205
St George's Free Church, 84, 125
St George's Hall, 147, 148
St George's School, 67
St John's Episcopal Chapel/Church, 84, 85, 89, 97, 131
St John's Free Church, 39
St Luke's Church, 115
St Mark's Church, Portobello, 205
St Mary's Roman Catholic Cathedral, 177
St Paul's Episcopal Chapel, 84, 89, 162, 193
St Peter's Episcopal Church, 30, 97
St Stephen's Church, 194

St Stephen's Free Church, 194
Sandford, Daniel Fox, 131
Sandford, Erskine, 127
schools, residential, 19, 23, 42, 45, 46, 62, 86, 101, 102, 103, 104, 206
Schulz, Adolph, 102
Schweitzer, Otto, 115
Scott, Adam, 192
Scott, Andrew, 183
Scott, Charles, 19
Scott, Sir Walter, 11, 12, 20, 27, 45, 56, 74, 87, 138
Scott, William, 22
Scottish Education Act (1872), 75, 130
Scottish Institution, 7, 13, 46, 48, 59, 103, 154, 166, 175
Scottish Meteorological Society, 46
Scottish National Portrait Gallery, 194, 209
Scottish Naval & Military Academy, 101, 178
Secretary for Scotland, 163
Selby Wright, Ronald, 38
Shand, Alexander (Baron), 98
Shephard, Thomas, 195
Simpson, Sir James Young, 58, 203
Simpson, Sir Walter, 158
Simson, James, David, 155
Sinclair, Catherine, Emilia, Sir George, 174
Sinclair, Sir John, 137
Skene, James, 45
Skene, William Forbes, 185
Skinner, Basil, 141
Smith, Alexander, Donald, William, 7
Smith, Ann, Euphemia, Marion, 60
Smith, David, 7, 60
Smith, E. Johnston, 59
Smith, George, 137
Smith, John, 196
Smith, Madeleine, 32, 113
Smith, Sydney, 27
Smith, Thomas, 20
Smith, Tom, 60
Society of Antiquaries, 80, 188, 209
Somerville, Miss Elizabeth, 60
South Australia, Governor of, 155
Speirs, Graham, 157

222

Index